Central Problems in Social Theory

Central Problems in Social Theory

Action, structure and contradiction in social analysis

Anthony Giddens

University of California Press
Berkeley and Los Angeles

First published in the USA 1979 by
University of California Press
Berkeley and Los Angeles, California

Library of Congress Catalog Card Number
79-64667

ISBN 0-520-03975-0 (alk. paper)

Printed in the United States of America

5 6 7 8 9

The paper used in this publication meets the minimum
requirements of American National Standard for Information
Sciences—Permanence of Paper for Printed Library Materials,
ANSI Z39.48-1984. ∞

Philosophy and sociology have long lived under a segregated system which has succeeded in concealing their rivalry only by refusing them any meeting-ground, impeding their growth, making them incomprehensible to one another, and thus placing culture in a situation of permanent crisis.

Merleau-Ponty

Contents

Preface

I have organised this book as separate papers, rather than as chapters. Each paper may be read as a self-contained entity; but they are all concerned with aspects of a limited range of issues which I take to be of essential importance for social analysis. Those who are unacquainted with the arguments I outlined in *New Rules of Sociological Method* may find it helpful to read the concluding synthetic paper, 'The Prospects for Social Theory Today', first.

I should like to thank the following people, who have been of particular help to me in writing this book: David Held, Lesley Bower, Rob Shreeve, John Thompson and Sam Hollick.

Cambridge   A. G.
December 1978

Introduction

Some ten years ago, I conceived the project of examining the residue of nineteenth-century European social theory for contemporary problems of the social sciences. Virtually all my work since that date has been concerned with developing that project. It seemed to me then, and still seems to me now, that social science in the contemporary world bears the strong imprint of ideas worked out in the nineteenth and early twentieth centuries in Europe. These ideas must be radically overhauled today: any appropriation we make from nineteenth-century social thought has to be a thoroughly critical one. This judgement must include the texts of Marx. I have not altered the opinion implied in *Capitalism and Modern Social Theory*[1] – which I thought of as an exegetical preparation to an extended critique of nineteenth-century social thought – that there are no easy dividing-lines to be drawn between Marxism and 'bourgeois social theory'. Whatever differences might exist between these, they share certain common deficiencies deriving from the context of their formation; no one today, I think, can remain true to the spirit of Marx by remaining true to the letter of Marx.

This book represents a further continuation of the project referred to above: it is intended as both a methodological and a substantive text. In *New Rules of Sociological Method*,[2] and in some of the sections of *Studies in Social and Political Theory*,[3] I undertook critiques of two broad programmatic approaches in social theory, hermeneutics or forms of 'interpretative sociology', and functionalism. In the first paper of the present book, I complement these with a critical study of some main currents in structuralist thought. My object in the remainder of the book is to develop a theoretical position which, although informed by ideas drawn from each of these three approaches, differs from all of them. I refer to this position as the *theory of structuration*. The book is both a conclusion and a preface. It amplifies the statement of a methodological standpoint introduced in the two books just mentioned. But at the same time I see it as a preparation for a study of contemporary capitalism and socialism to be published subsequently, in which I shall develop themes only briefly introduced here.

The theory of structuration begins from an absence: the lack of a theory of action in the social sciences. I have already discussed this in some detail in *New Rules of Sociological Method*. There exists a large philosophical literature to do with purposes, reasons and motives of action; but it has to date made little impact upon the social sciences. In some part this is understandable, because the philosophy of action, as developed by British and American philosophers, has not paid much attention to issues that are central to social science: issues of institutional analysis, power and social change. But those traditions of thought which have concentrated upon such problems, particularly functionalism and orthodox Marxism, have done so from a point of view of social determinism. In their eagerness to 'get behind the backs' of the social actors whose conduct they seek to understand, these schools of thought largely ignore just those phenomena that action philosophy makes central to human conduct.

It is no use supposing that such an opposition between voluntarism and determinism can be overcome by simply bringing these rival types of approach together, conjoining one to the other. The problems involved are more deeply buried than that. The philosophy of action, I argue in this book, has typically suffered from two sources of limitation in addition to a failure to theorise problems of institutional analysis. An adequate account of human agency must, first, be connected to a theory of the acting subject; and second, must situate action in *time and space* as a continuous flow of conduct, rather than treating purposes, reasons, etc., as somehow aggregated together. The theory of the subject I outline involves what I call a 'stratification model' of personality, organised in terms of three sets of relations: the unconscious, practical consciousness, and discursive consciousness. The notion of *practical consciousness* I regard as a fundamental feature of the theory of structuration.

But if the established approaches to the philosophy of action have to be substantially modified in order to incorporate a notion of agency within social theory, the same applies to the conceptions of structure and system which have appeared so prominently in the sociological literature. The characteristic interpretation of 'structure' among functionalist writers differs in a basic way from that typical of structuralist thought. But in both bodies of thought the notions of structure and system are often used more or less interchangeably. I claim that not only is it important to distinguish between structure and system, but that each should be understood in a rather different way from how they are ordinarily taken. A major theme of the book is that, as in the theory of agency – and in order to show the interdependence of action and structure – we must grasp the *time–space relations inherent in the constitution of all social interaction*. The repression of time in social theory, I undertake to show, is an inevitable outcome of the maintenance of the distinctions between synchrony and diachrony, or statics and dynamics, which appear throughout the literature of structuralism and functionalism alike. According to the theory of structuration, an understanding of social systems as situated in time–space can be effected by regarding structure as non-temporal and non-spatial, as *a virtual order of differences* produced and reproduced in social interaction as its medium and outcome. *Unser Leben geht hin mit Verwandlung*, Rilke says: Our life passes in transformation. This is what I seek to grasp in the theory of structuration.

The point of view I advocate in these papers is strongly influenced by Heidegger's treatment of being and time: not so much as an ontology, but as a philosophical source for developing a conceptualisation of the time–space constitution of social systems. William James echoes aspects of Heidegger's view when he says of time: 'The literally present moment is a purely verbal supposition, not a position; the only present ever realised concretely being the "passing moment" in which the dying rearward of time and its dawning future forever mix their lights.'[4] The temporality of the interweaving of nature and society is expressed, I want to say, in the finitude and contingency of the human being, of *Dasein*, which is the only link between the continuity of 'first' and 'second nature'. The relentlessness of the 'passing-away' of time is captured by the linguistic affinity with the inevitable 'passing-away' of the human being. The contingency of *Dasein* is not merely in the association of being-in-time with being-in-space but, as Heidegger shows, in the very constitution of 'existents' (in social theory, the constitution of society in structuration). As he points out, if time were merely a succession of nows, contingently associated with spatial presence, it would be impossible to understand why time does not go backwards: but if time is the 'becoming of the possible', the 'progression' of time is clarified.

Heidegger and Wittgenstein are often associated with the so-called 'linguistic turn' in modern philosophy. Stated thus, I think this is misleading; it suggests some views, at any rate, to which I am opposed. I reject the conception that 'society is like a language', a theme which is found, in various forms, in both structuralism and in most interpretative sociologies. I try to make clear in the opening paper some of the difficulties that persistently appear in structuralist social thought; and I have criticised interpretative sociologies in this respect in *New Rules of Sociological Method*. I consider Wittgenstein's later philosophy to be exceptionally important for current problems of social theory, but not in the ways in which that philosophy has characteristically been understood by the 'post-Wittgensteinians'. I take the significance of Wittgenstein's writings for social theory to consist in the association of language with definite *social practices*. I do not find it particularly valuable to undertake the sort of detailed parallels between Marx and Wittgenstein attempted by Rossi-Landi and others; but I do want to propose that there is a direct continuity between Marx and Wittgenstein in respect of the production and reproduction of society as *Praxis*. Every form of language philosophy, I think, implies a stance (usually implicit) towards 'the limits of language': that which cannot be directly expressed in language, because it is what makes language possible. In Wittgenstein's later philosophy 'the limits of language' are made explicit, and made the basis of a semantic theory. Language is intrinsically involved with *that which has to be done*: the constitution of language as 'meaningful' is inseparable from the constitution of forms of social life as continuing practices.

I regard social practices, together with practical consciousness, as crucial mediating moments between two traditionally-established dualisms in social theory. One I have already alluded to, in relation to the contrast between voluntaristic and deterministic types of theory: it is the dualism of the individual and society, or subject and object; the other is the dualism of conscious/unconscious modes of cognition. In place of each of these dualisms, as a single conceptual move, the theory of structuration substitutes the central notion of the *duality of structure*. By the duality of structure, I mean the essential recursiveness of social life, as constituted in social practices: structure is both medium and outcome of the reproduction of practices. Structure enters simultaneously into the constitution of the agent and social practices, and 'exists' in the generating moments of this constitution.

As a leading theorem of the theory of structuration, I advance the following: *every social actor knows a great deal about the conditions of reproduction of the society of which he or she is a member.* Failure to acknowledge this is a basic insufficiency of functionalism and structuralism alike; and it is as true of Parsons's 'action frame of reference' as it is of other varieties of functionalist thought. The proposition that all social agents are knowledgeable about the social systems which they constitute and reproduce in their action is a logically necessary feature of the conception of the duality of structure. But it is one that needs to be carefully elucidated. There are various modes in which such knowledge may figure in practical social conduct. One is in unconscious sources of cognition: there seems no reason to deny that knowledge exists on the level of the unconscious. Indeed, a case can be made to the effect that the mobilisation of unconscious desire normally involves unconscious cognitive elements.[5] More significant for the arguments developed in this book are the differences between practical consciousness, as tacit stocks of knowledge which actors draw upon in the constitution of social activity, and what I call 'discursive consciousness', involving knowledge which actors are able to express on the level of discourse. All actors have some degree of *discursive penetration* of the social systems to whose constitution they contribute.

In the above paragraph, and at many points throughout the book, I bracket the validity claims implied in the term 'knowledge', although I normally choose deliberately to speak of 'knowledge' rather than 'belief'. The logical status of the knowledge applied by social actors in the production and reproduction of social systems, as I emphasise in the concluding paper,[6] has to be considered on two levels. On the methodological level, what I label 'mutual knowledge' is a non-corrigible resource which the social analyst necessarily depends upon, as the medium of generating 'valid' descriptions of social life. As Wittgenstein shows, to know a form of life is to be able in principle to participate in it. But the validity of descriptions or characterisations of social activity is a distinct issue from the validity of 'knowledge' as belief-claims constituted in the discourse of social actors.

The scope and nature of the discursive penetration that actors have of the social systems in which they participate is a matter of great importance to what I term the *dialectic of control* in collectivities. This is one aspect of what I try to show to be *an intrinsic relation between agency and power*. I conceptualise power relations in social systems as regularised relations of autonomy and dependence. Power relations are always two-way; that is to say, however subordinate an actor may be in a social relationship, the very fact of involvement in that relationship gives him or her a certain amount of power over the other. Those in subordinate positions in social systems are frequently adept at converting whatever resources they possess into some degree of control over the conditions of reproduction of those social systems. I do not mean by this to imply that social life can in some sense be reduced to struggles for power, important and chronic as such struggles may be; conflict and power are not logically, but contingently associated.

Restrictions and distortions of the discursive penetration that actors are able to achieve over the circumstances of their action relate directly to *the impact of ideology*. In discussing the question of ideology, I want to show that problems of ideology-critique have to be radically severed from the epistemological issues with which they have frequently been merged. Ideology is not a distinctive type of symbol-system, to be contrasted with others, such as science. As I conceptualise it, ideology refers to the *ideological*, this being understood in terms of the capability of dominant groups or classes to make their own sectional interests appear to others as universal ones. Such capability is therefore one type of resource involved in domination. I do not intend in this book to develop more than a minimal outline of how ideology-critique may be conceived, nor of how the tasks of social science as critical theory should be understood in the contemporary world; these I reserve for the volume to follow. This comment also applies in some considerable degree to the analysis of contradiction and conflict. I develop a concept of social contradiction in some detail, and indicate the range of its potential application, as a theoretical preface to a more exhaustive study of the contradictions of capitalism and state socialism. Such study must form the substance of a critical theory of contemporary society: a critical theory which has to confront the obvious fact that Marxism itself can be, and is, used as an ideological medium of domination.

The theory of structuration elaborated in the present book could be read as a *non-functionalist manifesto*. The importance of functionalist theories, I argue, including the various forms of Marxist functionalism, is that they have always concentrated attention upon the significance of the unintended consequences of action. Such an emphasis is highly important when contrasted to action philosophies, which for the most part have simply ignored unintended consequences. The escape of human history from human intentions, and the return of the consequences of that escape as causal influences on human action, is a chronic feature of social life. But functionalism translates that return into 'society's reasons' for the existence of reproduced social items. According to the theory of structuration, social systems have no purpose, reasons or needs whatsoever; only human individuals do so. *Any explanation of social reproduction which imputes teleology to social systems must be declared invalid*. But many of those who have declared their opposition to functionalism in principle are themselves prone to employ functionalist arguments in practice. It is one thing to reject functionalist views either on logical or on ideological grounds. It is quite another to do so while still acknowledging the cardinal significance of unintended consequences in the reproduction of social systems: to show what a non-functionalist social science actually involves.

In analysing the conditions of social reproduction, and therefore of stability and change in society, I attempt to show the essential importance of tradition and routinisation in social life. We should not cede tradition to the conservatives! The sedimentation of institutional forms in long-term processes of social development is an inescapable feature of all types of society, however rapid the changes they may undergo. Only by grasping this conceptually, rather than repudiating it, can we in fact approach the study of social change at all. The exclusion of time on the level of the *durée* of human agency has its counterpart in the repression of the temporality of social institutions in social theory – a repression effected largely by means of the division of synchrony from diachrony. On the basis of this division, sociologists have been content to leave the succession of events in time to the historians, some of whom as their part of the bargain have been prepared to relinquish the structural properties of social systems to the sociologists. But this kind of separation has no rational justification with the recovery of temporality as integral to social theory: history and sociology become methodologically indistinguishable.

'Sociology', as I have remarked elsewhere, is not an innocent term.[7] It is one closely identified, in its origins and current use, with the threefold set of associations I indicate in the concluding paper: naturalism, functionalism and the theory of industrial society. The term sociology is today so widely in use that it would be merely obstructive to attempt to drop it altogether. I have continued to use it in *New Rules of Sociological Method*, and in this book, to refer in a general way to the study of the institutions of the industrialised societies. But this differentiation from the other social sciences is at best a convenient inconvenience, and since many of the arguments I develop apply to all of them, I have often used the term 'social science' in a generic fashion.

1

Structuralism and the Theory of the Subject

'Functionalism' and 'structuralism' have been perhaps the leading broad intellectual traditions in social theory over the past thirty or forty years. Both terms have long since lost any precise meaning, but it is possible none the less to identify a number of core notions which each invokes. Functionalism and structuralism in some part share similar origins, and have important features in common. The lineage of both can be traced back to Durkheim, as refracted in the former instance through the work of Radcliffe-Brown and Malinowski, and in the latter through that of Saussure and Mauss.[1] Radcliffe-Brown and Malinowski reacted against speculative, evolutionary anthropology; Saussure against not too dissimilar notions held by his predecessors, the neo-grammarians. Each of these three authors came to place a stress upon synchrony, separating the synchronic from the diachronic. Each came to accentuate the importance of the 'system', social and linguistic, as contrasted with the elements which compose it. But from then on the characteristic emphases diverge. In functionalism, the guiding model of 'system' is usually that of the organism, and functionalist authors have consistently looked to biology as a conceptual bank to be plundered for their own ends. In the work of Saussure, of course, and subsequently in that of the Prague circle, structuralism began as an approach to linguistics; in the form of social theory, however, structuralism may be most cogently defined as the application of linguistic models influenced by structural linguistics to the explication of social and cultural phenomena.[2]

The contrast has been a consequential one for the development of social theory in the Anglo-Saxon world as compared with that in France: I shall attempt to indicate some of the more significant divergences in what follows. I shall not be concerned with an overall appraisal of structuralism – which after all, if interpreted broadly, brings to mind the contributions of a dazzling variety of different authors, including Barthes, Foucault, Althusser, Lacan, Piaget, Greimas, etc. – and shall confine my attention strictly to a limited number of issues raised by the following: Saussure's linguistic theory; Lévi-Strauss's account of myth; and the 'critique of the sign' at the hands of those who have sought to develop a novel theory of structuration (Derrida, Kristeva).

Several of the themes I propose to raise in this paper are not discussed here in the degree which they warrant, because they are further analysed or exemplified in subsequent papers in this book. My discussion is partial and selective, because I want to use this paper in conjunction with previously published critiques of hermeneutics and action philosophy on the one hand, and of functionalism[3] on the other, and because it is intended as a preface to the papers which comprise the bulk of the book. Moreover, until right at the end of this paper, I shall be concerned mainly with critical analysis, rather than singling out the virtues of structuralist thought.

Saussure: structural linguistics

Of the various doctrines of Saussure, those most central to later developments in structuralism and semiology are: the distinction of *langue* (language) and *parole* (speech); the arbitrary character of the sign; the notion of difference; the constitution of the sign through the conjunction of signifier and signified; and the separation of synchrony and diachrony. These have become so familiar that they require only a schematic commentary.

Saussure did not use the term 'structure', the latter having been introduced into continental linguistics by Trubetskoy; Saussure preferred 'system'. The systematic character of *langue*, for Saussure, is the chief factor distinguishing it from *parole*, from the spoken or written word. The separation of *langue* from *parole*, Saussure held, differentiates both 'what is social from what is individual', and 'what is essential from what is accessory and more or less accidental'.[4] Language is a social institution, and as such is not a creation of the individual speaker: the speaker 'passively assimilates', as Saussure puts it, the pre-existing forms that language assumes. By contrast to *langue, parole* is a 'heterogeneous mass' of disparate events. The vocal apparatus has become the principal instrument of language among human beings, but this has no bearing upon the most integral characteristics of *langue*: these characteristics derive from the human faculty of grasping and ordering a system of signs. Such a faculty is not confined to language, since signs can be other than linguistic: hence Saussure envisaged the possibility of a general science of signs, or semiology, of which linguistics would be one branch.[5]

The arbitrary nature of linguistic signs, and their constitution through difference, are the chief notions by means of which Saussure attempted to explicate *langue* as system. Each notion places an emphasis upon form at the expense of content, or more accurately expressed, upon the relational rather than the substantive. Saussure pointed to the arbitrary character of the sign in two ways. One was simply by comparing words across languages: although they have a similar meaning, the sounds expressed in the pronunciation of 'ox' in English and 'boeuf' in French share nothing in common with one another. In this sense, the arbitrariness of the sign 'is proved . . . by the very existence of different languages'.[6] But this is secondary to the demonstration that the sounds which form words in a language have no intrinsic connection with the physical objects that they designate: the utterance 'tree' is no more or less appropriate to a tree as an object than 'arbre' is. In view of the controversy that Saussure's assertion of the arbitrary quality of the sign – which he took to be 'indisputable' – has provoked, it is perhaps worth observing that he qualified it in various ways. Signs are not arbitrary, of course, as he was careful to emphasise, in respect of the individual speaker. Quite the reverse; the speaker has no choice but to follow what is already established in the language. Saussure also distinguished what he called 'radically arbitrary' from 'relatively arbitrary' signs: the latter are second-order words, constructed from the first. 'Neuf' is radically arbitrary, but 'dix-neuf' is only relatively so, since it is a composite term.

The principle of relative arbitrariness clearly only affects the internal composition of language; language as a whole is 'radically arbitrary' in relation to the object-world. It follows from this that the terms of language can only be defined *sui generis*: terms only acquire identity or continuity in so far as they are differentiated from one another as oppositions or differences within the totality that is *langue*. Saussure's famous 'Geneva-to-Paris train' example is worth quoting here because, as I shall indicate further later on, it bears a definite similarity to issues that Anglo-Saxon philosophers have discussed in the context of the philosophy of action. We say that the 'same' Geneva-to-Paris train leaves Geneva every day at 8.25 p.m., even if from one day to another the engine, coaches and personnel are different. What gives the train its identity, Saussure argued, is the ways in which it is differentiated from other trains: its time of departure, route, etc. Similarly in language the identity of linguistic units, whether these be vocalisations or written terms, depends upon the differences or oppositions that separate them from one another, not upon their intrinsic content. A 't', for example, may be written in various different ways; its identity is preserved not by a unity of substance but by its demarcation from other letters. Exactly the same applies to the sounds that comprise linguistic utterances. The idea of difference, as Saussure formulates it, thus completes the insulation of *langue* as a self-contained system: the 'value' of the components of language derive solely from the demarcations drawn between them. 'In language', according to Saussure, 'there are only differences. Even more important: a difference generally implies positive terms between which the difference is set up; but in language there are only differences without *positive terms*'.[7]

The constitution of identity negatively through difference applies to each of the two aspects of linguistic signs, signifier and signified. But their combination in the sign transforms the negative into the positive. The only positive feature that language possesses – but it is a very fundamental one – is the articulation of signifiers and signifieds in the process of speaking or writing. Language, for Saussure, is basically a vocal/auditory system on the level of the signifier, but in both utterances and in writing, the connections between signifiers and signifieds are organised in terms of linear sequences, unfolding in time. Although Saussure sometimes proceeded as though each signifier has a definite signified, a concept or 'idea', attached to it, he also made it plain that this is a misleading way of representing the association between the two. Such a view would imply that concepts were formed prior to and independently of the terms used to express them. The relation between signifier and signified is much more intimate than this; without being articulated via the values created by phonological difference, thought would be just an inchoate flux. Linguistic signs only come into being through the mutual connection of signifiers and signifieds in the temporal conjunctions effected in speaking and hearing, reading and writing.

Time is thus not, as is sometimes suggested, absent from Saussurian linguistics. The fact that Saussure made the serial or linear character of signifiers basic to all language, and related this to a continuity of signifieds which meet at definite points of articulation, means that his view is not as distant as might appear from those later developed by Lacan and Derrida. Saussure did not so much eliminate time from his theory, as distinguish radically between two forms of temporality: that which is involved in the syntagmatic order of language, and thus is the very condition of synchrony, and that which is involved in the evolution of features of *langue*. In the first sense, time is integral to Saussure's understanding of the systematic character of language, because it is vital to the notion of 'system' here that the whole is only available in its particular articulations. This notion is quite distinct from the conception of the whole that pertains in functionalism in social theory, based on the analogy of organic or mechanical systems. None the less, Saussure did accentuate strongly the independence of synchrony from diachrony. The distinction between the synchronic and diachronic viewpoints, according to him, 'is absolute and allows no compromise'; the diachronic perspective concerns phenomena 'that are unrelated to systems although they do condition them'.[8] To study the states of a system we must abstract completely from changes in its elements. This is related back to the distinction of *langue* and *parole*. Only synchrony allows us to grasp the nature of *langue*.[9] Diachrony operates on the level of the event, of the modifications in language brought about through speaking.

Limitations of Saussure's views

The critical evaluation of Saussure's views has a dual interest: as linguistic theory in itself, and as a model of language that has served to shape some characteristic perspectives of structuralism – although, of course, various of Saussure's ideas were rejected by the Prague group and by Lévi-Strauss. The critical reception of

Saussure's linguistics is by now well developed in the literature. I wish to consider briefly only certain points which have some fairly direct implications for problems of social theory. There are basic difficulties with each of the five elements of Saussure's work which I have distinguished above.

1. Among Saussurian themes, perhaps that most extensively debated has been the doctrine of the arbitrary character of the sign. Concentration of critical attention upon this element in Saussure's doctrines is not unjustified since, as I have indicated previously, the twin notions of arbitrariness and difference are the main constituting features that establish the systematic character of *langue*. The term 'arbitrary' is a provocative one, and there is no doubt that some of the confusions to which Saussure's doctrine has given rise derive from the misleading implications it suggests – although Saussure attempted to cover himself against certain of these by sometimes substituting 'unmotivated' for 'arbitrary'. 'Unmotivated', like 'arbitrary', however, is a voluntaristic term, suggesting just that factor of choice which Saussure denied that the speaker, the passive prisoner of language, possesses. The notion of arbitrariness, as Saussure employed it, seems to have been used to make at least two points, and it is worth separating these out. One is that to affirm that *langue* exists independently of, or cannot be explained in terms of, the intentional acts initiated by speakers on the level of *parole*; *langue* is not in any sense an intended product of the activity of the subjects who are the language speakers. I shall come to some of the issues this raises shortly. The second is to stress the conventional nature of the sign, in the sense in which 'convention' is ordinarily employed by British and American philosophers, and I shall consider this initially.[10]

We can see that there are major unresolved difficulties in Saussure's conception if we pose the question: what is it about signs that is held to be conventional or 'arbitrary'? Is it something about the nature of the signifier; or the nature of the signified in some way; or is it the connection between the two? Saussure seemed to be in no doubt; it is the final one of these: 'The bond between the signifier and the signified is arbitrary'.[11] But the examples he offered to document the claim *do not concern this bond*, they concern only the nature of the signifier. The sounds made by a speaker, or the marks inscribed on a page, have no 'intrinsic' or isomorphic resemblance to phenomena or events in the object-world. Benveniste, in a famous discussion, has expressed the relevant point well. The argument that Saussure makes

> is falsified by an unconscious and surreptitious recourse to a third term which was not included in the initial definition. This third term is the thing itself, the reality. Even though Saussure said that the idea of 'sister' is not connected to the signifier s-ö-r, he was not thinking any the less of the *reality* of the notion. When he spoke of the difference between b-ö-f and o-k-s, he was referring in spite of himself to the fact that these two terms applied to the same *reality*. Here, then, is the *thing*, expressly excluded at first from the definition of the sign, now creeping into it by a detour . . . [12]

What Saussure's argument comes down to then, in respect of the examples proffered to support his case at least, is that the relation between *signifier and object-world* is conventional, with the possible exception of a few onomatopoeic words (and, as he pointed out, such words or expressions are normally stylised or conventional anyway). Since he focused on the signifier/signified relation as arbitrary, he tended to elide the 'signified' and the '*object* signified' (or referred to) by a word or statement.

2. This had two consequences, whose implications have been far-reaching, even among those structuralist authors only diffusely influenced by Saussure. (a) Since the 'thing', to echo Benveniste, was banished from view by fiat as it were, Saussure did not develop a reasoned and extended case against ostensive definitions of meaning, as Wittgenstein was later to do. Problems of reference, indeed, disappear almost completely from Saussure's discussion; the whole burden of linguistic theory is made to turn on the relation between signifier and signified. (b) The status of the signified, which after all was often employed by Saussure as generally equivalent to 'meaning', and can hardly be supposed to be tangential to a theory of language, was left relatively obscure. Saussure variously described signifieds as 'mental images', 'ideas' and 'concepts', thus as properties of mind. Ideas or concepts participate in the process of semiosis, by combining with signifiers; but how ideas or concepts achieve any capability of referring to objects or events in the world is completely

unexplicated.[13] It may well be the case, as various interpreters of
Saussure have remarked, that the general implication of Saussure's
viewpoint is that it is not the word or sentence which 'stands for'
objects or events in the world, but rather that the whole system of
langue 'lies parallel to reality itself'.[14] However in what sense *langue*
might 'lie parallel to reality' is not at all clarified in Saussure's
analyses. The lack of clarity about the nature of the signified,
together with the associated tendency to merge signified and signified object, have had important residues, I shall argue, in the later
development of structuralist thought.

3. Related problems arise in respect of Saussure's attempt to
accentuate the purely formal qualities of language as constituted
through difference. Language is all form, with no substance; linguistic values stem solely from differences. This emphasis undoubtedly
enabled Saussure to advance considerably beyond the achievements of his predecessors in linguistics, by concentrating attention
on relations between linguistic values, rather than upon the terms of
language considered individually. But no system can be com-
prehended as pure form, as defined wholly internally: not even, it is
generally agreed since Gödel, a system of mathematics. When
Ogden and Richards say that Saussure's characterisation of difference conceals or suppresses a process of interpretation in the sign,[15]
they are making an essential observation – and one which bears
directly upon the distance which has subsequently separated structuralism from hermeneutics. Saussure's own example can be used to
substantiate the point at issue. The identity of the 'Geneva-to-Paris
train' cannot be specified independently of *the context in which the
phrase is used*; and this context is not the system of differences
themselves, such as Saussure mentions, but factors relating to their
use *in practice*. Saussure implicitly assumes the practical standpoint
of the traveller, or the time-tabling official, in giving the identity of
the train; hence the 'same' train may consist of quite distinct engines
and carriages on two separate occasions. But these do not count as
instances of the 'same' train for a railway repair engineer, or a
train-spotter. The example may be a trivial one, and is not particularly significant in itself, but its ramifications are very important,
and constantly emerge in later developments connected with the
thought of those close to or influenced by structuralism. The dam
that Saussure established to protect the system of *langue* from

semantic and referential ties to the world of objects and events is continually and necessarily breached.

4. Of the various dualisms which are so prominent in Saussure's thought, those of *langue/parole* and synchrony/diachrony stand in closest association with one another. *Langue* can only be isolated by synchronic analysis; to study diachrony is to revert to the level of *parole*. It does not need close inspection of Saussure's *Cours* – in the form in which it has come down to us, at any rate – to see that each distinction covers a range of oppositions: system/event; necessary/contingent; social/individual; formal/substantive, etc. The ambiguities involved in this probably help to account both for the fruitfulness of Saussure's ideas, and for the muddled character of much of the ensuing discussion of the *langue/parole* and synchrony/diachrony oppositions. There is one principal way, however, in which the *langue/parole* differentiation has been shown to be inadequate in linguistic theory, and it has important implications in identifying the limitations of the separation of synchrony from diachrony. The basic inadequacy can be simply stated: Saussure did not show what mediates between the systematic, non-contingent, social character of *langue* on the one hand, and the specific, contingent and individual character of *parole* on the other. *What is missing is a theory of the competent speaker or language-user.* This has been recognised by Chomsky on the level of syntactics. Saussure, he points out, saw *langue* primarily as a repository of 'word-like elements' and 'fixed phrases', thus counterposing the established, given nature of *langue* with the free and voluntary form of *parole*. Hence he was unable to grasp what Chomsky calls the 'rule-governed creativity' of sentence formation in the day-to-day use of language.[16]

5. In relating this type of criticism to Saussure's distinction between synchrony and diachrony, we can return to some similarities between structuralism and functionalism. Saussure took pains to stress that the differentiation between synchrony and diachrony is one made by the linguist for purposes of analysis. Hence it is no objection to his view to affirm, as some have done, that language is constantly in a state of mutation; Saussure often acknowledged that such is the case. The same holds for functionalist authors in the social sciences who have distinguished between synchrony and

diachrony, or statics and dynamics: they have normally advanced this solely as a methodological division, and are not vulnerable to the criticism that societies are constantly undergoing processes of change. The real point concerns whether it is justified to claim that a linguistic system or a social system can be studied in abstraction from change, while at the same time the nature of that system can be adequately grasped. And this claim is not, in fact, one which can be sustained. The recursive character of language – and, by generalisation, of social systems also – cannot be understood unless we also understand that the means whereby such systems are reproduced, and thus exist *as* systems, contain within them the seeds of change. 'Rule-governed creativity' is not merely (as Chomsky's linguistics suggests) the employment of fixed, given rules whereby new sentences are generated; *it is at the same time the medium whereby those rules are reproduced and hence in principle modified.*

Treated as the *duality of structure*, I shall be returning to this notion on numerous occasions throughout this book. It will be one of my main claims that both structuralist and functionalist theories characteristically lack a conception of the duality of structure; and that, as regards the former of these, this is in some part traceable to the general influence of Saussure.

Lévi-Strauss: structural anthropology

In the writings of Lévi-Strauss, structuralism and functionalism are in some part reunited. One of the major sources which Lévi-Strauss has drawn upon is the work of Durkheim[17] and, to a lesser extent, that of Radcliffe-Brown and Malinowski. But he has only done so in a highly critical vein, and is indebted to a wide range of other thinkers also. Besides the very general influence of Rousseau, Marx and Freud, the most important writers in the evolution of Lévi-Strauss's thought have been Saussure, Trubetskoy and Jakobson. The work of the latter two authors is the avenue through which Lévi-Strauss has approached the ideas of Saussure, and he accepts basic elements in their critical assessment of their predecessor. Nevertheless a number of Saussurian themes are prominent in Lévi-Strauss's writings, albeit often in considerably modified form. These include the following: the priority of the collective and universal over the individual and contingent; an emphasis on the relational at the expense of the isolated unit; and acceptance of the application of the sign to non-linguistic phenomena: that is, the programme of semiology. The implication of the latter point, as construed by Lévi-Strauss, is not just that concepts employed by linguistics can be applied to the study of social and cultural phenomena; but that these are 'phenomena whose inmost nature is the same as that of language'.[18]

Lévi-Strauss's writings divide into various main areas in terms of their subject-matter: the study of kinship systems, the earliest of his preoccupations; the theory of primitive classification and totemism; and the analysis of the logic of myth. Of these I shall touch here only on the latter, which in its content is generally recognised to be the most persuasive sector of Lévi-Strauss's work, and one in which the theoretical precepts of his approach are developed in their most sophisticated fashion. Three such precepts are particularly relevant to the general impact of Lévi-Strauss's thought on the social sciences and philosophy: his understanding of the notion of 'structure' itself, his conception of the unconscious, and his approach to history.

Structures, for Lévi-Strauss, involve models posited by the anthropological observer. They are not representations of social activity or ideas, but are a mode of delving below the surface phenomena of social life to discover underlying relations whereby it is ordered, in a similar way to that in which combinatory elements are uncovered in linguistics. Lévi-Strauss early on fashioned his approach after the so-called 'phonological revolution' in linguistic theory, according to which elements of culture can be treated as analogous to phonemes, whose significance can only be grasped in their mutual relations. Structures: (a) consist of interconnected elements, 'none of which can undergo changes without effecting changes in all the other elements': in other words, they are systems; (b) involve transformations, whereby equivalences in divergent materials can be explicated; (c) make possible the prediction of how modifications in one element will alter the model as a whole.[19] Lévi-Strauss has been sensitive to the charge of formalism which attended Saussure's idea of difference, and accepts the gist of Benveniste's critique of the arbitrary nature of the sign. The aim of structuralist analysis is to recover the content of 'intelligible reality'; 'content and form', he argues, 'are not separate entities, but complementary points of view essential for the deep understanding of one and the same object of study'.[20] In specific contrast to the formalism of Propp, Lévi-Strauss holds that structures cannot be defined independently of their content, for the perception of structure is at the same time the identification of content. For Lévi-Strauss, this is a point with broad implications, which among other things distance him from positivism; scientific knowledge is not induced from sensory observations, but involves the construction of schemes whereby those observations are rendered intelligible.

Lévi-Strauss has frequently offered qualifications to the applicability of structural models. It is 'patently absurd', he says, to suppose that the structuralist method can achieve 'an exhaustive knowledge of societies',[21] even of those which are 'cold' or relatively immobile. He has often described his work as 'tentative' and as an 'initial statement', and has kept his reserve in the face of the more expansive claims that have been made for structuralism as a philosophy or as a 'new conception of the world'.[22] While he has disavowed the terms 'method' or 'philosophy', he has been prepared to endorse that of epistemology as an accurate designation of his concerns.[23] This no doubt reflects both his conviction that 'socio-logic' has to be made the basis of sociology and anthropology, and his absorption with the unconscious as the source of signification. The chief object of Lévi-Strauss's work is to identify what he variously calls 'unconscious psychical structures' or the 'unconscious teleology of mind' that underlie human social institutions. Although he bows in the direction of Freud, it seems evident enough that Lévi-Strauss's unconscious is not Freud's unconscious, and owes more to Trubetskoy and Jakobson than to Freud. The unconscious, for Lévi-Strauss, is the source of the basic structuring principles that govern language; language, as Lévi-Strauss puts it, 'is human reason, which has its reasons . . . of which man knows nothing'. ('Totalisation non réfléxive, la langue est une raison humaine qui a ses raisons, et que l'homme ne connaît pas.')[24] The study of the unconscious, which reflects basic operations in the structure of the brain, reveals the mechanisms of signification that lie beneath the conscious activity of the human subject. This 'Kantianism without a transcendental subject' does not so much – as later authors have tried to do – offer a theory of the origins of human subjectivity, as place an *epoché* upon the subject so far as anthropology is concerned.

Lévi-Strauss's views on the relation between structural analysis and history are complex and occasionally quite obscure. But the main thesis he seeks to advance is forcibly and bluntly put. History, understood as the attempt to describe or account for occurrences in time, does not enjoy the epistemological primacy often accorded to it: historical analysis is only one code among other codes, based on the interpretative mode expressing the contrast of 'before' and 'after', or 'preceding' and 'succeeding'. The concluding section of *La pensée sauvage* takes Sartre's writings as a leading example of a general tendency in Western thought to accord a dominant role to historical consciousness. 'Sartre', Lévi-Strauss remarks, 'is certainly not the only contemporary philosopher to have valued history above the other human sciences and formed an almost mystical conception of it.'[25] History, in the sense of the succession of events, is not the primary medium through which human experience is organised, nor is historical understanding the form in which the most basic elements of social life can be disclosed.[26] Lévi-Strauss brackets history, in each of the senses of the term (temporal occurrence, and accounts of such occurrence), in much the same way as he does the thinking and acting subject: in order, as he sees it, to penetrate more deeply to the foundations of human experience, especially as expressed in those societies which have 'an obstinate fidelity to the past conceived as a timeless model, rather than a stage in the historical process'.[27]

Myths, 'machines for the suppression of time', are peculiarly apposite objects of study to this end. In comparing the structure of myth with a musical score, Lévi-Strauss intends much more than just an analogy. An orchestral score 'suppresses' time by encapsulating it within a sphere that makes possible an indefinite number of actual performances. It would be inaccurate to say that music is pure form, since Lévi-Strauss does not recognise the possibility of such a phenomenon; but the structuring principles of music express properties of mind that are prior to the organisation of thought or activity in words. The temporal dimension of music, as of myth, is what Lévi-Strauss sometimes calls 'reversible' or 'non-cumulative', in contrast to the 'statistical' or 'cumulative' character of historical time. Music and myth express *langue*, or the unconscious, in its most accessible form. Both music and myth, when considered as 'narratives' – as actually played or told – operate through the connection of two orders of relation, horizontally and vertically. Both combine what Saussure called the syntagmatic and the associative; or, more broadly, Jakobson's metonymic and metaphoric dimensions.

Only a few further elements in Lévi-Strauss's discussions of myth are worth mentioning here. There are some variations between his earlier and later treatments of myth, but the overall themes are quite consistent. The principle of binary opposition as the origin of structures is both held to in Lévi-Strauss's earlier studies of myth, and defended throughout *Mythologiques*. In these latter volumes, Lévi-Strauss clarifies why myths cannot be studied in isolation: each myth is a sign rather than a complete order of signification. In decoding myths we have to proceed by means of a 'spiral move-ment', whereby each myth is used to provide clues for elucidating the structure of another, and so on. Binary opposition is used both as a way of identifying the structural components of myth, and at the same time as a mode of confirming the structural analysis in the 'spiralling' technique: an initial structural axis is identified, and substantiated by the disclosure of another axis to which it itself is in opposition. The antimony between nature and culture is the central opposition that Lévi-Strauss discusses throughout his work. But it is a crucial part of Lévi-Strauss's theory that this antimony is itself cultural, and is thus represented quite differently in divergent cultures.[28]

Lévi-Strauss: structure and subjectivity

When contrasted to functionalism as developed in modern Ameri-can sociology, Lévi-Strauss's work brings into clear focus the dual influence of Durkheim in the social sciences. Each has elaborated one thread of the Durkheimian theorem of the superiority of society over the individual. But whereas the functionalists have concen-trated upon practical activity, Lévi-Strauss concentrates on cogni-tion; and while functionalism, especially as worked out by Parsons, has developed the theme of society as moral consensus, Lévi-Strauss has drawn primarily upon Durkheim's 'sociological Kan-tianism'. For each, society 'has its reasons of which its members know little'. In the case of functionalism, these are the imperatives of societal co-ordination, the imperatives of normative order; for Lévi-Strauss they are the organising mechanisms of the uncon-scious.

The *langue/parole*, or code/message, distinctions have had no impact on the development of functionalism, although functionalist thought has not altogether lacked contact with linguistics more generally (as in the work of Malinowski). Since these distinctions have been very important to the notion of 'structure' that has evolved within structuralism, it is not surprising that the term has been employed quite differently by modern functionalists. For the latter, structure is basically a descriptive term, employed by analogy with anatomy as equivalent to something like 'fixed pattern'. Structure here has no connection with movement whatsoever: it is an arrangement of dry bones that are only made to rattle at all by the conjoining of structure with function. Function is the explanatory concept, the means whereby part is related to whole. The counterpart to the functionalists' structure/function division in Lévi-Strauss's structuralism is the differentiation of structure and event; structure plays an explanatory role only because it is linked to the idea of transformations.

Neither the functionalists nor Lévi-Strauss clearly distinguish structure from system, and it could be said that one or other of these notions is redundant to both schools of thought. There is no 'anatomy' in social life apart from its 'physiology': hence in functionalism structure and system become interchangeable terms.[29] It is apparent from the definition of structure quoted earlier that something similar is true of Lévi-Strauss's usage: apart from the notion of transformations, each of the other elements referred to are simply characteristics of systems. I shall want to argue later in the book, although not in this paper, that a distinction between structure and system is highly important to social theory.

Lévi-Strauss's writings have met with a critical reception at the hands of British and American anthropologists (especially those inclined to functionalism), many of whom regard the empirical support for his claims as less than completely convincing. I shall not be concerned with this type of criticism here, although there is no doubt that to some extent it stems from a positivist reading of Lévi-Strauss, which misunderstands the method he seeks to apply. I shall want to consider only certain conceptual limitations of Lévi-Strauss's structuralism – limitations which he in some part admits, but which stem from more than the restrictions he places upon structural analysis. The relevant issues can be dealt with quite briefly.

1. The first concerns Lévi-Strauss's treatment of the structuring properties of the unconscious. I want to argue that the same gap between the unconscious properties of mind and the conscious, purposive activity of human subjects appears in Lévi-Strauss as intervenes between *langue* and *parole* in Saussure; and that this is at the origin of a primary source of difficulty in Lévi-Strauss's structuralism. In the final volume of *Mythologiques (L'Homme nu)*, Lévi-Strauss specifically confronts charges that he eliminates the conscious self-understandings of social actors from structural analysis. While recording again his rejection of those versions of the subject found in existentialist phenomenology (in existentialism, 'contemporary man becomes enclosed in a self-enclosed tête-à-tête, and falls down in ecstasy before himself'),[30] Lévi-Strauss affirms that his exclusion of reflexivity is only a methodological bracketing.

> One must admit [he writes] that only subjects speak, and that every myth ultimately has its origin in an individual creation. This is undoubtedly true, but in order to move to the level of myth, it is necessary precisely that a creation does not remain individual; and that in the course of this transition it essentially discards those features with which it was contingently marked at the outset, and which can be attributed to the temperament, talent, imagination, and personal experience of the author.[31]

Could there be a clearer restatement, however, of the Saussurian contrast of *langue* and *parole*, transferred to a social context? The activity of human subjects is 'individual' and 'contingent', as compared to the supra-individual character of the collective, represented by myth. The logical chasm which separates the 'individual' from the 'social' is as great as it ever was for Durkheim or Saussure.

I wish to claim that this inadequacy is one which marks structuralist thought from Saussure onwards, and which is closely connected to the lack of a conception of the duality of structure. Structuralist thought has no mode of coping with what I shall call *practical consciousness* – non-discursive, but not unconscious, knowledge of social institutions – as involved in social reproduction.

One of the few places where Lévi-Strauss discusses questions relevant to practical consciousness is in a passage in *The Raw and the Cooked*, where he writes as follows:

Although the possibility cannot be excluded that the speakers who create and transmit myths may become aware of their structure and mode of operation, this cannot occur as a normal thing, but only partially and intermittently. It is the same with myths as with language: the individual who conscientiously applied phonological and grammatical laws in his speech, supposing he possessed the knowledge and virtuosity to do so, would nevertheless lose the thread of his ideas almost immediately.[32]

There is a confusion here between *discursive consciousness*, or that which can be brought to and held in consciousness, and *practical consciousness*; a confusion which derives from the idea (already implicit in the Saussurian polarities) that either something is conscious (discursively available), or else it is unconscious. There is a vital sense in which all of us *do* chronically apply phonological and grammatical laws in speech – as well as all sorts of other practical principles of conduct – even though we could not formulate those laws discursively (let alone hold them in mind throughout discourse). But we cannot grasp the significance of such practical knowledge if we interpret it separately from human consciousness and agency, or what I shall call the *reflexive monitoring of conduct* that is central to human activity: if we place an *epoché* upon the conscious and the practical.[33]

2. We can give this criticism more concrete form by considering Lévi-Strauss's evaluation of Mauss's theory of gift exchange. Mauss's theory, he claims, involves elements of a 'phenomenological' kind, that have to be discarded. We must not be deflected by the experience or ideas of the participants in such exchanges themselves, but have to treat the gift exchanges as a 'constructed object' governed by 'mechanical laws' of reciprocity, and separated from 'statistical time'. However, as Bourdieu has pointed out, far from clarifying the nature of the gift, treating the process of exchange as a formal structure in this way eliminates essential features of what a gift is. In Bourdieu's words:

The observer's totalising apprehension substitutes an objective structure fundamentally defined by its *reversibility* for an equally objectively *irreversible* succession of gifts which are not mechanically linked to the gifts they respond to or insistently call for: any really objective analysis of gifts, words, challenges or even women must allow for the fact that each of these inaugural acts may misfire, and that it receives its meaning, in any case, from the response it triggers off, even if the response is a failure to reply that retrospectively removes its intended meaning.[34]

The removal of the temporal components of the gift, in Lévi-Strauss's analysis, represses the fact that, for the gift exchange to occur, the counter-gift must be given at a later time, and must be different from the initial gift; *only in such ways is a 'gift' distinguished from a 'swap' or a 'loan'.* A whole range of strategic possibilities, moreover, in the practical activity of the gift exchange exist, and exist only, because of the irreversible time dimension. The point is not merely that these are complementary to Lévi-Strauss's interpretation of exchange as a code, but that they are not conceptually *recoverable* from the latter.

3. These observations connect directly to the encounter between structuralism and hermeneutics.[35] Saussure's structural linguistics was able to avoid direct exposure to problems of hermeneutics because the idea of difference as pure form, coupled with the doctrine of the arbitrary nature of the sign, made language into an insulated system of relations. Lévi-Strauss has accepted that this conception is untenable, and does not attempt to separate form wholly from content. But this actually prevents him from carrying over the implications of the 'phonological revolution' into anthropology with the degree of 'closure' that he seems to claim. The issues that have always dominated hermeneutics – the contextuality of meaning and problems of translation[36] – are dealt with by Lévi-Strauss only in terms of the 'context' of structure itself, defined objectively. The example of the gift shows that this is deficient: what counts as a 'gift' cannot be defined internally to the structural analysis itself, which presumes it as an already constituted 'ordinary language concept'. In this regard Ricoeur is surely correct when he argues that Lévi-Strauss's structural analyses of myth, far from excluding 'meaning as a narrative', bound to the contexts of its reproduction, actually presuppose it.[37] Structural analysis presupposes hermeneutics in so far as the latter is taken to be concerned with the interpretation and repair of meaningful communication, grounded in the intersubjectivity of practical day-to-day life.

4. At this juncture we may briefly revert to Lévi-Strauss's treatment of history and his approach to epistemology – issues that are closely

connected, since the latter is the basis of his view of the former. Lévi-Strauss's argument that the dominant modes of thought established in modern Western culture are in some key respects discrepant from the conceptual operations of the primitive *bricoleur* at first sight would appear again to lead back to hermeneutics. If this is not the direction which Lévi-Strauss takes, it is because of the structural homology of mind which he considers underlies all human thought, whatever the 'substance' that it employs. This is a 'sociological Kantianism' (rather than an explicit epistemology), like its Durkheimian prototype, since it expressly lacks a transcendental subject. Lévi-Strauss consequently has to deny that there is any privileged access to the structure of myth, either by those concerned in transmitting it or by the anthropological observer. It makes no difference, according to him, whether 'the thought processes of the South American Indians take shape through the medium of my thought, or whether mine takes place through the medium of theirs'.[38]

Now this might be a defensible standpoint if Lévi-Strauss's structural constitution of those 'thought processes' could be corroborated or validated in a manner comparable to that of linguistic hypotheses. But, as Culler shows, no such corroboration can be forthcoming. The approach of the linguist draws upon the recursive properties of language as part of the process, and as the means whereby, these properties are made available for study. The linguist draws upon his or her own competence, or that of others, as a speaker of a particular language, in both *devising* and *validating* characterisations of it.[39] The study of myth cannot draw recursively on its object in this way; Lévi-Strauss's 'spiralling' procedure is not a substitute for it – although it is the closest that he comes to acknowledging the hermeneutic circle. His standpoint hence oscillates between relativism and dogmatism, in respect of the structural oppositions he claims to identify in myth. There is no way to rebut the charge made by critics that, quite contrary to his own assertions, his analyses reflect categories of Western society imposed upon other cultures.[40]

5. Since it resolutely brackets any kind of reflexive understanding as only a 'surface manifestation' of deeper cognitive forms, Lévi-Strauss's structural anthropology has no mode of reflecting upon its own origins, as itself the product of a particular set of socio-cultural circumstances, as Sartre and other critics have emphasised. 'His-

tory', as reflexive consciousness applied to the development of human society, is not just one code among others. Nor can that 'code' be adequately explicated through the synchronic/diachronic division that Lévi-Strauss inherits from Saussure, as modified by Jakobson.[41] Jakobson's discussion of historical phonology is less distant from Saussure's view than it is sometimes presumed to be. Diachrony is held by Jakobson to produce imbalances that lead to readjustments on the level of synchrony, hence connecting the two. But history here is still understood as a succession of synchronic systems; diachrony and synchrony are not reconciled, nor is the separation of synchrony from diachrony seriously undermined.[42]

Derrida's critique of the sign

The influence of Lévi-Strauss over the development of semiotics in the 1950s and 1960s was considerable, however critical some of the leading figures in that field may have been of his work in certain respects. Structures were usually in that period treated as given codes, examined within closed and discrete systems. Barthes's early formulations of semiotics, for example, cover a range of systems of signs that are treated as so many separate instances of myth, which are only in a very general way claimed to reflect features of modern bourgeois culture. His analysis of eating, for instance, quite closely echoes the type of interpretation offered by Lévi-Strauss. The dishes arranged on a menu are regarded as expressing basic opposi- tions – 'savoury'/'sweet', etc. – that are combined syntagmatically in the sequence that constitutes the meal.[43] However, Barthes prop- osed that a mythology of modern society has to incorporate a critical stance, thus partly recovering the meaning of myth as 'false con- sciousness' from which Lévi-Strauss dissociated himself. There are two principal respects, according to Barthes, in which myth can be shown to act to conceal a system of class domination in contempor- ary capitalism. One is that, in myth, what are expressions of definite social forms become represented as natural and 'inevitable' occurr- ences; the other is that myth eclipses the conditions of its produc- tion.

In these points there is already a reversal of the characteristic emphases of Lévi-Strauss, and a movement away from structure towards structuration as an active historical process. As continued and radicalised further by Barthes, Derrida and the 'Left Heideggerians' of the *Tel Quel* group, this trend of thought is both highly critical of the structuralism of Saussure and Lévi-Strauss and yet at the same time a continuation of it. Lévi-Strauss adopted from Saussure a version of the *langue/parole* differentiation, reformulated as a distinction between code and message. The other authors mentioned above, however, are much more concerned with the relation of signifier and signified as elements of signification.

At first sight Lévi-Strauss and Heidegger appear as quite alien to one another, and it might seem as if there is a complete break in continuity marked by Derrida's interest in the second thinker. However there are certain overall – although admittedly distant – similarities between the views of Lévi-Strauss and Heidegger. Lévi-Strauss's belief that the concept of 'man', as distinct from 'nature', is a creation of European culture subsequent to the Renaissance, and his distancing from notions of 'self' and 'consciousness', have some resemblance to Heidegger's attempt to break with traditional views of philosophy as anchored in the knowing subject. Lévi-Strauss's 'Being' is not that of Heidegger, but the assertion of the former that the objective of structural anthropology is 'to understand Being in relation to itself, and not in relation to oneself'[44] has a certain loose affinity with the standpoint developed by Heidegger. For Heidegger, 'language speaks', and human subjectivity is constituted through the pre-given categories of language; for Lévi-Strauss 'Les mythes se pensent dans les hommes, et à leur insu'.[45]

What has been called by one commentator (Jameson) the 'most scandalous aspect of structuralism', its aggressive anti-humanism, represents, not the denial of subjectivity, but a demand for an account of its origins. In Lévi-Strauss, following the 'geological' analogy, such an account progresses no further than the attempt to disclose the operation of unconscious elements that govern cognition. The subject is recovered in the analysis only as a set of structural transformations, not as an historically located actor. Structural analysis in this conception is limited to a deciphering process. In a sense, this culminates in the same sort of dilemma as Husserl's transcendental phenomenology, save that the perspective is reversed. Husserl, having bracketed intersubjectivity in order to uncover the categories of knowledge in the ego, was unable satisfactorily to reconstitute it phenomenologically. Lévi-Strauss, having placed an *epoché* upon reflexive consciousness and history, so as to uncover unconscious structures, appears unable conceptually to retrieve the purposive subject – even as regards his own work, which is portrayed as the encounter of abstract categories of mind. Lévi-Strauss's critique of humanism thus remains undeveloped, as compared with that of Althusser, Foucault and Derrida, all of whom however refuse the appellation 'structuralist'.

In emphasising the 'structuring of structure',[46] as a continual process of production, Derrida breaks in a radical way both with Saussure's distinctions between *langue* and *parole* and between synchrony and diachrony. His concern with the signifier/signified relation, and with difference, still connects back to Saussure, but necessarily in altered form. The decisive contribution of Saussure's linguistics, according to Derrida, was to show, against previously established philosophical traditions, the inseparability of signifier from signified: that they are 'two sides of one and the same production'.[47] Saussure was not able to pursue the full implications of this, because he still retained the established notion of the sign, treating the signified as a determinate 'idea' or a 'meaning' fixed by the conjunction of word and thought. He thus left open the possibility that the signified could exist as the 'pure concept' or 'pure thought', independent of the signifier, much as idealist philosophers have traditionally argued. It is important to see that Derrida's critique of the 'metaphysics of presence' underlies his attack upon 'logocentricism' and his advocacy of the significance of writing, rather than vice versa. The integral fusion of signifier and signified entails that no philosophies which retain an attachment to 'transcendental signifieds' can be sustained; meaning is created only by the play of difference in the process of signification. 'Writing', as Derrida uses the term, does not refer to a script as such, to the physical 'presence' of inscriptions on a page, but *to the spacing inherent, in his view at any rate, in the notion of difference*. Difference, as articulated in a process of either speaking or reading, presumes a 'spatial' dimension which is also simultaneously a 'temporal' one, involved in the linearity of syntagmatic relations. 'Space', Derrida says, 'is "in" time; it is time's pure leaving-itself; it is the "outside-itself" as the self-relation of time.'[48]

Derrida's work can thus be seen as giving a new impetus to Saussure's formalism at the same time as it disavows the connection of that formalism with *langue* and synchrony: substance, or the 'concrete', is repudiated both on the plane of the sign (rejection of the 'transcendental signified'), and on that of the referent (an objectively given world that can be 'captured' by the concept). For each of these, which may be said to approximate respectively to idealism and positivism, Derrida substitutes the productivity of chains of signification. Like Heidegger, Derrida has to regard himself as within traditions of Western metaphysics which he tries also to step outside; hence his proclivity, like that of Heidegger, for terminological innovation which displays a distance from established categories of language. '*Différance*' indicates that difference involves an integration of the 'spatial' and the 'temporal' that I mentioned previously: to differ is to defer. Once the synchronic/diachronic contrast is abandoned, difference is recognised to exist only within the temporal process of deferring, the continual loss of the present to future and to past. Structuralism here comes face to face with its apparent adversary, historicism, and adopts it: the concepts that Derrida operates with are placed 'under erasure' to indicate the constant process of mutation which all signification implies.

The present, once grasped, is past: hence, for Derrida, signification only operates through the 'trace', the moment of difference that occurs within a signifying chain. The 'a' of *différance* – in French, at any rate – is not heard; it remains silent, Derrida points out, 'like a tomb'.[49] *Différance* is not a word or a concept, but the play of negation; it is *not*, has no existence, no 'being present'. All signs, and all texts, include traces of others.

> This chaining process means that each 'element' – phoneme or grapheme – is constituted from the trace which it carries in itself of other elements of the chain or the system ... There are only differences from differences and traces of traces ... *Différance* is thus a structure and a movement which can only be grasped in relation to the opposition of presence/absence. *Différance* is the systematic play of differences, of traces of differences, of the *spacing* whereby elements are connected to one-another.[50]

This is not, however, a recovery of history, any more than it is the case in Heidegger's philosophy. Derrida retains the view – which even if it is at odds with it, still has a resonance of Lévi-Strauss's conception – that 'history' is a metaphysic, and contains within it 'the motivation of an ultimate repression of difference'.[51] The identification of sequences of events of a determinate character remains wedded to a metaphysics of presence. For Derrida, art and the text are machines not for the suppression of time, but for its expression. The historicity of a work of art does not lie in the events, or their traces, which led up to its creation, but in the play of differences which are endlessly reinterpreted. A text, like writing more generally, displays most strikingly what would be called in another tradition the 'hermeneutic autonomy' of the object.

If a partial *rapprochement* between phenomenology, in its Heideggerian form, and structuralism has been attempted in the work of Derrida, another point of contact between the two philosophical traditions is also to be found in the writings of Kristeva, who has drawn upon Husserl. (Derrida has also written extensively, although critically, on Husserl.) Kristeva, like others associated with the *Tel Quel* group, is interested primarily in the theory of literature as productivity, but regards as one of her main objectives a reincorporation of the speaker within structuralist theory: 'One phase of semiology', she accepts, 'is now over: that which extends from Saussure and Peirce to the Prague School and structuralism . . . A critique of this "semiology of systems", and of its phenomenological foundations, can only be made if it begins from a theory of meaning, which must necessarily be a theory of the speaking subject.'[52]

This is still a 'de-centred' subject, explicitly contrasted to the Cartesian *cogito*, and Kristeva does not accept the main features of Husserl's phenomenological programme. However, according to Kristeva, Husserl's concept of intentionality, suitably modified, allows us to relate the signifier/signified differentiation to a theory of consciousness, by treating consciousness as made up of object – constituting mental acts. Consciousness, in other words, is not an amorphous 'substance', but is the predicative activity of a 'positioned' subject. However, the capacity of the subject to engage in such activity is not to be explicated through a phenomenological reduction, as in Husserl, but via the mastery of language: and we have to replace Husserl's abstract transcendental ego with a genetic account of the development of conscious identity as interdependent with, and reflecting the fractured nature of, the unconscious. Thus she emphasises 'the fundamental divergence that separates the phenomenological "lived experience" and its "impulses" from the productive and/or destructive Freudian semiotic impulses which are *prior* to the distinction between "subject" and "object"'.[53]

In pursuing the latter theme, Kristeva leans heavily upon Lacan's interpretations of psychoanalytic theory, as yielding an account of the 'production of the subject'. The psychoanalytic theory of psychic development connects the emergence of the 'I' with the entry of the child into signification, and thus with the signifier/signified relation. What Husserl called the 'thetic', and took to be an inherent property of mind, Kristeva treats as a stage in the development of the child: it is the stage at which the subject/object split becomes installed. The detachment of basic drives from the mother onto 'outside' objects coincides with the capacity of the child to distinguish itself symbolically as an 'I' from potential predicates. This is therefore at the same time the moment of signification, in which the sign becomes installed in place of a real relation. The child enters simultaneously into the twin dimensions of signification, the paradigmatic and syntagmatic, the first being structured about the symbolic relation 'speaking subject/outside', the second about that of 'subject/predicate'.[54]

Spacing, abstract and practical: Derrida and Wittgenstein

In this section I propose to draw some contrasts between Derrida's views and those of the later Wittgenstein, suggesting that Wittgenstein's philosophy helps illuminate some of the weaknesses which Derrida's standpoint shares with structuralist thought as a whole. Derrida's critique of the metaphysics of presence, and even his technique of deconstruction, can be seen to have important features in common with Wittgenstein's later philosophy. Both philosophers reject the view that meaning or the signified is an event, idea or mental process that in some way accompanies speech.

Différance is not an alien conception to Wittgensteinian philosophy: it could be said that for Wittgenstein meaning is created and sustained by the play of difference 'in use'. Now of course one should not exaggerate the similarities between Wittgenstein and Derrida on this point. Wittgenstein did not, as Derrida does, develop an explicit notion of difference as negation. Wittgenstein would not agree with Saussure that language is a system 'without positive terms'. But language to Wittgenstein is a system of differences in the sense that the meanings of words are not constituted through the nature of utterances or marks as isolated items, but only through the ways in which they acquire an identity through their differentiation as elements of language-games. Wittgenstein gives a good deal of emphasis, like Derrida, to *repetition* in the sustaining of linguistic identity. Wittgenstein's interpretation of language is not, as many commentators tend to present it, an a-temporal one; on the contrary, time is integral to it.[55] The meanings of terms *are never 'present' in their utterance or enunciation*, and 'exist' only in the continual process of their actualisation within forms of life: difference here is always also deferment, as it is for Derrida. According to Wittgenstein, much as Derrida argues, the traditional concerns of Western metaphysics have been bound up with the pursuit of illusory essences, the search to encompass the 'plenitude of the sign'. Signs do not express pre-formed meanings or concepts; words or utterances do not 'contain' ideas.

But the routes each then takes away from the metaphysical preoccupations of Western philosophy diverge. Wittgenstein's aphorism that such preoccupations arise when 'language goes on holiday' is not so much an argument against the misuse of words, as an emphasis upon the inevitable interweaving of language and the practical conduct of social life. I think one can argue that we can discover here one of the main continuities, and at the same time a basic contrast, between the work of Wittgenstein's early and later periods: in the coexistence of language with 'what cannot be said'. In the *Tractatus*, 'that whereof we cannot speak' appears as an abrupt finale, a blank void which looms when we have exhausted the logical elucidation of language. Now one way of reading the transition between Wittgenstein's earlier and later philosophies is to suggest that Wittgenstein came to the view that the 'limits of language' do not have to be consigned to such a void. Language is still seen to be intimately dependent upon the non-linguistic, or what cannot be put into words, 'what cannot be said'. But what cannot be said is no longer a mysterious metaphysic, that cannot even be talked *about*. What cannot be said is, on the contrary, prosaic and mundane. It is what has to be *done*: the meanings of linguistic items are intrinsically involved with the *practices that comprise forms of life*. This is a move of major significance, in my judgement, as compared to the orientation characteristic of structuralism, *in which 'that which cannot be said' is characteristically identified with the unconscious or, in Derrida, with writing.* It provides the main source of the following critical objections that can be made against Derrida's views.

1. A critique of Derrida cannot be most profitably approached via a reassertion of the priority of the spoken word over the written,[56] since Derrida does not use 'writing' in the ordinary sense. The thesis that writing is more fundamental to language than speaking, Derrida makes clear,[57] does not depend upon the proposition that the spoken word is an ephemeral event, while the text has a greater permanence. It depends upon the proposal that writing expresses *différance*, the spacing that alone makes the utterance possible. *Différance* is that which cannot be said, since it precedes and lends form to the act of speaking – or to that of the inscription of marks on paper. But here the prejudices of Saussurian linguistics return to haunt their critic: the spacing of Derrida's 'writing' derives only from the injection of the temporal into the spacing of the formal differences of *langue*.[58] *Différance* is *langue* interpreted as structuration; it does not reconnect, as Wittgenstein's analysis reconnects, what cannot be said with what has to be done. Derrida's *différance* acknowledges only the spacing of the signifier. Language is a 'situated product' only in the juxtaposition of the mark and traces of marks. For Wittgenstein, on the other hand, language is a situated product involved in the temporal, material and social spacing of language-games – or so I want to interpret Wittgenstein here.

2. In Derrida, as in other structuralist writers, the distinction between signifier and signified replaces that between meaning and reference which is prominent in Wittgenstein. The major limitation in virtually all structuralist thought is that it carries over – and compounds – the flaws inherent in Saussure's treatment of the signified, as deriving from the arbitrariness of the sign. Saussure employed the notion of the arbitrary character of the sign so as to create a gulf between sign and referent, the result of which, however, as I have stated, is that 'signified' sometimes means 'idea', 'concept' or 'thought', sometimes the referent or object. The connection between word and object is not to be found in any feature that the signifier shares with the object, including ostensive reference. Now the later Wittgenstein, of course, also rejects any notion that the nature of linguistic terms can be explicated either in terms of 'corresponding' features of the object-world, or in terms of

ostensive reference. But the Wittgensteinian identification of that which cannot be said as the *practical organisation of social life* entails that this rejection does not lead in the direction of an attempted retreat *from the object to the idea.* Whatever the obscurities that may be involved in the account of reference that is implied in the later Wittgenstein's philosophy, it is clear that, for Wittgenstein, to know a language is to have knowledge of an object-world as a relation of practice.[59] To know a language is to be able to participate in the forms of life within which it is expressed, and which it expresses. Wittgenstein's discussion of 'social spacing' as the origin of signification opens out to the conjunction of *langue* and *langage* (rather than just *parole*) in a way in which structuralism does not – offering, indeed necessitating, a bridging of the analysis of language and hermeneutics. For the 'spacing' of language appears in the organisation of differing social practices, not in the abstract order of the signifier/signified relation. Hermeneutics, or *problems of the mediation of language-games as semantic orders*, are as basic to the Wittgensteinian conception as the notion of the constitution of meaning within the relational systems of forms of life.

If Quine and Davidson are right, there may be a closer tie between meaning and reference than Wittgenstein was apparently prepared to acknowledge,[60] but this is not really relevant to the argument at this point. The retreat from reference on the part of structuralist thought has proved to be as incapable of repair within the language of structuralism itself, as the recovery of intersubjectivity was for Husserl in the transcendental phenomenological reduction. Nowhere is this clearer than in Derrida. Writing is purified structuration, bereft of any possibility of the recovery of context or of the semantic. The 'deconstruction' of texts is supposed to demonstrate their character as productivity, but such production turns out to be nothing more than the play of 'pure difference'. Writing, in Derrida's formulation, breaks with everything that might relate a text to an object-world: the 'horizon of communication as communication of consciousness'; the 'semantic or hermeneutic horizons . . . as . . . horizons of meaning'; and 'the concept of context'. This break is declared to follow from the spacing that 'constitutes the written sign' – held 'to be found in all language'.[61]

3. The identity that permits difference is thus quite explicitly taken by Derrida to derive from the constitution of codes themselves,

whether inscribed or spoken. The internal identity of codes is what separates them from any connotation of reference. But this reiterates, in a new guise, the problem that arose in respect of Saussure's attempt to constitute difference as pure form. Derrida seems not to notice, or chooses to ignore, that even to mention the identity of a code presumes some component of reference: *that which designates the elements of the code as belonging together*, as being 'vocalisations', 'marks', etc. The argument that codes or writing are constituted by their 'internal identity' is used by Derrida to dismiss the relevance of reference altogether. The spacing of writing makes for its endless repeatability and 'dissemination': 'the unity of the signifying form only constitutes itself by virtue of its iterability, by the possibility of its being repeated in the absence ... of its "referent" '.[62]

This appears to assimilate the lack of a referent 'present' at the time of an utterance with the absence of any connotation of reference at all as involved with the 'signifying form'.[63] The two are obviously not the same. Reference stubbornly intervenes even in the most formal identification of codes of spacing themselves. If this can be forgotten, or left out of account, it is because of the persistent assimilation which writers influenced by Saussurian concepts have made between referent and signified. This was presaged, as I have already noted, by Saussure's own tendency to merge the two, as a result of the impetus provided by the doctrine of the arbitrariness of the sign.

4. Derrida's denunciation of the 'presence' of the idea as the essence of signification leads him to retreat from the signified as far as possible, into the signifier. He does not take the more radical step of rejecting the signifier/signified distinction altogether. If Wittgenstein's account of meaning is along the right lines, however, the signifier/signified distinction must be discarded. For the nature of language, and of meaning more generally, cannot be explicated in terms of a twofold notion of this sort. The problem – which as I have tried to indicate, can be traced right through from Saussure – does not concern the signifier. One of the most important and illuminating contributions from the structuralist literature has been to demonstrate that any type of material form can participate in semiosis, that is, can 'carry' meaning. The problem concerns the signified. The 'withdrawal from the object' into the internal play of differ-

ence, which Saussure initiated, cannot be accomplished; hence the nature of the signified has either been left in obscurity, or the term has been used ambiguously to include both concept and object signified. For Wittgenstein, signifier, concept and object signified are to be explicated in terms of their incorporation within the practices which compose forms of life. 'Don't look for the meaning, look for the use' does not imply that meaning and use are synonymous, but that the sense of linguistic items can only be sought in the practices which they express and in which they are expressed.

The de-centring of the subject

Rejection of the signifier/signified distinction has immediate implications for the critical assessment of Lacan's 'structuralist reading' of psychoanalysis, which has strongly influenced the latter-day development of the 'theory of the subject' within structuralist philosophies. I shall address these implications directly elsewhere, and shall consider here only general themes related to the 'de-centring of the subject'.

The 'scandalous' rejection of humanism characteristic of the structuralist literature has its origins in a mistrust of consciousness or 'subjectivity'. This was presaged in Saussure's formulation of the priority of *langue* over the individual, subjective character of *parole*. To this we must add the impact of Marx, Nietzsche and Freud as radical critics of the claims of the Cartesian *cogito*: each can be seen as questioning, in a profound way, the reliability of consciousness as 'transparent to itself'. The structuralists' demystification of the claims of consciousness is dominated by the thesis that subjectivity is constituted in and through language. As Ricoeur puts it, 'the pure act of the *cogito* is empty, and remains to be mediated by the world of signs and the interpretation of those signs'.[64] The implications of such a standpoint are several, and important. Instead of taking consciousness as a given, it stresses the need for a genetic account of its production; consciousness is not regarded as a unitary or indivisible substance, but as a fractured and fragile set of processes; and the constitution of the 'I' is acknowledged to come about only through the 'discourse of the Other', that is through signification.

These notions are developed in an interesting way in Kristeva's work, which departs quite substantially from the emphases of either

Lévi-Strauss or Derrida. Both in the mode in which she utilises a phenomenological treatment of intentional consciousness, and in her interpretation of the 'positioning of the subject', she moves away from earlier versions of structuralism. But even in her writings we do not find an adequate analysis of human agency in the sense in which that term is normally understood by Anglo-Saxon philosophers of action. Her 'predicating subject' is still not far removed from the unconscious/conscious dualism, conceived above all as a linguistic relation, that dominates structuralist theories of the subject. Such theories have usually tended to retain elements of the Cartesianism they have sought to reject: the 'I think' is shown to express linguistic structures that precede or underlie the self-consciousness or reflexive capacities of the subject. As Lacan expresses it: 'the S [signifier] and the s [signified] of the Saussurian algorithm are not on the same level, and man only deludes himself when he believes his true place is at their axis, which is nowhere.'[65] But subjectivity here appears only as a series of moments brought about by the intersection of signifying structures. The reflexive, acting subject is but dimly recovered in such an analysis.

In criticising Searle's theory of speech acts, in conformity with her general standpoint, Kristeva argues that speech acts 'should be seen as signifying practices', and interpreted within 'a general theory of signifying activity'.[66] But replacing the notion of 'act' with that of 'practice' is specious if the analysis does not at the same time incorporate the emphasis that speech-act theory shares with Wittgenstein's view. *There are no signifying practices; signification should rather be understood as an integral element of social practices in general.*

We must actually repudiate the *cogito* in a more thoroughgoing way than Kristeva does, while acknowledging the vital importance of the theme that being precedes the subject–object relation in consciousness. The route to understanding this is not to be found through a sort of reconstituted *cogito*, but through the connection of *being and action*.

It is relevant to sketch in at this point the general outlines of a theory of the acting subject that is developed in much more detail in the following paper. This view depends upon stressing the importance of the 'reflexive monitoring of conduct' as a chronic feature of the enactment of social life. In this conception, reasons and intentions are not definite 'presences' which lurk behind human social activity, but are routinely and chronically (in the *durée* of day-to-day existence) instantiated in that activity.[67] The intentional character of human actions is: (a) not to be seen as an articulation of discrete and separate 'intentions', but a continuous flow of intentionality in time; and (b) not to be treated as a set of conscious states that in some way 'accompany' action. Only in the reflexive act of attention are intentions consciously articulated: normally within discourse.[68] The reflexive monitoring of action draws upon 'tacit knowledge' which, however, can only partially and imperfectly be expressed in discourse. Such knowledge, which is above all practical and contextual in character, is not unconscious in any of the senses in which that term is usually employed in the structuralist literature. *Language appears here as a medium of social practice*; the practical nature of 'stocks of knowledge' is well emphasised both by Schutz and Wittgenstein. The stocks of knowledge applied in the production and reproduction of social life as a skilled activity are largely 'unconscious' in so far as social actors can normally only offer a fragmentary account of what they 'know' if called upon to do so; but they are not unconscious in the sense given to that term by structuralist writers.

The significance of the reflexive monitoring of action against a background of tacit knowledge – phenomena at the core of all day-to-day social activity, but alien territory to structuralism – is well pointed up by Bourdieu's discussion of the gift relationship, alluded to earlier. It is only if one succumbs to what might be called a *genetic sociological fallacy* that an account of human agency appears as incompatible with the unconscious in the Freudian sense. The fallacy is to assume that, because the subject, and self-consciousness, are constituted through a process of development – and thus that the reflexive actor is not a 'given' either to philosophy or to social science – they are merely epiphenomena of hidden structures. The de-centring of the subject is quite as noxious as the philosophies of consciousness which are attacked if it merely substitutes a structural determination for subjectivity.

Texts

One of the major emphases that structuralism shares with hermeneutic phenomenology[69] is the insistence that a gulf divides the

text, as a particular articulation of language, from whatever intentions an author may have had in writing it. In Lévi-Strauss, mythology is regarded as peculiarly apposite to structural analysis because
myths 'have no author', and 'exist only as they are incarnated in a
tradition'.[70] Derrida specifically associates the autonomy of the text
with the separation of 'writing' from 'communication', and thereby
from its author; the supposition that knowledge of the author can in
any significant way illuminate the meanings generated by the text is
dismissed as another example of the metaphysics of presence.[71] The
interpretation of a text, the *Tel Quel* group emphasises, cannot be
treated as the identification of a core of meaning supplied by its
author, which relates that meaning to the 'con-text' of its creation.
There is no reading of a text, but only readings, the result of the
inherent productivity of writing or, in Derrida's words, 'its essential
drift'.

The relevance of authors' intentions to the interpretation of texts,
and more broadly to the interpretation of meaning, has of course
been much discussed in various disciplines, ranging from literary
criticism to the history of ideas.[72] I do not want to consider here the
problem of the role authors' intentions may play in validating
critical interpretations of texts. I want rather to take issue with the
conceptualisation of intentional activity that has been presumed in
such literature. Much of this literature must, from this regard, be
deemed obsolete in the light of the Wittgensteinian critique of
traditional notions about the purposive character of human action.
Intentions or purposes have been regarded, in other words, as
discrete mental events that are in some way correlated with the
creation of texts. It is important to see that Wittgenstein's rejection
of this view also extends to another element of the 'metaphysics of
presence' that Derrida also repudiates: the existence of a finite set
of 'rules of interpretation' governing interpretations of meaning.
The 'rule-following' which Wittgenstein identifies designates practices which express the recursive character of social life, and which
are constituted only in and through those practices; such rules are
therefore never fixed or given presences.

It is just through this recursiveness that we can grasp the nature of
social practices as in a continual process of production and reproduction. Social practices from this standpoint do not 'express' the
intentions of social actors; nor on the other hand do they 'determine' them. *Intentions are only constituted within the reflexive*

monitoring of action, which however in turn only operates in conjunction with unacknowledged conditions and outcomes of action. (For fuller discussion, see below, pp. 56–9.) From this point of view we can begin to recover the text, not just as involving the inherent productivity of language, but as itself a situated production, without on the other hand denying the 'autonomy of the text'. Structuralism *has not generated accounts of the interpretative work that is presumed in the everyday constitution of intersubjectivity.* A concentration upon the internal structuring of the text, stripped of referential components, replaces the participatory and practical interpolation of meaning within the conduct of language-games. Hence intersubjectivity is drawn upon in an unacknowledged way, tacitly presumed by textual analysis, but not theorised. This is undoubtedly in some part simply because of the central place which the text has assumed in structuralist thought: or rather, a particular type of conception of texts 'con-structed' as relational forms, separated from what Husserl called 'the naive intersubjectivity which is the unarticulated basis of the life-world'.

It should be noted that the view I am proposing is not identical to the conception of 'literary competence' suggested by Culler in criticising structuralism. Culler proposes that literary competence can be seen as consisting of tacit 'sets of conventions for reading literary texts', and as a 'rule-governed process of producing meanings'.[73] We can certainly accept, with Culler, that authors and readers bring more to a text than their knowledge of a language. They bring knowledge of a variety of social conventions: or, more accurately put, their very knowledge of language is inseparable from the social practices in the context of which language is constituted and reconstituted. However knowledge cannot be grasped simply as a rule-like semantics. Culler's proposal amounts to a sort of ethno-semantics of the reading of literary texts, if 'ethno-semantics' is understood in the manner of Goodenough and Lounsbury.[74] According to Goodenough, the task of ethno-semantics is to elucidate the content of culture, where 'a society's culture consists of whatever it is one has to know or believe in order to operate in a manner acceptable to its members'; and where this knowledge is explicated as definite sets of statable rules.[75] But to complement the typical structuralist emphasis upon the primacy of the semiotic with an accentuation of the importance of semantic rules is not satisfactory unless we attempt also to comprehend *the meshing of rules and practices in day-to-day activities.* This demands acknowledging the significance of 'ethno-methods' as the means whereby accountability is sustained: ethno-methods that are tacitly relied upon by every structuralist theorist of the text who, no matter what he or she might argue about texts that are subject to analysis or 'de-construction', still supposes that the text in which those arguments are expressed is intelligible to an indefinite audience.

Let me summarise the main elements of my view.

1. The production of a text, like the production of a social practice, is not the outcome of an 'intention', or an 'aggregate of intentions'. Rather, the intentional character of the activities concerned has to be treated as a chronic feature of the reflexive monitoring of action. A text is therefore not to be regarded as a 'fixed form', which is then somehow related *en bloc* to particular intentions; it should be studied as the concrete medium and outcome of a process of production, reflexively monitored by its author or reader.

2. Inquiry into the process of production of a text has to investigate the whole range of what I call in the following paper the 'rationalisation of action':[76] not merely its intentional component, but the reasons and motives that are involved in that production as a skilled accomplishment. The 'knowledge' that is thereby drawn upon by an author will be largely tacit and practical in character: mastery of a certain style, awareness of particular features of an expected or potential audience, etc. Moreover, this leaves a large conceptual space for the operations of the unconscious.

It follows from my earlier arguments that the distinction Kristeva makes between 'pheno-text' and 'geno-text' is not, as it stands, an adequate basis for understanding these phenomena. Her identification of the *chora* that is at the origins of semiosis seems valuable, but intervening between the subterranean 'operations' of the unconscious and the pheno-text are the constituting features of practical consciousness.[77]

3. All this bears upon what an 'author' *is*, as an acting subject. An author is neither a bundle of intentions, nor on the other hand a series of 'traces' somehow deposited within the text. Foucault says that writing 'is primarily concerned with creating an opening where the writing subject endlessly disappears'.[78] But to study the production of the text is at the same time in a definite sense to study the production of its author. The author is not simply 'subject' and the

text 'object'; the 'author' helps constitute him- or herself through the text, via the very process of production of that text. The importance of this is easily seen if we contrast the emergence of the 'personalised' author of the modern novel or poem with the 'anonymous' authors of myth or of medieval legend.

4. To argue that texts can be illuminatingly studied as situated productions is to insist that there are connections between the two ways in which 'meaning' is ordinarily employed in English: what someone means to say, write or do, and what that which is said, written or done means.[79] But this does not imply a return to a form of subjectivism. One of the main tasks of the study of the text, or indeed cultural products of any kind, must be precisely to examine the divergencies which can become instituted between the circumstances of their production, and the meanings sustained by their subsequent escape from the horizons of their creator or creators. These meanings are never 'contained' in the text as such, but are enmeshed in the flux of social life in the same way as its initial production was. Consideration of the 'autonomy' of the text, or the escape of its meaning from what its author originally meant, helps reunite problems of textual interpretation with broader issues of social theory. For in the enactment of social practices more generally, *the consequences of actions chronically escape their initiators' intentions in processes of objectification.*

The foregoing considerations allow us to take a position in respect of current rhetoric about the disappearance of the subject, or the 'end of the individual'. The pressing task facing social theory today is not to further the conceptual elimination of the subject, but on the contrary to promote *a recovery of the subject* without lapsing into subjectivism.[80] Such a recovery, I wish to argue, involves a grasp of 'what cannot be said' (or thought) as *practice*. Advocacy of the need to complete the dissolution of the subject reads ironically when taken against the background of Anglo-American sociology which, with some exceptions (most notably, symbolic interactionism), has hitherto been dominated by positivism. For positivistic philosophies lack any account of the reflexive subject, just as they lack a theorisation of institutions and history. The 'I' of Cartesian philosophy does not even appear in positivism, as a result of its phenomenalist premises: one might point out that the most radical and thoroughgoing attempt to erase the subject is found, not in structuralism, or in Deleuze and Guattari's *Anti-Oedipe*, but in Mach's positivism. Failure to see this is reinforced by the tendency of structuralist authors to lump together the Cartesian *cogito*, the various forms of idealism, together with positivism or empiricism, as all forms of philosophy founded in the subject. In their endeavour to dissolve the subject, structuralism and positivism thus have an important element in common, and in the context of the social sciences in the English-speaking world it is all the more necessary to insist that the de-centring of the subject must not be made equivalent to its disappearance. Any form of social theory which merges the de-centring of the subject, as a philosophical tenet, with a propadeutic of the end of the individual as either a desirable or inevitable movement of contemporary social change, becomes subject to the charge of ideology that critics are so fond of levelling against structuralism. It is useful here to contrast Foucault with Adorno and Horkheimer. The end of the individual, perhaps, signals the final passing of the age of bourgeois liberalism: not however as a fruitful historical transition, but rather *as swamped by a spreading totalitarianism*. A critical appraisal of such a phenomenon is hardly possible if social theory succumbs to the very processes which it should be concerned to comprehend.

Structuralism: a résumé and a forward look

The importance of structuralist thought for contemporary social theory, I want to claim, consists primarily in certain major themes which it has helped to bring into prominence: themes whose further development, however, cannot be satisfactorily pursued from within structuralist premises, as I have identified them in this paper. There are altogether seven respects, I think, in which structuralist thought is of particular significance, especially when considered in the light of the typical preoccupations of Anglo-Saxon sociology. I shall outline these only cursorily here: but they inform all my concerns in the succeeding papers in this book.

First, structuralist theory *points to the significance of spacing through difference* in the constitution of both language and society. This is an emphasis involved, in varying ways, in the work of Saussure, Lévi-Strauss and Derrida. Derrida's conception of *différance* is of great interest to social theory. But Derridean *différance* is associated too closely with the spacing of writing; the conception of spacing that can be discerned in Wittgenstein is superior to this in referring to the involvement of language with social practices. Social practices occur not just as transformations of a virtual order of differences (Wittgenstein's rules), and differences in time (repetition), but also in *physical space*. I shall argue in the following paper that the theory of the structuration of social systems should be based upon this *threefold connotation of différance*.

Second, and closely associated with the first point, structuralist thought *attempts to incorporate a temporal dimension into the very centre of its analyses*. In Saussure this is found in the syntagmatic aspect of language, even if the pronounced division introduced by the separation of the synchronic from the diachronic severs this from processes of linguistic change. The syntagmatic/associative opposition is lacking in functionalism, which incorporates time only as diachrony or 'dynamics' (see pp. 210–14 below). Structuralist theory has been able to generate a concept of structuration via the overcoming of the synchronic/diachronic distinction in a way not open to functionalism.[81] We have to recognise the limitations of this. It has not led to a capacity to develop explanatory accounts of social change; and in Derrida, it eventuates in a form of historicism, that denies the possibility of history in its own name. In attempting to escape the 'metaphysics of presence' Derrida, like Heidegger, reaches a view which tends to exorcise historical explanation in the very acknowledgement that everything is chronically in a state of movement. In Lévi-Strauss, the notion that historical understanding is only one code among others also effectively prevents a recovery of that understanding as a means of explaining social change. Structuralist thought hence has not developed a 'self-understanding' of the conditions of its own production as an intellectual tradition, and is vulnerable to the sorts of attack it has frequently drawn from authors such as Lefebvre and Goldmann, for whom it is merely an ideology of advanced capitalism.[82]

Third, whatever objections might be made against Lévi-Strauss's interpretation of history, it contains some extremely valuable insights. As against historicism, which so radicalises historical mutation that it becomes impossible to escape from it – even in order to produce historical analyses – and which thus characteristically terminates in some or other form of relativism, Lévi-Strauss points out that *'distance in time' is in some important respects the same as 'ethnographic distance'*. Moreover, in emphasising the contrasts between those types of society which operate in 'reversible time' and which although 'surrounded by the substance of history ... try to remain impervious to it', as compared to those which 'turn it into the motive power of their development',[83] Lévi-Strauss helps to lay the ground for a theory of social reproduction.

Fourth, structuralist theory offers the possibility – not fully realised thus far – of formulating *a more satisfactory understanding of the social totality than that offered by its leading rival, functionalism.* According to the latter, society may be portrayed as a pattern of relations between 'parts' (individuals, groups, institutions). Saussure's structural linguistics, by contrast, suggests the notion that society, like language, should be regarded as a 'virtual system' with recursive properties. The elaboration of this point, however (or so I shall claim), demands a conceptual distinction that is found neither in structuralism nor in functionalism: a distinction between 'structure' and 'system'.

Fifth, we find in structuralism a move of major significance for social theory: *an attempt to transcend the subject/object dualism.* Although this is not unique to structuralist thought, and is approached from variant perspectives by hermeneutic phenomenology and in the philosophy of the later Wittgenstein, the structuralist authors have elaborated it most fully. We can acknowledge the importance of this contribution while still emphasising that little is gained if we merely replace subjectivism by some sort of objectivism. The subject/object dualism can only be satisfactorily repudiated if we acknowledge that this is not a dualism but a *duality*.

Sixth, the critique of humanism and the theme of the *de-centring of the subject* have to be approached with caution, but nevertheless are of essential importance to social theory. The de-centring of the subject implies an escape from those philosophical standpoints which have taken consciousness as either a given, or transparent to itself. This should not lead, however, to the disappearance of the reflexive components of human conduct, or to their treatment as some sort of epiphenomena of deeper structures. Reflexivity has to be reconstructed within the discourse of social theory not just in respect of the members of society whose conduct is the object of study, but also *in respect of social science itself as a form of human endeavour.*

Seventh, *structuralist theory has made permanent contributions towards the analysis of the production of cultural objects.* The further development of these contributions, however, and the accomplishment of the task of integrating semiotic studies more closely with other areas of social theory, demands abandoning most if not all the oppositions that have been taken over from Saussure: those of *langue/parole*, synchrony/diachrony and signifier/signified; and discarding the conception of the arbitrary character of the sign. In their place, we may expect to develop a theory of codes, and of code production,[84] grounded in a broader theory of social practice, and reconnected to hermeneutics.

2

Agency, Structure

The principal issue with which I shall be concerned in this paper is that of connecting a notion of human action with structural explanation in social analysis. The making of such a connection, I shall argue, demands the following: a theory of the human agent, or of the subject; an account of the conditions and consequences of action; and an interpretation of 'structure' as somehow embroiled in both those conditions and consequences.[1]

Theories of action versus institutional theories

'Action' and 'structure' normally appear in both the sociological and philosophical literature as antinomies. Broadly speaking, it would be true to say that those schools of thought which have been preoccupied with action have paid little attention to, or have found no way of coping with, conceptions of structural explanation or social causation; they have also failed to relate action theory to problems of institutional transformation. This is most obviously true of the Anglo-Saxon philosophy of action, both in its Wittgensteinian form and in versions less directly influenced by Wittgenstein. Notwithstanding the great interest of Wittgenstein's later philosophy for the social sciences in respect of the relations between language and *Praxis*, we rapidly come up against its limits in respect of the theorisation of institutions. Institutions certainly appear in Wittgensteinian philosophy, and in a rather fundamental way. For the transition from the ideas of the earlier Wittgenstein to the later is effectively one from nature to society: language and social convention are shown in the *Philosophical Investigations* to be inextricably intertwined, so that to explicate one is to explicate the other. But as expressed in forms of life, institutions are analysed only in so far as they form a consensual backdrop against which action is negotiated and its meanings formed. Wittgensteinian philosophy has not led towards any sort of concern with social change, with power relations, or with conflict in society. Other strands in the philosophy of action have operated at an even further distance from such issues, focusing attention almost exclusively upon the nature of reasons or intentions in human activity.[2]

Within more orthodox sociological traditions, symbolic interactionism has placed most emphasis upon regarding social life as an active accomplishment of purposive, knowledgeable actors; and it has also been associated with a definite 'theory of the subject', as formulated in Mead's account of the social origins of reflexive consciousness. But the 'social' in Mead's formulation is limited to familial figures and the 'generalised other'; Mead did not elaborate a conception of a differentiated society, nor any interpretation of social transformation. Much the same is the case with the subsequent evolution of this tradition, which has not successfully developed modes of institutional analysis. One of the results has been a partial accommodation between symbolic interactionism and functionalism in American sociology: the former is held to be a 'micro-sociology', dealing with small-scale 'interpersonal' relations, while more embracing 'macro-sociological' tasks are left to the latter.

Functionalism and structuralism are alike in according a priority to the object over the subject or, in some sense, to structure over action. Functionalist authors have normally thought of this in terms of 'emergent properties' of the totality, which not only separate its characteristics from those of its individual members, but cause it to exert a dominant influence over their conduct. The difficulties Durkheim experienced with this notion, in so far as his writings are regarded from the point of view of their connections with functionalism, rather than with structuralism, are well known. Durkheim wished to emphasise that the characteristics of the social whole are separate from those of individual agents, and accentuated various senses in which 'society' is external to its individual members: every person is born into an already constituted society, and every person is only one individual in a system of association involving many others. But neither in his earlier writings nor in his later works did Durkheim manage to conceptualise the external or objective character of society in a plausible fashion. Durkheim's earlier position is exemplified in *The Rules of Sociological Method*, and associated externality with constraint. Two errors can be discerned in this standpoint. It was a mistake to understand social constraint as similar to physical constraint, and it was a mistake to regard constraint at all as a criterion of the 'social' or the 'institutional'. Taken together, these led to a conception of subject and object which even Durkheim had to admit has serious deficiencies. Society becomes a kind of inhibiting environment in which actors move, and which makes its presence felt through the pressurising effects which condition their conduct. The analogies to which Durkheim appealed in order to illustrate the 'external power' of social facts in his earlier work are clearly deficient. He sometimes compared the properties of society, as contrasted with those of its members, to the combination of elements in nature. The association of oxygen and hydrogen to form water creates properties which are not those of its constituent elements, or derivable from them; the same holds true of the relation between society and its constituent actors.[3] But such an analogy only works for those very types of perspective Durkheim set out to criticise, such as utilitarian individualism. If individuals, as fully formed social beings, came together to create new social properties by the fact of their association, as in contract theories of society, the analogy might hold; to support Durkheim's case, it does not.

Subsequently Durkheim came to modify his notion of constraint, stressing the moral nature of social facts, and thereby separating physical constraint from the sorts of pressures exerted by society over its members. It is this 'later Durkheim' – who recognised that moral phenomena are both positively motivating as well as constraining in his original sense – who was the main inspiration for Parsons. Parsons's 'action frame of reference' is much more indebted to Durkheim than to the others whose work he claimed to have synthesised in *The Structure of Social Action*.[4] Parsons understands action in relation to what he calls 'voluntarism', and has sought to reconcile the latter with a recognition of the 'emergent properties' of social systems. The reconciliation is achieved through the influence of normative values on two levels: as elements of personality and as core components of society. As 'internalised' in personality, values provide the motives or need-dispositions which impel the conduct of the actor; while on the level of the social system, as institutionalised norms, values form a moral consensus that serves to integrate the totality. 'Voluntarism' here thus becomes largely reduced to making space in social theory for an account of motivation, connected via norms to the characteristics of social systems. The conduct of actors in society is treated as the outcome of a conjunction of social and psychological determinants, in which the former dominate the latter through the key influence attributed to normative elements. This effectively excludes certain essential components of the theory of action, as I shall conceptualise it later.[5]

The antimony I have just sketched in also figures prominently in Marxist philosophies. In some part this is traceable to the ambiguous content of Marx's own writings. The Hegelian inheritance in Marx, with its connotation of active consciousness and the coming-to-itself of the subject in history, mingles uneasily and in an unresolved way in Marx's works with an allegiance to a deterministic theory in which actors are propelled by historical laws. The distance between the Lukács of *History and Class Consciousness* and the Marxism of Althusser gives ample evidence of the widely discrepant readings which Marx's texts can engender; although a more apposite comparison, I shall suggest below, is perhaps made between Althusser's views and the phenomenological Marxism of Paci. It has been pointed out often enough that there are similarities between Parsons's functionalism and Althusser's version of Marxism. Such similarities are not difficult to discern: Parsons's theory of the internalisation of values has distinct parallels with Althusser's reworking of the notion of ideology; and the former's identification of the functional problems facing social systems resembles Althusser's conception of the regions that compose social formations – even if for one author the 'determination in the last instance' is cultural, for the other economic. But the most important similarity is surely that, while both systems of thought are concerned to overcome the subject–object dualism – Parsons via the action frame of reference and Althusser through his 'theoretical anti-humanism' – each reaches a position in which subject is controlled by object. Parsons's actors are cultural dopes, but Althusser's agents are structural dopes of even more stunning mediocrity. (For further discussion of Althusser on structural causality, see pp. 155–60.) The 'true subjects' of Althusser's *mise en scène*, as he candidly admits, are the 'places and functions' that agents occupy.[6]

Paci's project is diametrically opposed to that of Althusser in so far as he attempts to provide a reading of Marx informed primarily by the later writings of Husserl.[7] Paci's theme is precisely the alienation of human subjectivity within capitalism. Like Lukács, he concentrates a good deal of his attention upon problems of reification, or objectification-as-reification, and it must be considered one of the most important contributions of phenomenologically-informed types of Marxism that they pose the issue of reification as central to the critique of ideology: something which is impossible to accomplish in Althusser's scheme.[8] But Paci's work is largely concerned with radicalising Husserl's *Crisis of European Sciences* as a critique of the reifying character of technical reason. His basic position is closely tied to phenomenology, and is open to some of the objections that Althusser and others influenced by structuralism have quite legitimately levelled against such styles of thought.

These things having been said, Marx's writings still represent the most significant single fund of ideas that can be drawn upon in seeking to illuminate problems of agency and structure. Marx writes in the *Grundrisse* that every social item 'that has a fixed form' appears as merely 'a vanishing moment' in the movement of society. 'The conditions and objectifications of the process', he continues, 'are themselves equally moments of it, and its only subjects are individuals, but individuals in mutual relationships, which they equally reproduce and produce anew . . .'[9] These comments express exactly the standpoint I wish to elaborate in this paper.

Time, agency, practice

I shall argue here that, in social theory, the notions of action and structure *presuppose one another*, but that recognition of this dependence, which is a dialectical relation, necessitates a reworking both of a series of concepts linked to each of these terms, and of the terms themselves.

In this section I shall consider some issues concerning the theory of action, before attempting to connect agency with a conception of structural analysis. I shall draw upon the analytical philosophy of action, as developed by British and American philosophers over the past two decades. But I shall want to say that, as characteristically formulated by such writers, the philosophy of action has a number of notable *lacunae*. One, which I have already mentioned, is my main concern in what follows: the analytical philosophy of action lacks a theorisation of institutions. Two other considerations, I shall claim, are vital to such a theorisation. The first is the incorporation of *temporality* into the understanding of human agency; the second is the incorporation of *power* as integral to the constitution of social practices.

I regard as a fundamental theme of this paper, and of the whole of this book, that social theory *must acknowledge, as it has not done previously, time–space intersections as essentially involved in all social existence*. All social analysis must recognise (and itself takes place in) not just a double sense of *différance*, but a threefold one, as I have already indicated in a preliminary way in the previous paper. Social activity is always constituted in three intersecting moments of difference: temporally, paradigmatically (invoking structure which is present only in its instantiation) and spatially. All social practices are *situated* activities in each of these senses.

I shall take up problems of time–space relations in some detail in a subsequent paper in the book (see pp. 198–233). At this juncture I shall confine my attention to temporality ad problems of agency. No author has illuminated these problems as much as Heidegger. In surveying the claims of Kant's transcendentalism, Heidegger notes that the Kantian *a priori* implies the mutuality of time and being: that which makes the thing what it is 'pre-cedes' the thing. But the effect of Kant's philosophy is to translate the underlying theorem of Classical philosophy – that what is real is time and space – into the proposition that *appearances* are in time and space. Leibnitz's view is in this respect more satisfactory; Leibnitz held that we cannot treat time and space as receptacles 'containing' experience, because it is only possible to understand time and space in relation to objects and events: time and space are the modes in which objects and events 'are' or 'happen'. Similarly, for Heidegger *seiend* is a verb form: every existent is a be-ing that is temporal. As one commentator puts it: 'Being appears to us, in time, as the Becoming of the Possible . . . futurity comes into our ken in terms of possibilities . . . the question of time is transcendentally the ontology of the possible.'[10] What Heidegger appears to ignore – and it is this which makes strongly historicist readings of his work possible – is the necessary insertion of a paradigmatic dimension in time–space relations. In the approach to social theory developed below, I shall argue that time, space and 'virtual time–space' (or structure) – the threefold intersection of difference – are necessary to the constitution of the real. Or, to express the point in another way: the syntagmatic, which both differs and defers, necessitates the paradigmatic, although the latter is recursively dependent upon the former.

A. N. Whitehead says somewhere that 'What we perceive as the present is the vivid fringe of memory tinged with anticipation'. Heidegger stresses the link between *Andenken* (memory: literally, 'think-on') and *denken* (think) in holding that the experience of time is not that of a succession of nows, but the interpolation of memory and anticipation in the present-as-Being. Neither time nor the experience of time are aggregates of 'instants'. This emphasis is important for various reasons. One, which bears directly upon the treatment of action by analytical philosophers, concerns the conceptualisation of acts, intentions, purposes, reasons, etc. In ordinary English usage, we speak as if these were distinct unities or elements in some way aggregated or strung together in action. Most British and American philosophers of action have accepted this usage unquestioningly. In so doing they have unwittingly abstracted agency from its location in time, from the temporality of day-to-day conduct. What this literature ignores is the reflexive moment of attention, called into being in discourse, that breaks into the flow of action which constitutes the day-to-day activity of human subjects.[11] Such a moment is involved even in the constitution of 'an' action or of 'an act' from the *durée* of lived-through experience.[12]

'Action' or agency, as I use it, thus does not refer to a series of discrete acts combined together, but to *a continuous flow of conduct*. We may define action, if I may borrow a formulation from a previous work, as involving a 'stream of actual or contemplated causal interventions of corporeal beings in the ongoing process of events-in-the-world'.[13] Certain comments need to be made about this. First, the notion of action has reference to the activities of an agent, and cannot be examined apart from a broader theory of the acting self. It is necessary to insist upon this apparent tautology, because in a substantial part of the philosophical literature the nature of action is discussed primarily in relation to a contrast with 'movements': the characteristics of the actor as a subject remain unexplored or implicit.[14] The concept of agency as I advocate it here, involving 'intervention' in a potentially malleable object-world, relates directly to the more generalised notion of *Praxis*. I shall later treat regularised acts as *situated practices*, and shall regard this concept as expressing a major mode of connection between action theory and structural analysis. Second, it is a necessary feature of action that, at any point in time, the agent 'could have acted otherwise': either positively in terms of attempted intervention in the process of 'events in the world', or negatively in terms of forbearance. The sense of 'could have done otherwise' is obviously a difficult and complex one. It is not important o this paper to attempt to elaborate a detailed justification of it. It is a mistake, however, to suppose that the concept of action can be fully elucidated in this respect outside of the context of *historically located modes of activity*.[15]

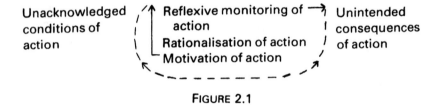

Unacknowledged conditions of action   Reflexive monitoring of action   Rationalisation of action   Motivation of action   Unintended consequences of action

FIGURE 2.1

Figure 2.1 portrays what could be regarded as a 'stratification model' of action: a model whose implications however cannot be properly worked out separately from the discussion of the properties of structure that I shall provide in a subsequent section. The reflexive monitoring of conduct refers to the intentional or purposive character of human behaviour: it emphasises 'intentionality' *as process*. Such intentionality is a routine feature of human conduct, and does not imply that actors have definite goals consciously held in mind during the course of their activities. That the latter is unusual, in fact, is indicated in ordinary English usage by the distinction between meaning or intending to do something, and doing something 'purposefully', the latter implying an uncommon degree of mental application given to the pursuit of an aim.[16] When lay actors inquire about each other's intentions in respect of particular acts, they abstract from a continuing process of routine monitoring whereby they relate their activity to one another and to the object-world. The distinctive feature about the reflexive monitoring of human actors, as compared to the behaviour of animals, is what Garfinkel calls the accountability of human action. I take 'accountability' to mean that the accounts that actors are able to offer of their conduct draw upon the same stocks of knowledge as are drawn upon in the very production and reproduction of their action. As Harré expresses this, 'the very same social knowledge and skill is involved in the genesis of action and accounts . . . an individual's ability to do each depends upon his stock of social knowledge'.[17] But we must make an important emendation to the point of view Harré appears to take. The 'giving of accounts' refers to the *discursive* capabilities and inclinations of actors, and does not exhaust the connections between 'stocks of knowledge' and action. The factor missing from Harré's characterisation is *practical consciousness*: tacit knowledge that is skilfully applied in the enactment of courses of conduct, but which the actor is not able to formulate discursively.

The reflexive monitoring of behaviour operates against the background of the rationalisation of action – by which I mean the capabilities of human agents to 'explain' why they act as they do by giving reasons for their conduct – and in the more 'inclusive' context of practical consciousness. Like 'intentions', 'reasons' only form discrete accounts in the context of queries, whether initiated by others, or as elements of a process of self-examination by the actor. It is very important to emphasise that the reflexive monitoring of action includes the monitoring of *the setting of interaction*, and not just the behaviour of the particular actors taken separately. This is shown by Garfinkel to be a basic feature of the ethno-methods involved in the day-to-day constitution of social interaction.[18] The rationalisation of action, as a chronic feature of daily conduct, is a normal characteristic of the behaviour of competent social agents, and is indeed the main basis upon which their 'competence' is adjudged by others. This does not mean that reasons can be linked as directly with norms or conventions as some philosophers have claimed or implied. Reasons do not just include the citing of or the appeal to norms: to suppose that such is the case actually draws the philosophy of action back towards the Parsonian action frame of reference, since conduct then becomes driven by 'internalised' normative imperatives.[19]

The reasons actors supply discursively for their conduct in the course of practical queries, in the context of daily social life, stand in a relation of some tension to the rationalisation of action as actually embodied within the stream of conduct of the agent. The least interesting or consequential aspect of this concerns the possibilities of deliberate dissimulation that exist: where an actor claims to have acted for reasons that he was not in fact guided by. More important are the grey areas of practical consciousness that exist in the relation between the rationalisation of action and actors' stocks of knowledge; and between the rationalisation of action and the unconscious. The stocks of knowledge, in Schutz's terms, or what I call the *mutual knowledge* employed by actors in the production of social encounters, are not usually known to those actors in an explicitly codified form; the practical character of such knowledge conforms to the Wittgensteinian formulation of knowing a rule. The accounts actors are able to provide of their reasons are bounded, or subject to various degrees of possible articulation, in respect of tacitly employed mutual knowledge.[20] The giving of reasons in day-to-day activity, which is closely associated with the moral accountability of action, is inevitably caught up in, and expressive of, the demands and the conflicts entailed within social encounters. But the articulation of accounts as reasons is also influenced by unconscious elements of motivation. This involves possibilities of rationalisation in the Freudian sense, as the dislocating effects of the unconscious upon conscious processes of rational accounting.

Motivational components of action, which I take to refer to the organisation of an actor's wants, straddle conscious and unconscious aspects of cognition and emotion. The whole weight of psychoanalytic theory suggests that motivation has an internal hierarchy of its own. I shall argue in a subsequent paper that a conception of the unconscious is essential to social theory, even if the resultant schema I shall develop departs in some ways from classical Freudian views. But the unconscious, of course, can only be explored in relation to the conscious: to the reflexive monitoring and rationalisation of conduct, grounded in practical consciousness. We have to guard against a reductive theory of institutions in respect of the unconscious: that is, against a theory which, in seeking to connect the forms of social life to unconscious processes, fails to allow sufficient play to autonomous social forces – Freud's own 'sociological' writings leave a lot to be desired in this respect.[21] But we must also avoid a reductive theory of consciousness: that is, one which, in emphasising the role of the unconscious, is able to grasp the reflexive features of action only as a pale cast of unconscious processes which really determine them.

The philosophy of action, as developed by Anglo-Saxon authors, has skirted issues that are indicated at each side of Figure 2.1. So far as the unconscious is concerned, this neglect expresses more than just an acceptance of Wittgenstein's suspicions about the logical status of psychoanalysis.[22] Rather it is a consequence of a preoccupation with the relations between reasons and intentional conduct; most authors, if they refer to 'motives' at all, use the term as equivalent to reasons. A theory of motivation is crucial because it supplies the conceptual links between the rationalisation of action and the framework of convention as embodied in institutions (although I shall argue subsequently (see pp. 216–19) that large areas of social behaviour can be regarded as not directly motivated). But a theory of motivation also has to relate to the unacknowledged conditions of action: in respect of unconscious motives, operating or 'outside' the range of the self-understanding of the agent. The unconscious comprises only one set of such conditions, which have to be connected to those represented on the other side of the diagram: the unintended consequences of action.

If action philosophy has largely avoided questions of the unconscious, it has also displayed virtually *no interest in the unintended consequences of intentional conduct.*[23] This is certainly responsible in some part for the gulf that has separated the philosophy of action from institutional theories in social science. If functionalist writers have been unable to develop an adequate account of intentional conduct,[24] they have nevertheless been quite rightly concerned with the escape of activity from the scope of the purposes of the actor. The unintended consequences of action are of central importance to social theory in so far as they are systematically incorporated within the process of reproduction of institutions. I shall discuss the implications of this in some detail later. But it is worthwhile pointing out at this juncture that one such implication is that the unintended consequences of conduct relate directly to its unacknowledged conditions as specified by a theory of motivation. For in so far as such unintended consequences are involved in social reproduction, they become conditions of action also.[25] To follow this through further, however, we must turn to the concept of structure.

Time, structure, system

In social science, the term 'structure' appears in two main bodies of literature: that of functionalism, which is often in contemporary versions called 'structural-functionalism'; and the tradition of thought that has embraced it most completely, structuralism. So far as the first of these is concerned, 'structure' normally appears in conjunction with 'function'. Spencer and other nineteenth-century authors who employed these terms did so often in the context of fairly bluntly-expressed schemes of biological analogies. To study the structure of society is like studying the anatomy of the organism; to study its functions is like studying the physiology of the organism. It is to show how the structure 'works'. Although more recent functionalist authors have become wary of employing direct or detailed biological parallels, the same sort of presumed relation between structure and function is readily apparent in their works. Structure is understood as referring to a 'pattern' of social relationships; function, to how such patterns actually operate as systems. Structure here is primarily a descriptive term, the main burden of explanation being carried by function. This is perhaps why the literature of structural-functionalism, both sympathetic and critical, has been overwhelmingly concerned with the concept of function, barely treating the notion of structure at all. It is in any case indicative of the degree to which the critics of functionalism have taken over the parameters of their opponent.

In structuralism, by contrast, 'structure' appears in a more explanatory role, as linked to the notion of transformations. Structural analysis, whether applied to language, to myth, literature or art, or more generally to social relationships, is considered to penetrate below the level of surface appearances. The division between structure and function is replaced by one between code and message. At first sight, structure in this usage, and other concepts associated with it, seem to have little or nothing in common with the notions employed by functionalist authors. But as I have tried to demonstrate in the previous paper, although internally diverse traditions of thought, structuralism and functionalism do share certain overall themes and characteristics, a fact which in some part reflects the influence of Durkheim over each. Two common features are worth reiterating here: one is the initial commitment of each to a distinction between synchrony and diachrony, or statics and dynamics; the other is their mutual concern not only with 'structures' but with 'systems'. These are obviously in each case connected perspectives, because the methodological isolation of a synchronic dimension is the basis for the identification of the characteristics of structure/systems. The differentiation of synchrony and diachrony is a basic element of structuralism and functionalism alike; but both have generated attempts to transcend it. So far as the latter is concerned, the most interesting and important of such attempts involves complementing the notion of function with a conception of dysfunction, thus treating social processes in terms of a tension between integration and disintegration. I have commented on the deficiencies of this view elsewhere.[26] Within structuralist thought, the attempt to overcome the synchronic/diachronic distinction has produced an emphasis upon structuration, or as Derrida puts it, 'the structuring of structure'. For reasons I have specified in the foregoing discussion of structuralism, such notions of structuration tend to remain 'internal' to designated components of structural relations.

I shall elaborate below a conception of structuration that is directly linked to the account of human agency mentioned previously. But first it is necessary to consider briefly the relation between structure and system. While both terms appear in the respective literatures of structuralism and functionalism, the distinction between them in each is an unstable one, so that the one tends to collapse into the other. Saussure used the term 'system' rather than 'structure', meaning by the former the set of dependencies between the elements of *langue.* The introduction of 'structure' by Hjelmslev and the Prague group did not so much create a complementary concept to that of system, as substitute the former for the latter. The subsequent history of structuralism suggests that one or other of the terms is redundant, since their usage overlaps so much: system often appears as a defining characteristic of structure.[27] In functionalism there seems at first sight to be a basis for distinguishing between structure and system, following the structure/function contrast. Structure could be taken to refer to 'patterns' of social relationships, system to the actual 'functioning' of such relationships. This is indeed a distinction that often is made in functionalist writings. But it is not surprising that it is not one which is clearly sustained, resting as it does upon a supposed parallel with a differentiation between anatomy and physiology in the study of the organism. The 'structure' of an organism exists 'independently' of its functioning in a certain specific sense: the parts of the body can be studied when the organism dies, that is, when it has stopped 'functioning'. But such is not the case with social systems, *which cease to be when they cease to function*: 'patterns' of social relationships only exist in so far as the latter are organised as systems, reproduced over the course of time. Hence in functionalism also, the notions of structure and system tend to dissolve into one another.

The concept of structuration I wish to develop depends upon making distinctions between structure and system (without questioning that these have to be closely connected); but it also involves understanding each of the terms differently from the characteristic usages of both structuralism and functionalism.

I want to suggest that *structure, system* and *structuration*, appropriately conceptualised, are all necessary terms in social theory. To understand why a use can be found for each of these notions, we have to return to the theme of temporality I introduced earlier. In functionalism and structuralism alike, an attempt is made to exclude time (or more accurately, time–space intersections) from social theory, by the application of the synchrony/diachrony distinction. However, social systems are 'taken out of time' in differing fashion in the two types of theoretical tradition. In functionalism, and more generally in Anglo-Saxon sociology and anthropology, the attempt to bracket time is made in terms of 'taking a snapshot' of society, or 'freezing' it at an instant. The logical defects of such a view should be obvious, and it only retains whatever plausibility it has because of the implicit comparison that lies behind it. The anatomy of a body, or the girders of a building, the sort of imagery that is involved with this conception of structure, are perceptually 'present' in a sense which 'social structure' is not. Consequently, in this mode of thinking the synchrony/diachrony distinction is unstable. Time refuses to be eliminated. (For further considerations on this, see pp. 198–201 below.) The term 'social structure' thus tends to include two elements, not clearly distinguished from one another: the *patterning of interaction*, as implying relations between actors or groups; and the *continuity of interaction* in time. Thus Firth writes in *Elements of Social Organisation* that 'The idea of the structure of society . . . must be concerned with the ordered relations of parts to a whole, with the arrangement in which the elements of social life are linked together.' But then later he adds, talking of 'structural elements running through the whole of human behaviour', that these consist 'really in the *persistence or repetition* of behaviour', in the '*continuity* in social life'[28] (emphasis added).

What this comes down to is an implicit recognition of a syntagmatic dimension (patterning in time–space) and a paradigmatic dimension (continuity-producing, virtual order of elements) in social analysis – although no account is provided of how these interconnect. Now this differentiation (although with certain confusions, see pp. 24–8 above) is just that employed by Lévi-Strauss, and one might therefore suppose that Lévi-Strauss's conception of structure might be simply adopted in place of the idea of 'social structure' typically employed in functionalist versions of social science. And I do want to suggest a usage of 'structure' that is closer to that of Lévi-Strauss than to functionalism. But there are at least five limitations that compromise the usefulness of Lévi-Strauss's notion.

1. Lévi-Strauss holds that structure connotes a model constructed by the observer, and in his words 'has nothing to do with empirical reality'.[29] I do not want to accept this curious mixture of nominalism and rationalism that Lévi-Strauss appears to advocate. I shall argue that structure has a 'virtual existence', as instantiations or moments; but this is not the same as identifying structure merely with models invented by sociological or anthropological observers. Although I shall not defend the claim, I regard the concepts I formulate below as compatible with a realist epistemology.

2. Lévi-Strauss's structuralism lacks a concept of structure-as-structuration. Processes of structuration, in other words, are treated by Lévi-Strauss, in the mode suggested by his persistent allusion to musical scores, as combinatory forms produced by an external player (the unconscious, in Lévi-Strauss's sense). But a theory of structuration that is concerned with all types of social processes and modes of reproduction, while not disavowing unconscious mental operations, must allocate a central place to discursive and practical consciousness in the reproduction of social practices.

3. Lévi-Strauss's approach appears ambiguous in regarding structure as relations between a set of inferred elements or oppositions, and as rules of transformation that produce equivalences across sets. The same sort of ambiguity tends to appear in mathematical concepts of structure, which usually treat structure as a matrix of admissible transformations of a set. 'Structure' can be understood either as the matrix, or the laws of transformation, but usually tends to merge the two together. I shall not regard structure as referring in its most basic sense to the form of sets, but rather to the *rules (and resources)* that, in social reproduction, 'bind' time. Thus 'structure',

as applied below, is first of all treated as a generic term; but structure*s* can be identified as sets or matrices of rule-resource properties.

4. The notion of structure applied by Lévi-Strauss is associated with the basic shortcomings I have identified in structuralist thought generally, in respect of semantic spacing as *Praxis*. I shall argue that, strictly speaking, there are no such things as 'rules of transformation'; *all social rules are transformational*, in the sense that structure is not manifested in empirical similarity of social items.[30]

5. If structure exists (in time–space) only in its instances, it must include, it seems to me, reference to phenomena that are completely foreign to Lévi-Strauss's attempt to overcome formalism by emphasising form as the realisation of content: phenomena relating to *power*. I want to say that, in the senses in which I shall elaborate conceptions of domination and power, these concepts are logically presupposed by that of agency, and by the agency/structure connections characterised below.

As I shall employ it, 'structure' refers to 'structural property', or more exactly, to 'structuring property', structuring properties providing the 'binding' of time and space in social systems. I argue that these properties can be understood as rules and resources, recursively implicated in the reproduction of social systems. Structures exist paradigmatically, as an absent set of differences, temporally 'present' only in their instantiation, in the constituting moments of social systems. To regard structure as involving a 'virtual order' of differences, as I have already indicated, does not necessitate accepting Lévi-Strauss's view that structures are simply models posited by the observer. Rather, it implies recognising the existence of: (a) knowledge – as memory traces – of 'how things are to be done' (said, written), on the part of social actors; (b) social practices organised through the recursive mobilisation of that knowledge; (c) capabilities that the production of those practices presupposes.

'Structural analysis' in the social sciences involves examining the structuration of social systems. The connotation of 'visible pattern' which the term 'social structure' ordinarily has, as employed in Anglo-American sociology, is carried in my terminology·by the notion of system: with the crucial proviso that social systems are patterned in time as well as space, through continuities of social reproduction. A social system is thus a 'structured totality'. Structures do not exist in time–space, except in the moments of the constitution of social systems. But we can analyse how 'deeply-layered' structures are in terms of the historical duration of the practices they recursively organise, and the spatial 'breadth' of those practices: how widespread they are across a range of interactions. The most deeply-layered practices constitutive of social systems in each of these senses are *institutions*.

It is fundamental to understand that, when I speak of structure as rules and resources, I do not imply that we can profitably study either rules or resources as aggregates of isolated precepts or capabilities. From Saussure to Wittgenstein to Searle the game of chess appears in the philosophical literature as a reference point for illustrating features of linguistic and social rules. But, as I shall suggest below – especially in the way in which they are employed by philosophical authors – such game analogies can be highly misleading. Rules tend to be regarded as isolated formulae, to be related to particular 'moves'. Nowhere in the philosophical literature, to my knowledge, are either the history of chess (which has its origins in warfare), or actual games of chess, made the focus of study. Such study would, however, be much more relevant than the usual analogies for elucidating the standpoint I wish to suggest, which regards rules as media and outcome of the reproduction of social systems. Rules can only be grasped in the context of the historical development of social totalities, as recursively implicated in practices. This point is important in a twofold sense. (a) *There is not a singular relation between 'an activity' and 'a rule'*, as is sometimes suggested or implied by appeal to statements like 'the rule governing the Queen's move' in chess. Activities or practices are brought into being in the context of overlapping and connected sets of rules, given coherence by their involvement in the constitution of social systems in the movement of time. (b) Rules cannot be exhaustively described or analysed in terms of their own content, as prescriptions, prohibitions, etc.: precisely because, apart from those circumstances where a relevant lexicon exists, *rules and practices only exist in conjunction with one another*.

Rules and resources

The connections between the three concepts in Figure 2.2 can be quickly stated at the outset. Social systems involve regularised

STRUCTURE	Rules and resources, organised as properties of social systems. Structure only exists as 'structural properties'.
SYSTEM	Reproduced relations between actors or collectivities, organised as regular social practices.
STRUCTURATION	Conditions governing the continuity or transformation of structures, and therefore the reproduction of systems.

FIGURE 2.2

relations of interdependence between individuals or groups, that typically can be best analysed as *recurrent social practices.* Social systems are systems of social interaction; as such they involve the situated activities of human subjects, and exist syntagmatically in the flow of time. Systems, in this terminology, have structures, or more accurately, have structural properties; they are not structures in themselves. Structures are necessarily (logically) properties of systems or collectivities, and *are characterised by the 'absence of a subject'.* To study the structuration of a social system is to study the ways in which that system, via the application of generative rules and resources, and in the context of unintended outcomes, is produced and reproduced in interaction.

Each of these notions demands further elaboration, however, beginning with rules and resources. The idea of 'rule' of course, has been much discussed in the recent philosophical literature, and it is important to enter some major qualifications as to its use.

1. I reject the distinction which is frequently made between 'con-stitutive' and 'regulative' rules (which can be traced back to Kant).[31] All social rules have both constitutive and regulative (sanctioning) aspects to them. The sort of prescription which is usually offered as an instance of a regulative rule is, for example, 'don't take the goods of another'; as contrasted to something like the aforementioned 'rule governing the Queen's move' in chess. But the first enters into

the constitution of ideas of 'honesty', 'propriety', etc.; while the latter implies sanctions ('you mustn't/can't move the piece like that').

2. We have to be very careful about using the rules of games – like chess – as illustrative of the characteristics of social rules in general. Only certain features of 'knowing a rule' are best exemplified in this way, because games like chess have clearly fixed, formalised rules that are established in a lexicon, as well as because the rules of chess are not generally subject to chronic disputes of legitimacy, as social rules may be. To know a rule, as Wittgenstein says, is to 'know how to go on', to know how to play according to the rule. This is vital, because it connects rules and practices. Rules generate – or are the medium of the production and reproduction of – practices. A rule is thus not a generalisation of what people do, of regular practices. These considerations are important in respect of the arguments of those authors (such as Ziff) who have been inclined to discard the notion of rule in favour of that of dispositions.[32] The usual basis of this view is the idea that rules are foreign to most areas of social life, which are not organised prescriptively. One version is given by Oakeshott, who writes that, in language and in practical social life:

> No doubt . . . what is learnt (or some of it) can be formulated in rules and precepts; but in neither case do we . . . learn by learning rules and precepts . . . And not only may a command of language and behaviour be achieved without our becoming aware of the rules, but also, if we have acquired a knowledge of the rules, this sort of command of language and behaviour is impossible until we have forgotten them as rules and are no longer tempted to turn speech and action into the applications of rules to a situation.[33]

This, however, identifies knowing rules with knowing how to formulate rules, which are two different things. 'To know how to go on' is not necessarily, or normally, to be able to formulate clearly what the rules are. A child who learns English as a first language, when he or she can speak the language, knows the rules of English usage, whether or not he or she can formulate any of them. Oakeshott's argument does not compromise the general usefulness of 'rule', although it does focus attention upon the Wittgensteinian emphasis on the practical character of rule-following.

3. Pursuing the implications of point 2, we may say that Wittgenstein's references to the rules of children's games are more illuminating in some key respects than discussions of games with fixed and determined rules like chess. He makes, in fact, virtually the same point as Oakeshott, when arguing that the rules involved in most forms of life resemble the former more than they do the latter: 'remember that in general we don't use language according to strict rules – it hasn't been taught us by means of strict rules, either'. In children's games, at least those which are practised by children's groups themselves, or transmitted informally from generation to generation, there is no lexicon of formal rules, and it may be an essential characteristic of the rules which do exist that they cannot be strictly defined. Such is the case, Wittgenstein argues, with most of the concepts employed in ordinary language. We cannot clearly delimit them in a lexical sense: 'not because we don't know their real definition, but because there is no real "definition" to them. To suppose that there must be would be like supposing that whenever children play with a ball they play a game according to strict rules.'[34] The point made in the previous paper (p. 43) with regard to ethno-semantics is worth repeating at this juncture. The operations of practical consciousness enmesh rules *and* the 'methodological' intepretation of rules in the continuity of practices.[35] Garfinkel's conception of the interpretative work which is always temporally involved in accountability is very important here. What Garfinkel calls 'ad hoc' considerations – the 'etcetera clause', 'let it pass', etc. [*sic*] – are chronically involved in the instantiation of rules, and are not separate from what those rules 'are'.

In emphasising the importance of resources as structural properties of social systems, I mean to stress the centrality of the concept of power to social theory. Like 'rule', power is not a description of a state of affairs, but a capability. I think it true to say that few of the major thinkers or traditions of thought in sociology have accorded power as focal a place in social theory as is warranted. Those who have recognised the essential importance of power, like Nietzsche and Weber, have usually done so only on the basis of a normative irrationalism which I want to repudiate (although I shall not give the grounds for this here). If there is no rational mode of adjudging 'ultimate value' claims, as Weber held, then the only recourse open is that of power or might: the strongest are able to make their values count by crushing others.[36] More common are those standpoints

which either treat power as secondary to the meaningful or normative character of social life, or ignore power altogether. Such is the
case, for example, with the works of authors in traditions of
phenomenology (Schutz) or Wittgensteinian social thought
(Winch), just as much as with traditions to which they are opposed
in other respects (the functionalism of Durkheim or Parsons). It is
even true, in a certain, although a quite different, sense, of Marxism,
in so far as Marx connected power directly to class interests, with the
possible inference that when class divisions disappear, relations of
power do also.

Among the many interpretations of power in social and political
theory, two main perspectives appear. One is that power is best
conceptualised as the capability of an actor to achieve his or her will,
even at the expense of that of others who might resist him – the sort
of definition employed by Weber[37] among many other authors. The
second is that power should be seen as a property of the collectivity:
Parsons's concept of power, for instance, belongs to this latter
category.[38] I wish to claim, however, that neither of these modes of
conceiving power is appropriate in isolation; and that we should
connect them together as features of the duality of structure. I shall
treat resources as the 'bases' or 'vehicles' of power, comprising
structures of domination, drawn upon by parties to interaction and
reproduced through the duality of structure. Power is generated by
definite forms of domination in a parallel way to the involvement of
rules with social practices: and, indeed, as an integral element or
aspect of those practices. (For an extended discussion of power and
domination, see pp. 88–94 below.)

The theory of structuration

The concept of structuration involves that of the *duality of structure,*
which relates to the *fundamentally recursive character of social life,
and expresses the mutual dependence of structure and agency.* By the
duality of structure I mean that the structural properties of social
systems are both the medium and the outcome of the practices that
constitute those systems. The theory of structuration, thus formulated, rejects any differentiation of synchrony and diachrony or
statics and dynamics. The identification of structure with constraint
is also rejected: structure is both enabling and constraining, and it is

one of the specific tasks of social theory to study the conditions in the organisation of social systems that govern the interconnections between the two. According to this conception, the same structural characteristics participate in the subject (the actor) as in the object (society). Structure forms 'personality' and 'society' simultaneously – but in neither case exhaustively: because of the significance of unintended consequences of action, and because of unacknow-ledged conditions of action. Ernst Bloch says, *Homo semper tiro*: man is always a beginner.[39] We may agree, in the sense that every process of action is a production of something new, a fresh act; but at the same time all action exists in continuity with the past, which supplies the means of its initiation. *Structure thus is not to be conceptualised as a barrier to action, but as essentially involved in its production:* even in the most radical processes of social change which, like any others, occur in time. The most disruptive modes of social change, like the most rigidly stable forms, involve structura-tion. Hence there is no need, nor any room, for a conception of de-structuration such as that suggested by Gurvitch.[40] A notion of de-structuration is only necessary if we retain the idea that structure is simply equivalent to constraint, thereby counterposing structure and freedom (as Gurvitch does, and as Sartre does also).

It is important to accentuate this last point, because some authors who have emphasised the contingency of social life have done so only at the cost of adopting an overly voluntaristic viewpoint. One such example, its interesting contributions notwithstanding, is Shackle's economics. Shackle argues against determinism in human economic activities, stressing their temporal and contingent charac-ter: but he is led by this to attach an excessive importance to what he calls 'decision' in human social life. The past is dead and 'deter-mined', but the present is always open to the free initiative of human actors.[41] Commendable as this perspective may be in some ways, it hardly allows us to grasp how the past makes itself felt in the present, even while the present may react back against the past. In this respect, Shackle's view seems to share a good deal in common with that elaborated by Sartre in *The Critique of Dialectical Reason* – indeed, it would not be too inaccurate to regard Shackle's work as a kind of Sartrean economic theory. For in spite of his accentuation of the importance of history to the understanding of the human condition, Sartre preserves a gulf between past and present, in the sense that while the past is 'given and necessary' the present is a realm of free, spontaneous creation: in that sense he fails to escape from a dualism of 'materiality' and '*Praxis*'.

According to the notion of the duality of structure, rules and resources are drawn upon by actors in the production of interaction, but are thereby also reconstituted through such interaction. Structure is thus the mode in which the relation between moment and totality expresses itself in social reproduction. This relation is distinct from that involved in the relation of 'parts' and 'wholes' in the co-ordination of actors and groups in social systems as posited in functionalist theory. That is to say, the differences which constitute social systems reflect a dialectic of presences and absences in space and time. But these are only brought into being and reproduced via the virtual order of differences of structures, expressed in the duality of structure. The differences that constitute structures, and are constituted structurally, relate 'part' to 'whole' in the sense in which the utterance of a grammatical sentence presupposes the absent corpus of syntactical rules that constitute the language as a totality. The importance of this relation of moment and totality for social theory cannot be exaggerated, since it involves a dialectic of presence and absence which ties the most minor or trivial forms of social action to structural properties of the overall society (and, logically, to the development of mankind as a whole).

It is an essential emphasis of the ideas developed here that institutions do not just work 'behind the backs' of the social actors who produce and reproduce them. Every competent member of every society knows a great deal about the institutions of that society: such knowledge is not *incidental* to the operation of society, but is necessarily involved in it (see pp. 248–53 below). A common tendency of many otherwise divergent schools of sociological thought is to adopt the methodological tactic of beginning their analyses by discounting agents' reasons for their action (or what I prefer to call the rationalisation of action), in order to discover the 'real' stimuli to their activity, of which they are ignorant. Such a stance, however, is not only defective from the point of view of social theory, it is one with strongly-defined and potentially offensive political implications. It implies a *derogation of the lay actor*. If actors are regarded as cultural dopes or mere 'bearers of a mode of production', with no worthwhile understanding of their surroundings or the circumstances of their action, the way is immediately laid open for the supposition that their own views can be disregarded in any practical programmes that might be inaugurated. This is not just a question of 'whose side (as social analysts) are we on?'[42] – although there is no doubt that social incompetence is commonly attributed to people in lower socio-economic groupings by those in power-positions, or by their associated 'experts'.

It is not a coincidence that the forms of social theory which have made little or no conceptual space for agents' understanding of themselves, and of their social contexts, have tended greatly to exaggerate the impact of dominant symbol systems or ideologies upon those in subordinate classes: as in Parsons or Althusser. A good case can be made to the effect that only dominant class groups have ever been strongly committed to dominant ideologies.[43] This is not just because of the development of divergent 'sub-cultures' – for example, working-class culture as compared to bourgeois culture in nineteenth-century Britain – but also because *all social actors, no matter how lowly, have some degree of penetration of the social forms which oppress them.*[44] Where partially closed, localised cultures become largely unavailable, as is increasingly the case within advanced capitalism, scepticism about 'official' views of society often is expressed in various forms of 'distancing' – and in humour. Wit is deflationary. Humour is used socially both to attack and to defend against the influence of outside forces that cannot otherwise easily be coped with.

One must not overestimate the degree of conviction with which even those in dominant classes, or other positions of authority, accept ideological symbol-systems. But it is not implausible to suppose that, in some circumstances, and from some aspects, those in subordinate positions in a society might have a greater penetration of the conditions of social reproduction than those who otherwise dominate them. This is related to the *dialectic of control* in social systems that I shall analyse later (pp. 145–50, below). Those who in a largely unquestioning way accept certain dominant perspectives may be more imprisoned within them than others are, even though these perspectives help the former to sustain their position of dominance. The point at issue here has a definite similarity to Laing's thesis about schizophrenia: that notwithstanding the distorted nature of schizophrenic language and thought, in some respects the schizophrenic person 'sees through' features of day-to-day existence which the majority accept without demur.

These things having been said, we have to enter major qualifications about what is implied in the proposition that every competent actor has a wide-ranging, yet intimate and subtle, knowledge of the society of which he or she is a member. First, 'knowledge' has to be understood in terms of both practical and discursive consciousness: and even where there is substantial discursive penetration of institutional forms, this is not necessarily, nor normally, expressed in a propositional manner. Schutz in a sense makes this point when he calls typifications 'cookery book knowledge', and contrasts cookery book knowledge to the sort of abstract, theoretical knowledge called for by the relevances of the social scientist.[45] But this does not distinguish satisfactorily between practical consciousness, which is knowledge embodied in what actors 'know how to do', and discourse, that is, what actors are able to 'talk about' and in what manner or guise they are able to talk about it.

Second, every individual actor is only one among others in a society: very many others, obviously, in the case of the contemporary industrialised societies. We have to recognise that what an actor knows as a competent – but historically and spatially located – member of society, 'shades off' in contexts that stretch beyond those of his or her day-to-day activity. Third, the parameters of practical and discursive consciousness are bounded in specifiable ways, that connect with the 'situated' character of actors' activities, but are not reducible to it. These can be identified from Figure 2.1: the unconscious conditions of action and the unintended consequences of action. All of these phenomena have to be related to problems of ideology, a task which I undertake in a following paper.

Structural properties of social systems

Social systems, by contrast to structure, exist in time–space, and are constituted by social practices. The concept of social system, understood in its broadest sense, refers to reproduced *interdependence of action*: in other words, to 'a relationship in which changes in one or more component parts initiate changes in other component parts, and these changes, in turn, produce changes in the parts in which the original changes occurred'.[46] The smallest type of social system is dyadic. We must beware, however, of the idea that dyadic systems show the workings of more inclusive social systems in miniature, such that the former can be used as a basis of theorising the properties of the latter – the sort of procedure Parsons used in *The Social System*.[47] One of my reasons for adopting a distinction between *social integration* and *system integration* below is in order to recognise contrasts between various levels of the articulation of interaction.

The term 'system' cannot be left an unexamined one, any more than those of agency and structure. The concept of system has entered sociology from two main sources. On the one hand, the notion of system, whether going by that name or some other (for example, structure!) has always been an important element of functionalism where, as I have suggested before, it has rarely strayed far from organic analogies. The social system is conceived of in terms of parallels with physiological systems. The other source of provenance is from 'systems theory', which is not clearly distinguishable from 'information theory' or 'cybernetics', all of which have largely arisen outside the social sciences.

In an influential discussion, Bertalanffy distinguishes three aspects of systems theory. 'General system theory' is concerned with exploring similarities between totalities or wholes across the range of natural and social sciences. According to Bertalanffy, one of the main trends in modern thought in general involves the rediscovery of wholes as compared to aggregates, of autonomy as opposed to reduction.[48] Such a rediscovery, he admits, has received a direct impetus from developments in modern technology, which forms the second category, 'systems technology'. Systems technology does not just refer to computers, automated machines, etc., but also to the incorporation of human beings, or their activities, within designed control systems. Information theory and cybernetics were created mainly in association with such technological developments. Finally, there is 'systems philosophy', which is concerned with broad philosophical implications of systems theory. Bertalanffy himself regards systems philosophy as having a major importance in the modern context, seeing it as generating an appropriate philosophy to replace logical positivism: systems philosophy can provide a new basis for achieving the unity of science striven for by the logical positivists.[49]

I shall have nothing to say about the third of these categories, which is not in my opinion of any particular interest. But the second is crucial: for, understood as a series of technological advances, systems theory has already had a great practical impact upon social life, an impact whose full implications will only be felt in the future.

Any theoretical appropriation of concepts from systems theory within the social sciences must hold firm against collapsing the first category into the second. Systems theory in the second sense is a potent ideological force in the contemporary world;[50] only by maintaining the distinction between first and second categories is it possible to submit systems technology to ideology-critique. But sustaining this possibility, I think, also involves resisting the sort of claims that ertalanffy and others have made about the applicability of general systems theory to human conduct. The position I propose to adopt here is close to that elaborated by Richard Taylor: the reflexive monitoring of action among human actors cannot be adequately grasped in terms of principles of teleology applicable to mechanical systems.[51] Purposive behaviour is usually treated by systems theorists in terms of feed-back.[52] I shall accept below Buckley's argument that systems involving feed-back processes are worthwhile distinguishing from the system mechanisms usually given prominence within functionalism, which are of a 'lower' kind.[53] But I shall also want to differentiate feed-back system processes from a 'higher' order of reflexive self-regulation in social systems.

Functionalist authors have always accentuated the closeness of the connections between biology and sociology: the boldest and most comprehensive version of this still being Comte's hierarchy of the sciences. To question the naturalistic framework associated with this sort of position, and to refuse any special technical sense to the term 'function', as I do throughout this book, is not to deny that there may be significant continuities between the natural and social sciences. It is rather to reconceptualise the form those continuities might take (cf. pp. 257–9, below). In respect of problems discussed in this paper, the most relevant sources of connection between biological and social theory do not involve the functional analogies so strongly represented in the history of sociology, but rather concern recursive or *self-reproducing* systems. There are two related types of theory involved here. One is the theory of automata,[54] as modelled in the Turing machine. But this is not of as much interest to the conceptualisation of social reproduction as recent conceptions of cellular self-reproduction (autopoiesis) – although it is probably too early to say just how close the parallels with social theory might turn out to be. The chief point of connection is undoubtedly recursiveness, taken to characterise autopoietic organisation. Autopoietic organisation can be understood as relations between the production of components which 'participate recursively in the same network of productions of components which produced these components . . .'[55] Varela proposes that the theoretical issues which have recently emerged in the cybernetics of autopoietic systems suggest a logical framework close to dialectics. The attempt of Russell and Whitehead to reduce the theory of numbers to set-theoretical format foundered upon the definition of the null set, or zero, as the class of all classes that are not members of themselves, which led to contradictory consequences. Russell and Whitehead thus prohibited self-referential expressions. But the phenomenon of self-indication is a logical property of theoretical characterisations of autopoietic organisation: which suggests that contradiction is also.[56] However this may be in biological systems, I shall want to argue in detail in a following paper that the self-regulating properties of social systems must be grasped via a theory of *system contradiction*.

Social integration and system integration

I have earlier argued that systems of social interaction, reproduced through the duality of structure in the context of bounded conditions of the rationalisation of action, are constituted through the interdependence of actors or groups. The notion of integration, as employed here, refers to the degree of interdependence of action, or 'systemness', that is involved in any mode of system reproduction. 'Integration' can be defined therefore as regularised ties, interchanges or *reciprocity of practices* between either actors or collectivities. 'Reciprocity of practices' has to be understood as involving regularised relations of relative autonomy and dependence between the parties concerned (see below, pp. 92–3). It is important to emphasise that, as employed here at any rate, *integration is not synonymous with 'cohesion', and certainly not with 'consensus'*.

The division between social and system integration, and that between conflict and contradiction, are introduced as a means of coping with basic characteristics of the differentiation of society (see Figure 2.3). We can define social integration as concerned with *systemness on the level of face-to-face interaction*; system integration

SOCIAL INTEGRATION	Reciprocity between actors (relations of autonomy/ dependence)
SYSTEM INTEGRATION	Reciprocity between groups or collectivities (relations of autonomy/dependence)

FIGURE 2.3

as concerned with *systemness on the level of relations between social systems or collectivities.*[57] This distinction is the nearest I shall come in this book to admitting the usefulness of a differentiation between 'micro-' and 'macro-sociological' studies. The special significance of face-to-face interaction, however, is not primarily that it involves small groups, or that it represents 'society in miniature'. We must be particularly wary of this last connotation, in fact, because it carries the implication that the more inclusive social system or society can be understood as the social relationship writ large. 'Face-to-face interaction' rather emphasises the significance of *space and presence* in social relations: in the immediacy of the life-world, social relations can be influenced by different factors from those involved with others who are spatially (and perhaps temporally) absnt.

Systemness on the level of social integration typically occurs through the reflexive monitoring of action in conjunction with the rationalisation of conduct. I shall discuss later how this connects with normative sanctions and with the operations of power. But it is extremely important, for the point of view developed throughout this book, to emphasise that the systemness of social integration *is fundamental to the systemness of society as a whole.* System integration cannot be adequately conceptualised via the modalities of social integration; none the less the latter is always the chief prop of the former, *via the reproduction of institutions in the duality of structure.* I shall have a lot more to say about this below (pp. 210–22). The duality of structure relates the smallest item of day-to-day behaviour to attributes of far more inclusive social systems: when I utter a grammatical English sentence in a casual conversation, I contribute to the reproduction of the English language as a whole. This is an unintended consequence of my speaking the sentence, but one that is bound in directly to the recursive-

ness of the duality of structure. In this example social and system
integration are the same process, and if all processes of system
reproduction were of this nature, there would be no need to
distinguish between social and system integration at all. But the
unintended consequences of action stretch beyond the recursive
effects of the duality of structure: this introduces the further series
of influences that can be understood in terms of system integration,
and it is to these that the differentiations in Figure 2.4 refer.

SYSTEM   =   interdependence of action
conceived as   (1) homeostatic causal loops
                 (2) self-regulation through feed-back
                 (3) reflexive self-regulation

FIGURE 2.4

As employed by functionalist authors, the interdependence of
system parts is usually interpreted as homeostasis.[58] Homeostasis
may be regarded as involving the operation of causal loops, that is,
'circular' causal relations in which a change in one item initiates a
sequence of events affecting others, that eventually return to affect
the item that began the sequence, thus tending to restore it to its
original state. The use of the term 'system' in functionalist writings,
and its identification with homeostatic properties, makes it seem as
if the idea of homeostasis exhausts the meaning of interdependence
of action in system integration. But as critics of functionalism
influenced by systems theory have pointed out, homeostasis is only
one form or level of such interdependence: and one, borrowing
from a physiological or mechanical model, where the forces involved operate most 'blindly'.[59] It is not the same as self-regulation
through feed-back, and is a more 'primitive' process.

It seems evident enough that homeostatic causal processes are an
important feature of the reproduction of social systems – although I
hold that such processes cannot be adequately grasped using the
language of functionalism. Homeostatic features of social systems
may be distinguished from those which belong to a higher order,
involving self-regulation through feed-back via the operation of
selective 'information filtering'. In physical systems, the simplest
type of feed-back scheme involves three elements: receptor, control
apparatus and effector, through which messages pass. Feed-back

mechanisms may promote stasis: but, unlike homeostatic processes, they can also be directional, propelling controlled change. A fairly direct parallel can be drawn between such feed-back effects and processes involved in social systems. But reflexive self-regulation is a distinctively human phenomenon, with many important implications.

As a mode of illustrating the three levels of systemness, we may consider a so-called 'poverty cycle': for example, material deprivation → poor schooling → low-level employment → material deprivation. A poverty cycle forms a homeostatic loop if each of these factors participates in a reciprocal series of influences, without any one acting as a 'controlling filter' for the others. A homeostatic loop forms systemness of the following pattern:

We might discover such a loop if we trace out the influence of primary education upon the other elements mentioned above. If, however, we consider the influence of children's overall educational career upon the other factors, it might emerge that an examination taken on entry to secondary school is a crucial filter that exerts a controlling influence upon other elements in the cycle. (The validity of the particular example is not important.) In such a circumstance, the examinations can be regarded as the equivalent of an information control apparatus in a mechanical feed-back system. The feed-back effect here might govern a regularised process of directional change: such as a progressive transfer of children from working-class backgrounds into white-collar occupations, in conjunction with a relative expansion of the white-collar sector. Now let us suppose that, on the basis of studies of the community, school and work, the Ministry of Education applies knowledge of the poverty cycle to intervene in the operation of that cycle: in this case the reflexive monitoring of action rejoins the organisation of social systems, and becomes a guiding influence in it.

The expansion of attempts at reflexive self-regulation at the level of system integration is evidently one of the principal features of the contemporary world. Such a phenomenon underlies the two most pervasive types of social mobilisation in modern times: the 'legal-rational' social *organisation* and the secular *social movement*. But it is also highly important to recognise that attempts at reflexive

self-regulation also produce a further diffusion of feed-back processes, via the introduction of 'systems technology'. I have already
stressed that reflexive self-regulation understood purely as technical control – as is so vigorously argued by Habermas – may become a
potent ideological force.

I have argued that *institutions* may be regarded as practices which
are deeply sedimented in time–space: that is, which are enduring
and inclusive 'laterally' in the sense that they are widespread among
the members of a community or society. At this point I want to
introduce a distinction that I shall refer to quite often subsequently
in this book, between *institutional analysis* and the analysis of
strategic conduct. This does not correspond to the differentiation
between social and system integration, because I intend it to be
methodological rather than substantive. The point of the distinction
is to indicate two principal ways in which the study of system
properties may be approached in the social sciences: each of which
is separated out, however, only by a methodological *epoché*. To
examine the constitution of social systems as strategic conduct is to
study the mode in which actors draw upon structural elements –
rules and resources – in their social relations. 'Structure' here
appears as actors' mobilisation of discursive and practical consciousness in social encounters. Institutional analysis, on the other
hand, places an *epoché* upon strategic conduct, treating rules and
resources as chronically reproduced features of social systems.[60] It is
quite essential to see that this is only a methodological bracketing:
these are not two sides of a dualism, they express a duality, the
duality of structure. No such bracketing appears in naturalistic
sociologies, which tend to equate social causation and structural
constraint as synonymous notions. A classic example is Durkheim's
Suicide, in which suicidal conduct is treated as caused by factors
such as 'weak social integration' (in combination with psychological
causes). Durkheim's account lacks any mode of understanding
suicidal behaviour, and the social interaction in which it is meshed,
as reflexively monitored conduct.[61]

Contrast the character of Durkheim's sociology with that of
Goffman. Goffman implicitly brackets institutional analysis in
order to concentrate upon social interaction as strategic conduct.
Much of Goffman's work may be read as investigating the tacit
stocks of knowledge that are employed by lay actors in the production of social encounters. Goffman analyses 'knowledge' in the

Wittgensteinian sense of 'knowing rules'; the feeling of sharp illumination that the reader often experiences in reading Goffman derives from his making explicit what, once he has pointed them out, we recognise to be ingredients of practical consciousness, normally employed in an unacknowledged way in social life. On the other hand, Goffman's sociology, like Wittgensteinian philosophy, has not developed an account of institutions, of history or structural transformation. Institutions appear as unexplained parameters within which actors organise their practical activities.[62] This is therefore in the end more than a methodological 'bracketing': it reflects the *dualism* of action and structure that has been noted earlier. Being limited in this sense, Goffman's sociology also ignores the possibility of recognising the dialectic of presence/absence that connects action to the properties of the totality: for this involves the need to generate an *institutional theory of everyday life*.

The duality of structure in interaction

Let us now give more concrete form to the duality of structure in interaction, following on from what has been outlined above.

What I call here the 'modalities' of structuration represent the central dimensions of the duality of structure in the constitution of interaction. The modalities of structuration are drawn upon by actors in the production of interaction, but at the same time are the media of the reproduction of the structural components of systems of interaction. When institutional analysis is bracketed, the modalities are treated as stocks of knowledge and resources employed by actors in the constitution of interaction as a skilled and knowledgeable accomplishment, within bounded conditions of the rationalisation of action. Where strategic conduct is placed under an *epoché*, the modalities represent rules and resources considered as institutional features of systems of social interaction. The level of modality thus provides the coupling elements whereby the bracketing of strategic or institutional analysis is dissolved in favour of an acknowledgement of their interrelation.

The classification given in Figure 2.5 does not represent a typology of interaction or structures, but a portrayal of dimensions that are combined in differing ways in social practices. The communication of meaning in interaction does not take place separately

INTERACTION	communication	power	sanction
(MODALITY)	interpretative scheme	facility	norm
STRUCTURE	signification	domination	legitimation

FIGURE 2.5

from the operation of relations of power, or outside the context of normative sanctions.[63] All social practices involve these three elements. It is important however to bear in mind what has been said previously in respect of rules: no social practice expresses, or can be explicated in terms of, a single rule or type of resource. Rather, practices are situated within intersecting sets of rules and resources that ultimately express features of the totality.

The distinction between interpretative schemes, as concerning the communication of meaning, and norms, as concerning the sanctioning of conduct, can be clarified by considering Winch's discussion of rule-following in his *Idea of a Social Science*. According to Winch, 'rule-following' conduct can be identified with 'meaningful action'. The criterion of behaviour which is rule-following is to be found in whether one can ask of that behaviour if there is a 'right' and 'wrong' way of doing it.[64] Now this conflates two senses of rule-following or, rather, *two aspects of rules that are implicated in the production of social practices*; that relating to the *constitution of meaning*, and that relating to *sanctions* involved in social conduct. There are right and wrong ways of using words in a language, a matter which concerns those aspects of rules involved in the constitution of meaning; and there are right and wrong modes of conduct in respect of the normative sanctions implicated in interaction. Although it is important to separate them out conceptually, these two senses of right and wrong always intersect in the actual constitution of social practices. Thus 'correct' language use is always sanctioned; while the relevance of sanctions to conduct other than speech is inevitably connected with the identification of that conduct on the plane of meaning. The first sense, to adapt an example discussed by MacIntyre,[65] is that in which an expression like 'going for a walk' is used rightly or wrongly in relation to a particular activity: that is, what is to *count* as 'going for a walk' in the language as practised in day-to-day life. The second is the sense in which 'going for a walk' is involved with norms of 'correct', 'desirable' or 'appropriate' conduct: going for a stroll along the pavement in this aspect differs from wandering along the middle of the road in disregard of the conventions or laws governing traffic behaviour (and personal safety). The point of distinguishing these two senses of 'rule' (and rejecting the idea that these are two *types* of rule, constitutive and regulative) implicated in social practices, is precisely in order to be able to examine their interconnection. The identification of acts, in other words, interlaces in important ways with normative considerations (and vice versa). This is most obvious and most formally codified in law where, as regards sanctions that are applied, a great deal hinges on distinctions between 'murder', 'manslaughter', etc.

It is not enough just to stress the need in social theory to relate the constitution and communication of meaning to normative sanctions; each of these has in turn to be linked to power transactions. This is so in the twofold sense indicated by the term duality of structure. Power is expressed in the capabilities of actors to make certain 'accounts count' and to enact or resist sanctioning processes; but these capabilities draw upon modes of domination structured into social systems.

By 'interpretative schemes', I mean standardised elements of stocks of knowledge, applied by actors in the production of interaction. Interpretative schemes form the core of the mutual knowledge whereby an accountable universe of meaning is sustained through and in processes of interaction. Accountability, in Garfinkel's sense, depends upon the mastery of ethno-methods involved in language use, and it is essential to grasp the point, made by Garfinkel and in rather different form by Habermas, that such mastery cannot be adequately understood as 'monological'. This involves more than the proposition (made by Habermas) that a satisfactory approach to semantics cannot be derived from Chomsky's syntactics: it points to features of the relation between language and the 'context of use' that are of essential importance to social theory. In the production of meaning in interaction, context cannot be treated as merely the 'environment' or 'background' of the use of language. *The context of interaction is in some degree shaped and organised as an integral part of that interaction as a communicative encounter.* The reflexive monitoring of conduct in interaction involves the routine drawing upon of physical, social and temporal context in the sustaining of accountability; but the drawing upon of context at the same time recreates these elements as contextual relevances. The 'mutual knowledge' thus employed and reconstituted in social encounters can be regarded as the medium whereby the interweaving of locutionary and illocutionary elements of language is ordered.

As with other aspects of context, the communication of meaning in processes of interaction does not just 'occur' over time. Actors sustain the meaning of what they say and do through routinely incorporating 'what went before' and anticipations of 'what will come next' into the present of an encounter.[66] Indexical features of interaction thus imply *différance* in Derrida's sense. But the language-use is also grounded in other, referential features of context, which border on 'what cannot be said'. Ziff's analysis of context is important here.[67] Some linguists have argued that language can in principle be separated from all features of context, because such features can themselves be expressed in language: a view which converges with some of the central notions of structuralism. This would entail that the uptake of an utterance such as 'The pen on the desk is made of gold', as used and understood in an everyday context of communication, could be analysed into a statement or set of statements describing the contextual elements mutually known by the participants, and necessary to the indexical properties of the utterance. Hence, it is claimed, for 'the pen on the desk', we could substitute 'the only pen on the desk in the back room of number 2A Millington Road, Cambridge at 11.30 on 9 May 1978'. However, the claim is not, in fact, a defensible one. The substitute sentence does not actually verbalise the contextual characteristics used to produce the mutual understanding of the original utterance and its referential features. None of the participants in the interaction, to understand the utterance, need to know such facts as the address of the house they are in, or the time or the date at which the utterance was made. Also, as Ziff points out, it would be a mistake to presume that, even if the first sentence, as involved in the everyday practical use of language, could be replaced by the terms of the second, there would be a gain in precision of meaning; there would not.

The foregoing considerations do not, of course, cover the problems that would have to be confronted if one were to attempt to work out a semantic theory adequate for the social sciences. It is important to repeat, however, that the approach to the production

of meaning in interaction suggested here attributes equal consequence to each of the senses in which 'meaning' is used in ordinary
English usage: what an actor means to say/do, and what the
meaning of his utterance/act is. This is of some considerable significance in the light of the tendency of theories of meaning to have a
reductive character: to try to reduce meaning either to what
speakers mean or intend to say, or conversely to suppose that what
speakers mean to say is irrelevant to the elucidation of the nature of
meaning. The division in some part separates those who have been
primarily concerned with utterances, or act-identifications, on the
one hand, as compared on the other hand to those who have been
preoccupied with the interpretation of texts. Some authors in the
first category (for example, Grice) have attempted to elaborate a
theory of meaning in terms of communicative intent; some in the
second category (critics of the 'intentional fallacy') have sought to
eschew reference to communicative intent altogether as relevant to
the characterisation of meaning. In contrast to each of these, I
regard the meanings of communicative acts – that is, acts in which
one element of the reflexive monitoring of conduct includes the
intent to communicate with another – as in principle distinguishable
from other meanings that may be attributed to those acts. The latter
derive from, and are sustained in, the differences expressed in the
practices of language-games; but such practices, as the active
accomplishment of human subjects, are organised through and in
the reflexive monitoring of conduct. The interplay of meaning as
communicative intent, and meaning as *différance*, represents the
duality of structure in the production of meaning.

Norms and practices

In turning from interpretative schemes to norms, it is perhaps
worthwhile emphasising again that the differentiation between the
two is an analytical, not a substantive one: the conventions whereby
the communication of meaning in interaction is achieved have
normative aspects, as do all structural elements of interaction. This
is in fact indicated by the double sense of 'accountability' in
ordinary language. The giving of 'accounts' of conduct is intimately
tied in to being 'accountable' for them, as the normative component
of the rationalisation of action.[68]

The normative character of social practices can be anchored in what Parsons calls the 'double contingency' of social interaction.[69] In other words, the reactions of each party to a process of interaction depend upon the contingent responses of the other or others: the response of the other(s) is thus a potential sanction upon the acts of the first and vice versa. The double contingency of interaction connects, however, not only to the normative institutionalisation of conduct, as Parsons argues, but to the actualisation of power. Normative sanctions are a generic type of resource drawn upon in power relations.

The normative constitution of interaction may be treated as the actualisation of *rights* and the enactment of *obligations*. The double contingency of interaction, however, entails that *the symmetry between these may be factually broken in actual social conduct.* This is one crucial area in which the contingency of 'double contingency' tends to evaporate from Parsons's action frame of reference: for him the normative institutionalisation of reciprocal sets of expectations (structured as roles) controls the activities of actors in processes of interaction. From the point of view of the theory of structuration developed here, however, the norms implicated in systems of social interaction have at every moment to be sustained and reproduced in the flow of social encounters. What from the structural point of view – where strategic conduct is bracketed – appears as a normatively co-ordinated legitimate order, in which rights and obligations are merely two aspects of norms, from the point of view of strategic conduct represents *claims*, whose realisation is contingent upon the successful mobilisation of obligations through the medium of the responses of other actors.

The operation of sanctions through the double contingency of interaction is essentially distinct from the consequences which ensue from 'technical prescriptions', in which the tie between an act and its sanction is of a 'mechanical' kind. That is to say, in prescriptions such as 'avoid drinking contaminated water', the sanction – the risk of being poisoned – involves consequences that have the form of natural events. Durkheim acknowledged this distinction in separating what he called 'utilitarian' from 'moral' sanctions. But the way in which he formulated the distinction, treating moral sanctions as the very prototype of social relations, prevented him from theorising a quite basic sense in which norms can be regarded, in a 'utilitarian' manner by agents – a manner that has to be related conceptually to the contingent character of the realisation of normative claims. There is a range of possible 'shadings' between acceptance of a normative obligation as a moral commitment, the type case for Durkheim, and conformity based on the acknowledgement of sanctions that apply to the transgression of normative prescriptions. In other words, the fact that the normative features of social life involve the double contingency of social interaction does not necessarily relegate a 'utilitarian' mode of orientation towards sanctions to non-social causal consequences of behaviour. An actor may 'calculate the risks' involved in the enactment of a given form of social conduct, in respect of the likelihood of the sanctions involved being actually applied, and may be prepared to submit to them as a price to be paid for achieving a particular end. The theoretical significance of this seemingly obvious point for problems of legitimation and conformity is considerable – in two respects. One is that it draws the theory of legitimation away from the 'internalised value-norm-moral consensus' theorem that has been the hallmark of the 'normative functionalism' of Durkheim and Parsons.[70] The second is that it directs attention to the *negotiated* character of sanctions, relating the production of meaning to the production of a normative order. 'Calculative' attitudes towards norms can extend through to processes of 'presentation of self', 'bargaining', etc., in which actors who either conform or transgress normative prescriptions may negotiate in some degree what conformity or transgressin *are* in the context of their conduct, by means of that conduct, thereby also affecting the sanctions to which it is subject.

A classification of sanctions can be based upon the elements mobilised to produce the sanctioning effect, the latter to be effective always in some sense impinging upon actors' wants (conscious or unconscious) – even in the case of sanctions which involve the use of force. It follows however from what has been said previously, that it would be a mistake to suppose that sanctions only exist when actors overtly try to bring each other 'into line' in some particular fashion. The operation of sanctions, or 'sanctioning', is a chronic feature of all social encounters, however pervasive or subtle the mutual processes of adjustment in interaction may be. This applies, of course, to the production of meaning in a basic sense. The stocks of knowledge drawn upon in linguistic communication, including syntactical rules, have a strong 'obligating' quality, and could not operate outside a normative context any more than any other structural features of systems of interaction. Conformity to linguistic rules is basically secured as a means and an outcome of the everyday use of language itself, in which the main normative commitments are simply those of the sustaining of 'accountability' in Garfinkel's sense.

Power: relations of autonomy and dependence

As in the case of the other modalities of structuration, power can be related to interaction in a dual sense: *as involved institutionally in processes of interaction, and as used to accomplish outcomes in strategic conduct.* Even the most casual social encounter instances elements of the totality as a structure of domination; but such structural properties are at the same time drawn upon, and reproduced through, the activities of participants in systems of interaction. I have argued elsewhere that the concept of action is *logically tied* to that of power, where the latter notion is understood as transformative capacity.[71] This has usually only been obliquely recognised in the philosophy of action, in which it is common to talk of action in terms of 'can' or 'able to', or 'powers'. The literature concerned to analyse human agency in terms of 'powers', however, rarely if ever intersects with sociological discussions of relations of power in interaction. The relation between the concepts of action and power, on the level of strategic conduct, can be set out as follows. Action involves intervention in events in the world, thus producing definite outcomes, with intended action being one category of an agent's doings or his refraining. *Power as transformative capacity can then be taken to refer to agents' capabilities of reaching such outcomes.*[72]

Even a casual survey of the massive literature concerned with the concept of power and its implementation in social science indicates that the study of power reflects the same dualism of action and structure that I have diagnosed in approaches to social theory generally. One notion of power, found in Hobbes, in Weber in somewhat different form, and more recently in the writings of Dahl, treats power as a phenomenon of willed or intended action.[73] Here power is defined in terms of the capacity or likelihood of actors to achieve desired or intended outcomes. According to other authors, on the other hand – including such otherwise diverse figures as

Arendt, Parsons and Poulantzas – power is specifically a property of the social community, a medium whereby common interests or class interests are realised. These are effectively two versions of how power structures are constituted, and two versions of 'domination' (each of which *may* link the notion of power logically to that of conflict, but neither of which necessarily does so). The first tends to treat domination as *a network of decision-making*, operating against an unexamined institutional backdrop; the second regards domination as itself an institutional phenomenon, either disregarding power as relating to the active accomplishments of actors, or treating it as in some way determined by institutions.

As is well known, there have been various attempts to reconcile these two approaches, on the basis of exposing the limitations of the 'power as decision-making' approach.[74] The capability of actors to secure desired outcomes in interaction with others, according to Bachrach and Baratz, is only 'one face' of power; power has another face, which is that of the 'mobilisation of bias' built into institutions. The second is a sphere of 'non-decision-making'; of implicitly accepted and undisputed practices.

However the idea of 'non-decision-making' is only a partial and inadequate way of analysing how power is structured into institutions, and is framed in terms of the action approach that is supposedly subjected to critique. Non-decision-making is still basically regarded as a property of agents, rather than of social institutions.

Perhaps the best critical appraisal of these issues is that by Lukes.[75] Power, according to him, is more than merely schizoid; it does not just have two faces, but three. There is one key part of Lukes's argument which I shall reject at the outset: he says, following Gallie,[76] that power is an 'essentially contested' concept and 'ineradicably evaluative'. I think this view is either mistaken or unenlightening. It is mistaken if the implication is that some notions in the social sciences are *essentially* contested, while others are not, such that we could draw up an (uncontested?) list of essentially contested concepts, separate from others. The chronic contestation or disputation of concepts and theories in the social sciences is in some part due to the fact that these concepts and theories are caught up in what they are about, namely social life itself: a line of thought I shall develop in the concluding paper in this volume. The notion of power certainly tends to provoke particularly deep-seated controversies. But a range of other terms that also figure in an important way in this book – class, ideology, interests, etc. – are equally potent in this respect; and I would want to claim not just that a few especially contentious concepts such as these, but the whole conceptual apparatus of social theory is in some sense 'ineradicably evaluative'. These things do not, of course, necessarily compromise Lukes's suggestion that the three faces of power he analyses may be more or less closely related to differing political positions; however I want to contend that it is not in fact useful to distinguish three dimensions of power, as Lukes attempts to do.

Lukes accepts that the non-decision-making approach marks an advance over the decision-making one (or what he calls the 'pluralist' view). The former of these, as contrasted to the latter, is two-dimensional because it does not simply concentrate upon the enactment of decisions, but also points to ways in which issues are suppressed from being 'decisionable' at all. As Lukes says, quite rightly, the specific limitation of the two-dimensional view is that it is still too closely linked to the standpoint which it opposes. 'The basis of the [social] system', Lukes points out, 'is not sustained simply by a series of individually chosen acts, but also, most importantly, by the socially structured and culturally patterned behaviour of groups, and practices of institutions . . .'[77] Consequently in place of the two-dimensional view, Lukes introduces his three-dimensional concept. The three-dimensional view invokes the notion of interests: in conjunction with it, Lukes redefines power as the capability of one actor or party to influence another in a manner contrary to that other's interests. Now this does not seem to work. Or at least intuitively there seems no reason to suppose that power is only exercised where A affects B in a way contrary to B's interests – as compared to where A affects B in a way that is irrelevant to B's interests, or more importantly where A affects B in a way that accords with B's interests.[78] The second of these could only be excluded as a case of power if B always behaved in his own interests, regardless of anyone else's intervention; but people are not always inclined to act in accordance with their interests. I should want to say, as against Lukes, that the concept of interest, like that of conflict, has nothing logically to do with that of power; although substantively, in the actual enactment of social life, the phenomena to which they refer have a great deal to do with one another. But in any case appeal to interests is an odd twist in the argument, because adding the idea of interests to the 'one'- and 'two-dimensional' views, which is essentially Lukes's strategy, does not in fact address the problem of how to incorporate 'socially structured conduct' within a general treatment of power; for Lukes does not suggest that interests are a group or structural phenomenon rather than one to do with individual actors. Rather than adding on another 'dimension' to the decision-making and non-decision-making approaches, we need to do what Lukes advocates, but does not in fact accomplish; this implies attempting to overcome the traditional division between 'voluntaristic' and 'structural' notions of power.

Lukes has, however, attacked the problem directly in a subsequent publication.[79] Power in social theory, he argues, as I do, is centrally involved with human agency; a person or party who wields power *could* 'have acted otherwise', ånd the person or party over whom power is wielded, the concept implies, *would* have acted overwise if power had not been exercised. 'In speaking thus, one assumes that, although the agents operate within structurally determined limits, they none the less have a certain relative autonomy and could have acted differently.'[80] In representing structure as placing limitations or constraints upon the activities of agents, however, Lukes tends to repeat the dualism of agency and structure that I have spoken of in earlier papers. Hence he talks of 'where structural determinism ends and power begins',[81] and is unable satisfactorily to deal with structure as implicated in power relations, and power relations as implicated in structure.

This can only be achieved, I think, if it is recognised that power must be treated in the context of the duality of structure: if the resources which the existence of domination implies and the exercise of power draws upon, are seen to be at the same time structural components of social systems. The exercise of power is not a type of act; rather power is instantiated in action, as a regular and routine phenomenon. It is mistaken moreover to treat power *itself* as a resource as many theorists of power do. Resources are the media through which power is exercised, and structures of domination reproduced, as indicated in Figure 2.6.

The notion of resources, as structural components of social systems, figures as a key one in the treatment of power within the theory of structuration. The concept of power both as transformative capacity (the characteristic view held by those treating power in terms of the conduct of agents), and as domination (the main focus of those concentrating upon power as a structural quality), depends

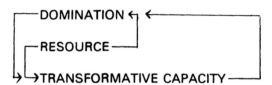

FIGURE 2.6

upon the utilisation of resources. I regard each view as implying the other, however. Resources are the media whereby transformative capacity is employed as power in the routine course of social interaction; but they are at the same time structural elements of social systems as systems, reconstituted through their utilisation in social interaction. This is therefore the correlate, in respect of power, of the duality of structure in respect of the communication of meaning and of normative sanctions: resources are not just additional elements to these, but include the means whereby the meaningful and the normative content of interaction is actualised. 'Power' intervenes conceptually between the broader notions of transformative capacity on the one side, and of domination on the other: power is a relational concept, but only operates as such through the utilisation of transformative capacity as generated by structures of domination.

To repeat what has been said before, understood as transformative capacity, power is intrinsically related to human agency. The 'could have done otherwise' of action is a necessary element of the theory of power. As I have tried to indicate elsewhere,[82] the concept of agency cannot be defined through that of intention, as is presumed in so much of the literature to do with the philosophy of action; the notion of agency, as I employ it, I take to be logically prior to a subject/object differentiation. The same holds for the concept of power. The notion of power has no inherent connection with intention or 'will', as it has in Weber's and many other formulations. It might at first seem somewhat odd to hold that an agent can exercise power without intending to do so, or even wanting to do so: for I wish to claim that the notion of power has no logical tie to motivation or wanting either. But it is not at all idiosyncratic: if it sounds so, it is perhaps because many discussions of the concept of power have taken place in a political context, where 'decisions' are clearly articulated in relation to ends that actors pursue. As with the sphere of agency more generally, those aspects of power encompassed by intentional actions, or within the reflexive monitoring of conduct, have a particular form; a range of notions such as 'compliance', 'bargaining', etc., apply only within such a context.

Although in the sense of transformative capacity power is implied in the very notion of action, I shall henceforth employ the term 'power' as a sub-category of 'transformative capacity', to refer to interaction where transformative capacity *is harnessed to actors' attempts to get others to comply with their wants.*Power, in this relational sense, concerns the capability of actors to secure outcomes where the realisation of these outcomes depends upon the agency of others. The use of power in interaction·thus can be understood in terms of the facilities that participants bring to and mobilise as elements of the production of that interaction, thereby influencing its course. Social systems are constituted as regularised practices: power within social systems can thus be treated *as involving reproduced relations of autonomy and dependence in social interaction.*[83] Power relations therefore are always *two-way*, even if the power of one actor or party in a social relation is minimal compared to another. Power relations are relations of autonomy and dependence, but even the most autonomous agent is in some degree dependent, and the most dependent actor or party in a relationship retains some autonomy.

Structures of domination involve *asymmetries of resources employed* in the sustaining of power relations in and between systems of interaction.

Resource   *Sanction*

AUTHORISATION   COERCION
⇕   ⇕
ALLOCATION   INDUCEMENT

FIGURE 2.7

In all institutionalised forms of social interaction, as I shall indicate in the following paper, there are two major resources which can be distinguished; we can add to these two main categories of sanction, as indicated in Figure 2.7. Authorisation and allocation may be associated with either or both types of sanctions: or as it may be better expressed, two *modes of sanctioning*. Obviously there is no clear-cut division between the types of sanctions, and they may be combined in varying ways. The distinction is essentially one between positive and negative sanctions, or rewards and punishments; but the threatened withholding of a promised reward can be a punitive gesture, and conversely the possibility of avoidance of or release from coercive measures can serve as an inducement.

It is important to emphasise that power should not be defined in terms of conflict, since the widely-employed Weberian definition of power, referred to earlier, has sometimes been read to imply that power and conflict are necessarily linked: as if power only exists, or is only exercised, when the resistance of others has to be overcome. It seems clear enough that this is not what Weber intended; however that may be, the formulation offered here carries no implication of this sort at all. The use of power, of course, often does stimulate conflict, or occurs in the context of struggle. This is not because of any kind of inevitable connection between power and conflict, but because of the substantive relations that often exist between power, conflict and interests. Interests I shall regard as founded in wants, regardless of whether an actor is conscious of those wants (that is, actors or groups may have interests of which they are unaware). Power and conflict, like power and the realisation of interests, are frequently, but nevertheless contingently, associated with one another. (For further discussion of the concept of interests, see pp. 188–90 below.)

Methodological individualism: a brief excursus

In conclusion, it might be useful to comment briefly about the bearing of the ideas advanced in this paper upon the debate over methodological individualism in social theory. There is, of course, no unitary view that can be identified as 'methodological individualism': the phrase has been used to cover a variety of different ideas. One version appears prominently in Weber's works, but I shall briefly consider here the formulation offered by Popper, who has been among the foremost advocates of such a view in modern times. Popper has described his standpoint succinctly as follows: 'all social phenomena, and especially the functioning of all social institutions, should always be understood as resulting from the decisions, actions, attitudes, etc. of human individuals ... we should never be satisfied by an explanation in terms of so-called "collectives".'[84] There are three key terms in this assertion that need some explanation: *individuals*, *collectives*, and what is implied in institutions *resulting* from decisions, etc. So far as the first of these is concerned, Popper's statement reflects a characteristic tendency in the literature of methodological individualism (pro and con) to assume that the term 'individual' stands in need of no explication. It might be thought a truism to hold that societies only consist of individuals – one reading that might be made of Popper's claim.[85] But it is only a truism (that is true in a trivial or uninteresting sense) if we understand 'individual' to mean something like 'human organism'. If 'individual', however, means 'agent' in the sense I have employed in this paper, the situation is quite different. The first part of Popper's statement then reflects the inadequacies of action theory that I have analysed above. Institutions do indeed 'result' from human agency: but they are the outcome of action only in so far as they are also involved recursively as the medium of its production. In the sense of 'institution' therefore, the 'collective' is bound to the very phenomenon of action.

The position adopted here can be summarised as follows:

1. Social systems are produced as transactions between agents, and can be analysed as such on the level of strategic conduct. This is 'methodological' in the sense that institutional analysis is bracketed, although structural elements necessarily enter into the characterisation of action, as modalities drawn upon to produce interaction.

2. Institutional analysis, on the other hand, brackets action, concentrating upon modalities as the media of the reproduction of social systems. But this is also purely a methodological bracketing, which is no more defensible than the first if we neglect the essential importance of the conception of the duality of structure.[86]

3

Institutions, Reproduction, Socialisation

In the preceding paper, I deferred consideration of problems of institutional analysis, and it is these I shall concentrate upon in the sections which follow. I distinguish 'institution' from 'social system' or 'collectivity'. Institutions, to quote Radcliffe-Brown, may be regarded as 'standardised modes of behaviour'[1] which play a basic part in the time–space constitution of social systems. The standardisation of behaviour in time–space, as I have emphasised in the foregoing discussion, involves its chronic *reconstitution* in contingent contexts of day-to-day social activity. Temporality enters into the reproduction of social systems in a threefold way:

1. In *the immediate nexus of interaction*, as contingently accomplished or 'brought off' by actors, social reproduction in its most elemental sense.
2. In the *reproduction of the personnel* of social systems, as beings with a finite life-span, *Sein zum Tode*, anchored of course in biological reproduction.
3. In the *reproduction of institutions*, sedimented in the *longue durée* of historical time.

In the concluding parts of this paper, I shall be concerned to show how these temporal contexts of social reproduction can be connected to an account of socialisation. In those sections of the paper I shall wish to develop further certain elements of the 'stratification model' of personality. But before taking up such issues, I want to expand the discussion of structure offered previously, and on this basis to outline a classification of institutions.

Signification and coding

In the study of signification, as a structural feature of social systems, the rules, or aspects of rules, that are of interest are *codes*, or modes of coding. The analysis of forms of domination involves considering the connections between what I shall call *authorisation* and *allocation*. The study of legitimation necessitates a grasp of modes of normative *regulation*, whereby 'legitimate orders' are sustained (see Figure 3.1).

SIGNIFICATION	Theory of coding
DOMINATION	Theory of authorisation and allocation
LEGITIMATION	Theory of normative regulation

FIGURE 3.1

In discussing the theory of signification I shall confine what I have to say to a fairly abstract or formal level. I wish to accentuate the importance of incorporating some of the central notions of semiotics within social theory. At the same time I want to stress the necessity of connecting these with a more satisfactory account of agency than is available within structuralist traditions, and with an examination of forms of domination and legitimation.

The sign may be accepted as the basic element of signification with the same reservations as those I have applied to structure: signs only exist as produced and reproduced in signification, just as structure only exists in and through processes of structuration. The theory of signification has to be freed from the subject/object dualisms that I earlier indicated have dogged most areas of the social sciences. In respect of signification, these dualisms have presented themselves in particularly acute fashion: in divergent conceptions of language, and in different philosophical standpoints. From the point of view of subjective idealism, language, and hence signification more generally, are understood as means or media of communication between actors: signs are transmitted information or meanings. What is missing here is a grasp of signification as a *constitutive feature of the context of communication itself.*[2] On the other hand, structuralist theories of language have taken signs as 'already-given' constituent properties of sign-systems. Sometimes this view has carried the implication that signs have 'fixed' or 'bounded' properties (even if only determined methodologically by the synchronic abstraction): thus tending to elide the distinction between signs and signals.[3] As against each of these views, we must once more substitute duality for dualism: signification, as concerning generative properties of structure, is linked recursively to the communication of meaning in interaction. Signification refers to structural features of social systems, drawn upon and reproduced by actors in the form of interpretative schemes. I therefore cannot agree with Eco when he defines semiotics as a 'discipline studying everything which can be used in order to lie', since the telling of lies necessarily applies to intentional action, and thus operates solely on the level of strategic conduct. The general character of Eco's position, however, conforms to that taken here: 'A signification system is an autonomous semiotic construct that has an abstract mode of existence independent of any possible communicative act it makes possible. On the other hand . . . *every act of communication to or between human beings . . . presupposes a signification system as its necessary condition.*'[4]

This should not be taken to indicate the attribution of a priority to the semiotic over the semantic, or acceptance of the Saussurian doctrines of the arbitrary character of the sign and the constitution of 'pure difference'. On the contrary, I consider that the semantic has priority over the semiotic.[5] The implication of this has to be made clear. It does not involve reducing meaning to the subjective level of communication, as is characteristically asserted by structuralist theorists who accord primacy to the semiotic; rather, meaning must be treated as grounded in the 'contexts of use' of language.[6] The valid core of the thesis of the arbitrary nature of the sign is to be located in the conventional character of signs: the differences which constitute signification are grounded in the 'spacing' of social practices. This does not as such resolve a traditional problem in the literature of semiotics: whether semiotics should be seen as an all-embracing study of signs or sign-systems, of which the study of language is just one part, or whether conversely it is more appropriately treated as a sub-category of linguistics. But my standpoint is more consonant with the latter type of view: it is plausible to suppose that the linguistic sign is, as Barthes says, the 'fatal relay' of all modes of signification, since language is such a permeating feature of human social activity. This does not, of course, prejudice recognising the most important contribution to emanate from semiotics: the emphasis that all kinds of contents, not just spoken or written words, can become caught up in signification.

Signs may be distinguished from both signals and symbols. I shall use 'symbol' in a manner to be defined later. A signal can be treated as a fixed stimulus that elicits a given interpretative response or range of responses. Signals hence can operate in purely mechanical systems, although they may be incorporated as elements of signification: as such they are obviously only of marginal importance when compared with the generic form of signs. I have argued previously that Saussure's dualism of signifier and signified should be recast. It is not helpful to speak of signifiers which in some way 'correspond to' or 'articulate with' signifieds, nor even 'signifying chains' that somehow articulate with chains of signifieds. Nevertheless, the notion of the articulation of chains of signifiers and signifieds does point the way beyond the presumption that signs are 'already-given' items in the way in which signals are.

The syntagmatic/paradigmatic distinction is directly relevant to this, since these relationships are multiform on a vertical as well as on a linear or temporal axis.[7] As structural properties of social systems, codes embody multivalent traits, and have in a certain sense to be read 'textually'. That is to say, the code-message concept, which is readily able to deal with the generation of communication within closed, mechanical systems, needs to be carefully elaborated when applied to the explication of communication in social interaction. We cannot simply identify pre-existing codes which generate messages, since the 'messages' also enter into the reconstruction of 'codes' in the duality of structure in interaction; but, more than this, in social interaction the 'messages' are always 'texts' in the sense in which they are generated from, and express a plurality of codes.

The notion of code, understood against such a backdrop, necessarily presupposes that of transformations. This applies of course as much to the syntactical rules involved in the production of linguistic signs as to other semiotic systems of direct interest to social analysis. There is good reason, however, to deny the thesis that all forms of coding can be ultimately grounded in binary oppositions, of whatever type.[8] Rather, binary oppositions come into focus through a methodological concentration upon one segment of difference, as constituted generally in networks of oppositions.

Resources: authorisation and allocation

In distinguishing authorisation from allocation, I mean to separate conceptually two major types of resource which constitute structures of domination, and which are drawn upon and reproduced as power relations in interaction. By 'authorisation' I refer to capabilities which generate command over *persons*, and by 'allocation' I refer to capabilities which generate command over *objects* or other material phenomena.

The analytical distinction between these is a highly important one, because it can help us to avoid some traditional shortcomings of the sociological literature: shortcomings which can be related to the influence of two broad streams of social and political thought.[9] In one such stream of thought, Marxism (it would be more accurate to make the qualification: certain forms of Marxism), domination is associated first and foremost with allocative resources (property). There is real force in the critical comments directed against such forms of Marxism that they fail to give sufficient attention to authorisation as a resource (authority). Authorisation tends to be treated reductively, as derivative of allocation. The consequence is not only a defective understanding of the political system of industrial capitalism, but an inability to confront the problem of the nature of authority in socialist societies. It is just this kind of critical comment which is typically levelled against Marxism by those writing from within an alternative tradition: that of the *theory of industrial society*. Here authorisation is not reduced to allocation, but the reverse: the second is regarded as a special case of the first.[10] Rather than accentuating the possible contrasts between capitalism and socialism, this type of approach minimises them; authorisation is presumed to have a more or less constant form in every industrial society. The significance of allocation as a medium of domination is correspondingly understated, in both an analytical and an historical sense. It is understated in the former sense because it is regarded as merely a sub-type of authorisation; and in the latter sense because power deriving from allocation (property) is seen to be of major importance only in the structure of domination during the period of classical or entrepreneurial capitalism. Hence this type of thinking has been closely associated with the managerialist argument about the separation of economic power from property ownership.

It is worth emphasising that each of these traditions of thought shares something in common, beyond their manifest differences. Both envisage the 'obsolescence of property', one as a result of revolutionary change, the other as a result of a more gradual process of evolution. In both, therefore, or so I should want to claim, there is an underestimation of the continuing importance of allocation as a generic feature of domination. This is undoubtedly in some part due to the assimilation which is characteristically made between 'property' and 'private property', with the implication that with the transcendence of the latter, property as a concept loses its relevance for social analysis. This is not the view I take here, although I acknowledge the central importance of differentiating private from collective property (as well as recognising further distinctions that could be made within these).

Legitimation and norms

I shall defer further discussion of these issues for the time being, and turn to a brief initial appraisal of problems of normative regulation. The theory of normative regulation occupies a peculiarly focal position in contemporary social analysis, largely as a result of the emphases brought into prominence in the sociology of Durkheim and of Parsons. I have traced these through and criticised them in some detail elsewhere.[11] It is not accidental that it has proved difficult within this type of theoretical tradition to find conceptual space for a notion of legitimation, in spite of Parsons's original endeavour to merge ideas adopted from both Durkheim and Weber. For Parsons essentially absorbed the Weberian concept of 'legitimate orders' within Durkheim's *conscience collective*, as part of the solution to the 'Hobbesian problem of order'.[12] The problem of order was defined by Parsons as concerned with how society can exist, with some degree of stability over time, in the face of the struggle of individual wills, the war of all against all. The effect of adopting this point of departure has been to tie Parsons's own theories, in a deep-rooted way, to a position in which interests are grasped primarily in terms of an *individual/society opposition*. The moral consensus which makes possible the unity of the social whole incorporates values 'internalise' as need-dispositions in personality, thus ensuring a fit between the individual and society. The theme of 'common values' replaces that of legitimation, in so far as the latter is understood as relating to the sectional interests of dominant groups (and hence to ideology).

The notion of legitimation is preferable to one of normative consensus for two reasons: first, it does not imply any particular degree of agreement over the value-standards actualised as rights and obligations; second, it allows a much clearer appreciation of the interplay between value-standards and sectional interests in society. By 'value-standards' I mean any kind of normative prescription that may be mobilised as a sanctioning feature of interaction. We have to regard as suspect any theory that holds that every relatively stable society necessarily rests upon a close parallelism between, or 'interpenetration' of, the value-standards involved in legitimation and the motives co-ordinated in and through the conduct of the members of that society. This is relevant to Parsons's account in respect both of his general interpretation of personality and the *consensus universel*, and to his appropriation of psychoanalytic theory as part of this scheme.

For Parsons, there is a clear convergence between Durkheim and Freud: elements of Freud's conception of personality development can be used to elucidate the 'value consensus – norm – internalised need-disposition' resolution of the problem of order. But this is a Freud largely purged of antagonism or tension. The main characteristics of human personality, Parsons argues, are 'organised about the internalisation of systems of social objects which originated as the role-units of the successive series of social systems in which the individual has come to be integrated in the course of his life history'.[13] This is specifically distinguished by Parsons from a view of the development of personality which involves the repression of instinctual drives; the formation of personality occurs through the internalisation of 'object-systems' which become progressively differentiated over time as the individual becomes more closely incorporated within society. The consequence of such an interpretation is to suggest an intrinsic harmony or compatibility between motivation and value-standards in an area where – if the main direction of Freud's thought is followed – there are inherent tensions of a fundamental kind.

There are other possible disjunctions between the conduct of actors in society and structures of legitimation which compromise the theorem of the necessary interpenetration of motivation and value consensus. For legitimate orders to have any binding force at all, of course, they must be embodied as structural conditions of action for at least a certain proportion of the members of a collectivity or a society. But the presumption that this must extend to the majority of such actors, for that collectivity or society to enjoy some stability of existence, is not warranted. The level of normative integration of dominant groups within social systems may be a more important influence upon the overall continuity of those systems than how far the majority have 'internalised' the same value-standards.

These considerations are not merely significant at the level of the overall society, or large-scale organisations, but apply to all circumstances of interaction. In any context of interaction, what is a legitimate value-standard for one actor may be just a 'factual' feature of the environment of action for another. This is actually a characteristic principle of the operation of sanctions, even where the normative elements involved are only relatively 'weak' in form.

Structural properties

I want to suggest that each of the three aspects of structure I have distinguished can be understood as ordered in terms of the *mediations* and *transformations* which they make possible in the temporal–spatial constitution of social systems. The most basic sense of mediation is that involved in the 'binding' of time and space themselves, the very essence of social reproduction. The binding of time and space, to anticipate a theme I shall develop further later, can be understood in terms of what can be called the 'presence-availability' of actors within social systems. All social interaction involves mediation in so far as there are always 'vehicles' that 'carry' social interchange across spatial and temporal gaps. In societies or communities of high-presence availability – in other words, where interaction is predominantly of a face-to-face kind – the mediating vehicles are those supplied by the faculties of physical presence. Writing and other media of communication (telephone, television, mechanised modes of transportation) bind much greater distances in time and space.

In the previous paper I have proposed the argument that there are no such things as rules of transformation: all social rules (codes and norms) are transformational. To say that rules are transformational, in the terminology I employ in this book, is to say that they generate an indefinite range of empirical contents, which have an identity with one another only in respect of their relation to those rules. While this may be obvious enough in respect of codes and norms, it is perhaps not so clear how resources involve either mediations or transformations. For resources (for example, wealth, property) might seem to exist in a temporal–spatial sense, in a way in which rules do not. But I want to say that the material existents involved in resources (a) are the content, or the 'vehicles', of resources in a parallel manner to the 'substance' of codes and norms, and (b) as instantiated in power relations in social systems, only operate in conjunction with codes and norms. (Allocation is only 'property' as instantiated in conjunction with rules of signification and legitimation.) The transformational character of resources is just as basic as that of rules: which is why I employ the term 'transformational capacity' as an intrinsic feature of human agency. Resources, however, provide the *material levers* of all transformations of empirical contents, including those involved in the operation of codes and norms.

The notions of transformation and mediation do not only apply to the structuring of interaction in real time–space, they are also essentially involved in analysing structures themselves. When mediation and transformation are taken together, they can be said to concern the *convertibility* of rules and resources. I shall provide an example of this here which is really only illustrative, but prepares the way in some degree for the more substantive discussion of social institutions that follows: the significance of private property as a structural component of modern capitalism. Some key structural relations instantiated in the capitalist system can be represented in virtual time–space as follows:

(1)   private property : money : capital : labour contract : profit

(2)   private property : money : capital : labour contract : industrial authority

(3)   private property : money : educational advantage : occupational position

Although private property is not in any way distinctive to modern capitalism, certain definite modes of the convertibility of private property are (which is, of course, relevant to the signification of 'private property' as such). The central structural components of the capitalist mode of production involve the convertibility relations indicated in (1). Money, the 'universal whore', as the medium of pure exchange-value provides for the convertibility of property rights into capital (in the context of the totality). The universalisation of the money economy is the condition of the emergence of capitalist society, as opposed to the existence of capitalistic sectors within agrarian production systems. As a universal standard of exchange-value, money permits both the transformation of private property into capital and, in association with this, facilitates the commodification of labour power as the only 'property' possessed by the wage-worker. The existence of property/money as capital in turn provides for the convertibility of capital into profit via the extraction of surplus value.

A linked range of transformation–mediation relations can be sketched in as structural components of the convertibility of private property into industrial authority in (2). The convertibility of the two structural properties at the right-hand 'end' of the set depends upon different transformations, of course, to those in (1). These transformations are however again in some degree particular traits of capitalism: the legitimation of authority in the capitalist enterprise is primarily organised through the labour-contract itself (as compared, for example, to the bond of fealty between feudal lord and serf). The structural relations indicated in set (3) simply illustrate another range of convertible elements. The transformation of money, or wealth more generally, into educational advantage obviously can take various forms; but in many contemporary societies a privileged education can still be directly purchased in private schools like any other commodity. The transformations of educational advantage into occupational position similarly can be instantiated in a variety of ways: again, some of these are fairly direct (for example, the 'old school tie').

The study of structures, as I have said before, is always the study of *structuration*. The caution that Eco counsels about the notion of code applies to all three components of structure I differentiate:

One can . . . maintain that it is not true that a code organises signs;

it is more correct to say that codes provide the rules which *generate* signs as concrete occurrences in communicative intercourse. Therefore the classical notion of 'sign' *dissolves* itself into a highly complex network of changing relationships. Semiotics suggests a sort of molecular landscape in which what we are accustomed to recognise as everyday forms turn out to be the result of transitory chemical aggregations and so-called 'things' are only the surface appearance assumed by an underlying network of more elementary units. Or rather, semiotics gives us a sort of photomechanical explanation of semiosis, revealing that where we thought we saw images there were only strategically arranged aggregations of black and white points, alternations of presence and absence . . .[14]

The isolation of structural sets of the sort I have discussed above is indispensable to the analysis of structuration, but we must always bear in mind that it is justified only on methodological grounds. Of course, the sets I have used as illustrations are portrayed in relatively simple form: more complex networks of structural relations could easily be represented and analysed in a similar way.

The identification of structures can in no sense be regarded as the only aim of sociological investigation. The instantiation of structure in the reproduction of social systems, as its medium and outcome, is the proper focus of sociological analysis. Each of the three sets mentioned above thus has to be interpolated as elements of cycles of social reproduction producing systemness in social relations. In the context of such interpolation, we can identify structural elements that are most deeply embedded in the time–space dimensions of social systems: in the following paper, in which I shall relate the analysis of structuration to system contradiction, I shall refer to such structural elements as *structural principles*. Structural principles govern the basic institutional alignments in a society.

Classification of institutions

To forestall misunderstanding, it is worth stressing again that the differentiation of signification, domination and legitimation is an analytical one. If signification is fundamentally structured in and through language, *language at the same time expresses aspects of domination; and the codes that are involved in signification have normative force.* Authorisation and allocation are only mobilised in conjunction with signifying and normative elements; and, finally, legitimation necessarily involves signification as well as playing a major part in co-ordinating forms of domination. These very connections, however, make the signification–domination–legitimation scheme a useful basis for a classification of institutions which emphasises their interrelation within the social totality.

S–D–L	Symbolic orders/modes of discourse
D(auth)–S–L	Political institutions
D(alloc)–S–L	Economic institutions
L–D–S	Law/modes of sanction

S = Signification
D = Domination
L = Legitimation

FIGURE 3.2

In Figure 3.2, the lines connecting signification–domination–legitimation are not, of course, causal connections, but merely indicate interdependence. The first letter in each line indicates direction of analytical focus. Thus when we focus upon those institutional forms through which signification is organised, we are concerned with the analysis of *symbolic orders* and *modes of discourse*. No such analysis can ignore the ways in which symbol-systems and modes of discourse are interwoven with forms of domination and legitimation. A parallel argument applies to the other types of institution: *political*; *economic*; and *legal/repressive*.

I distinguish 'sign' from 'symbol' in a manner close to that suggested by Ricoeur, who treats as a symbol 'any structure of signification in which a direct, primary, literal meaning designates, in addition, another meaning which is indirect, secondary, and figurative and which can be apprehended only through the first'. Symbols draw upon the 'surplus of meaning' inherent in signification as a whole: it seems reasonable to claim that such surplus of meaning can be grasped as the conjunction of metaphor and metonymy within symbolic orders.[15] The importance of such a conception of symbolism is considerable, when compared to that which ordinarily prevails in sociology, where *'symbol' is often used as merely equivalent to 'representation'*, and hence where symbols are presumed to have rigid boundaries. This is a static, conservative view of symbolism, which cannot satisfactorily explain the intimacy and subtlety whereby symbolic orders are geared in to processes of social change. If we accept, however, that symbolism relates, as Ricoeur says, 'the multiplicity of meaning to the equivocalness of being', we are able to see that the 'breakthrough of language towards something other than itself', marked by symbolism, expresses the potency of symbols in stimulating new meanings.[16] The metaphorical and metonymical associations of symbols are as important in science as in other types of discourse: metaphor, indeed, may be at the very root of innovation in scientific theories.[17]

There are numerous ways in which the 'political' and 'economic' are defined in the literature. In the scheme offered in Figure 3.2, I treat the realm of the political as being usefully understood in a generic sense as concerning the mobilisation of *authorisation* as a resource; and that of the economic as concerning the mobilisation of *allocative resources*. There are thus political and economic aspects of all social systems which have some enduring existence. So far as the sphere of the political goes, this usage differs from two common types of interpretation: that which links the political specifically to the emergence of the modern state[18] and that which associates the political inherently with the resolution of conflicts of values or interests. The first assumes that the term 'political' is intrinsically dependent upon the formation of a distinct 'polity'. Such a conception makes it difficult to acknowledge significant continuities between pre-state and state societies; it implicitly tends to take for granted a basic feature of liberal democratic government, the severing of polity and economy. The same principle applies in reverse as regards the economic, which is sometimes understood in such a way as to limit its sense to those societies which have a distinct and definite 'economy'. Some other definitions that are more inclusive are also strongly imbalanced towards capitalist society in so far as the economic is conceptualised as exchange relations. I reject these here, as well as those that have an affinity with the second of the conceptions of the political referred to above: I have in mind the sort of definition which equates the economic with struggles deriving from scarce resources (cf. Polanyi's critique of 'formal economics').

Similarly, I do not mean to confine the realm of legal institutions to those societies which have formalised statutes. Formalised laws differ from juridical rules generally in respect, as one author has expressed it, of 'clarity, fixity, finality'.[19] That is to say, statutes are set out as definite formulae, having fixed application, and holding in a universal fashion for those infractions which fall within them. But it is an obvious – and a much laboured – point in sociology that formalised items and procedures of law can only be studied in terms of their intersection with more diffuse normative elements in society: and, we must add, with the sanctions associated with them.

In further examining broad features of the institutions of the industrialised societies, we have to consider some basic problems of class analysis. In *The Class Structure of the Advanced Societies*, I elaborated a standpoint, in respect of such problems, which I still think essentially correct, even if in some other regards the work has a number of serious limitations.[20] 'Classes' have often been treated – in some traditions of social theory – as though they were groups or collectivities: most commonly, in those traditions claiming a lineage from Marx. On the other hand, there are contrasting approaches – most notably associated with Max Weber and those who have followed him – in which the term 'class' is used to refer to a category of aggregate qualities (chances in the market, or traits of occupations). Neither of these types of conceptualisation seems satisfactory. The first faces a range of familiar difficulties. Collectivities like a family, school, etc. seem relatively easy to identify, but classes do not. Thus those who take this approach have sometimes tended to argue that we can only speak of a 'class' when there is some degree of common class consciousness held by those who are members of that class – a view for which a certain amount of textual support can be mustered from Marx, but which is none the less clearly inconsistent with the main body of Marx's writings. Those who have adopted the second type of standpoint, on the other hand – including Weber – have encountered major difficulties in making any connection between class categories and actual forms of group organisation: thus the relation between Weber's notions of 'economic class situation' on the one hand, and 'social class', on the other, remains obscure.[21]

I therefore propose abandoning both of these approaches, suggesting that a theory of class can only be satisfactorily elucidated as involving the influence of an institutional order of 'class society' upon the formation of collectivities. Such an understanding of class structuration implies connecting (via what I would now call the duality of structure) a theory of class society, as an institutional form, with an account of how class relations are expressed in concrete types of group formation and consciousness. The origins of class society can be identified in certain structural characteristics of capitalist society alluded to previously: the formation of distinct spheres of economy and polity, whereby economic activity is 'insulated' from direct political control. There is hence an immediate and integral relation between the concepts of the capitalist state and of class society. The insulation of economy and polity, in terms of the classification of institutions offered above, is the fundamental feature of capitalist society: which also means, in our times, the dominant sector of world society. While its organisation is still rooted in structures of the nation–state, its ramifications are obviously international: the relations between states and multinational corporations within world commodity markets are its concrete expression (cf. below, pp. 225–6).

What applies as a theorem in respect of class domination also applies generically to any type of institutional analysis: an understanding of institutional forms can only be achieved in so far as it is shown how, as regularised social practices, institutions are constituted and reconstituted in the tie between the *durée* of the passing moment, and the *longue durée* of deeply sedimented time–space relations. This leads through to a point of major importance, already emphasised in a previous paper: the totality/moment relation is compatible with a variety of different 'layers' (to borrow a term from Gurvitch) of relations of autonomy and dependence between collectivities. The significance of such a stress is that it enables us to avoid difficulties that have always been associated with functionalist views of the whole, or more broadly, those views in which the whole is a 'present' combination of parts. Such approaches have only been able to deal with the participation of the part in the whole by assuming that the one shares certain of the features of the other: that there is an homology between them. One result of this is a tendency to move directly from part to whole in social analysis: to presume that the solution to the question 'what integrates the individual into society?' *ipso facto* explains what integrates society. This kind of conception (which receives additional reinforcement from the organic analogies that virtually always inform it, in a manifest or more buried way) effectively forecloses the possibility of treating society *as consisting of groups in tension*: as groups in relations of power and various levels of conflict. On the other hand, those forms of functionalism, such as that developed by R. K. Merton, which are more able to acknowledge the centrality of power and conflict in society, have relinquished an understanding of the totality as in some way implicated in its parts.[22] Thus for Merton the social whole can be analysed as only a 'net sum of functional consequences' of the interaction of individuals and collectivities.[23]

Functionalism and social reproduction

It is not enough merely to reject functionalist theories of the totality; we must also reject functionalist interpretations of social reproduction (in each of the senses in which I have earlier indicated that the concept of social reproduction may be understood). We have to make a distinction between two sorts of functionalism here, even if there are certain continuities and parallels between them. The functionalist conception of the whole as an organic unity is linked particularly to what is sometimes referred to as 'normative functionalism',[24] and includes certain main elements that can without much difficulty be traced through from Comte to Durkheim to Parsons. Such a view is obviously uncommon in Marxist traditions, which necessarily in some sense acknowledge the division of society into classes. Marxist–functionalist interpretations of social reproduction (or of economic reproduction, the reproduction of capital), on the other hand, are very common indeed. It is not hard to find in the Marxist literature theorems of an openly functionalist sort, however much their authors might disclaim any connotation of functionalism. Thus when Poulantzas writes that the state has 'the particular function of constituting the factor of cohesion between the levels of a social formation',[25] he offers a functional definition no different in form from many comparable ones that appear in the literature of non-Marxist social science. The state is not defined just in terms of what it does, or how it operates, but in terms of how what it does contributes to the 'needs of the system'. The interpretation of the nature of the state built upon this conceptualisation explains the state's activities through their functional indispensability or usefulness to the continued existence of the capitalist system. Much writing in contemporary Marxism centres about the analysis of reproduction, and the dominant tone is a functionalist one. Marx's analyses of simple and expanded reproduction quite readily lend themselves to functionalist readings, and have often been interpreted in such a fashion by those who have looked to them as a source of insight into the relations of capital and labour in capitalist development.[26]

Such traits are particularly prominent in the works of those influenced by Althusser: for Althusser's Marxism, as I have pointed out before, shares with 'normative functionalism' a blindness to the everyday fact that all social agents have an understanding, practical and discursive, of the conditions of their action. In both Althusserian Marxism and Parsonian sociology the reproduction of society occurs 'behind the backs' of the agents whose conduct constitutes that society. The involvement of actors' own purposive conduct with the rationalisation of action is lacking in each case: in Parsons's sociology as a result of the value consensus–norm–internalised need-disposition theorem, and in Althusser's writings as a consequence of his deterministic account of agency; hence the teleology of the system either governs (in the first) or supplants (in the second) that of actors themselves.

In place of each of these approaches I wish to insist that the only teleology involved in social systems is that comprised within the conduct of social actors.[27] Such teleology *always* operates within bounded conditions of the rationalisation of action. All social reproduction occurs in the context of 'mixes' of intended and unintended consequences of action; *every* feature of whatever continuity a society has over time derives from such 'mixes', against the backdrop of bounded conditions of rationalisation of conduct. In this conception, the notion of system *presupposes* that of social reproduction: reproduction is not a mysterious accomplishment that social systems manage to carry out via the activities of their 'members'.

It is important to make the argument clear at this point, and this is best done by providing an illustration. Consider Marx's discussion of the reserve army in the capitalist economy. Marx's argument can be read, and frequently has been read, in a functionalist vein. Capitalism has its own 'needs', which the system functions to fulfil. Since the system needs a reserve army, one comes into being. The argument is sometimes stated in reverse. Since the operation of capitalism leads to the formation of a reserve army, this must be because it needs one. Neither version of the reserve army argument can be defended. Not even the most deeply sedimented institutional features of societies come about because those societies need them to do so. They come about *historically*, as a result of concrete conditions that have in every case to be directly analysed; the same holds for their persistence.

The reserve army argument can be expressed as a homeostatic series of relations of social reproduction in conformity with the scheme outlined in the previous paper. That is to say, the existence of a pool of unemployed workers might be shown to form a causal loop with other factors in the production system. Now a functionalist would express this as the proposition, 'the function of the reserve army is to stabilise capitalist production'. But I want to ban the term 'function' from the social sciences – at least as having a technical sense of this sort. The term 'function', as it appears in the above proposition, is noxious in two senses.

1. In saying 'function' rather than 'effect' (within a causal loop), the interpreter implies that some sort of explanation has been offered of why the reserve army is there, or of how it contributes to the reproduction of the capitalist system. However the proposition in question is not an explanation of anything. It is at most a preliminary approach to an explanation of aspects of social reproduction. Such an explanation must show concretely what are the relations involved between each of the elements that comprise the causal loop.
2. Use of the term 'function' implies the traditional dichotomy between dynamics and statics: that the function of the reserve army can be analysed 'out of time'. But we cannot bracket time in studying social stability any more than we can in studying social change. The equation of time with change must be resisted.

In rejecting functionalist conceptions that social systems have 'needs' or 'reasons' of their own, which can be used to explain anything about what happens in or to them, there is one class of statements that I do not mean to exclude from social analysis. This is those of a counterfactual sort: 'what has to happen for given features of a social system to come about/persist/be altered'. We have to employ such conjectural propositions with some caution, because they may lend themselves to interpretation in a functionalist manner. Take as an example the statement: 'in order to persist in relatively stable form, the capitalist economy has to maintain a certain overall level of profit'. The force of 'has to' here is counterfactual: it involves identifying conditions that must be met if certain consequences are to obtain. The 'has to' is not a property or 'need' of the system, and has no explanatory force – *unless* actors within the system get to know about the conditions in question, and actively incorporate them in a process of reflexive self-regulation of system reproduction. (For further discussion of these issues, see below, pp. 210–16.)

All social reproduction is grounded in the knowledgeable application and reapplication of rules and resources by actors in situated social contexts: all interaction thus has, in every circumstance, to be contingently 'brought off' by those who are party to it. Change is in principle involved with social reproduction – again in both its basic sense and in its 'generational' sense – in its very contingency: social systems are chronically produced and reproduced by their constituent participants. *Change, or its potentiality, is thus inherent in all moments of social reproduction.* It is essential to see that any and every change in a social system logically implicates the totality and thus implies structural modification, however minor or trivial this may be. This is illustrated by linguistic change: modifications in the phonemic, syntactical or semantic character of words in language are effected through and in language use, that is through the reproduction of language; since language only exists in and through its reproduction, such modifications implicate the whole.

In relating institutions to social change, it is necessary to link the bases of group formation to system contradiction: in the capitalist societies this linkage is mediated in a fundamental way by class domination. The most deep-lying contradiction in industrial capitalism, or so I shall argue later, is that between private appropriation and socialised production (pp. 141–5, below): this contradiction is expressed institutionally in the relations of economy and polity referred to previously, which in turn are the institutional grounding of class structure. The relation between class structure and class formation, however, as I have already pointed out, is a complicated one. Although 'capitalist society' may be regarded as a generic type, involving a definite alignment of institutions, there can be wide variations in the types of class formation between different concrete societies. Two general types of factor influence such variations: the conjunction of particular forms of primary and secondary contradictions; and the conjunction of class with other bases of group formation.

If it be accepted that class refers above all to a mode of institutional organisation, rather than to collectivities as such, it follows that class domination does not exclude other influences upon the structuring of collectivities.[28] Other modes of domination may cut across class domination; or alternatively they may have the effect of accentuating rather than diminishing or weakening it. Two sources of schism that are particularly relevant here are those of ethnic differences (or their attribution) and sex divisions: although I do not propose to undertake any sort of general analysis of the conjunctions of class with ethnic or sexual domination in this context. As before, we have to be careful to avoid any functional arguments which suggest that, where ethnic or sexual domination does converge with modes of class domination, such convergence can be accounted for by its functional necessity for capitalist society. But there is no doubt that there are important convergences of both kinds in contemporary capitalism, and it is easy to find illustrations of them. Thus ethnic discrimination in many contemporary countries has the consequence of driving those subject to that discrimination into segmented labour markets, helping to consolidate the formation of distinct underclasses. This is hence a kind of 'double discrimination'. Something similar is true of the position of women at all levels of the labour force: indeed, for women of ethnic backgrounds subject to discrimination, there may exist a 'triple discrimination'.[29]

Problems of role theory

In (non-Marxist) functionalist theories of social systems, the concept of role has figured very prominently. Thus for Parsons, social systems consist in interconnected roles; and role 'is the primary point of direct articulation between the personality of the individual and the structure of the social system'.[30] But the notion of role has of course also been widely used by authors in traditions other than that of functionalism, most notably by those influenced by symbolic interactionism. The role concept has been subject to a variety of critiques.[31] I shall not comment upon these, but wish to mention three major types of objection which can be made against the use of the notion of role in social analysis. First, although the notion of role is often introduced in the literature as allowing some 'free play' for the social actor, that is, as avoiding the reduction of human behaviour to the determinism of social causes, for the most part role theory heavily emphasises the 'given' character of roles. It is the individual's 'performance' in the role which he or she might have some influence or mastery over, not the role itself. Role analysis hence often tends to perpetuate the action/structure dualism so strongly engrained in social theory: society supplies the roles to which actors adapt as best they might. Such an emphasis tends to persist even among some of those writers who allot a considerable conceptual space to human agency. According to Goffman, for example: 'In entering the position, the incumbent finds that he must take on the whole array of action encompassed by the corresponding role, so role implies a social determinism and a doctrine about socialisation. . . . Role then is the basic unit of socialisation. It is through roles that tasks in society are allocated and arrangements made to enforce their performance.'[32]

Second, the idea of role is often used in such a way as to presume both a unity of normative expectations that cohere to form the role, and a consensus in a social system about what those expectations are. The former of these assumptions tends to be encouraged by the conception that for each position in a social system, there is a corresponding role, or 'role set'. It betrays a particular, and deficient, view of society (and, one might add, of theatre[33]) according to which stability and the 'ordered regulation of expectations' are natural, and to which change is foreign. 'As much as I love the theatre, as much am I, for that very reason, its enemy' (Artaud). The linkage of role to normative consensus, which is a particularly central feature of Parsons's sociology, has been debated by those role theorists (for example Merton, Dahrendorf, Goode) who wish to distance themselves from the consensual character of the Parsonian portrayal of society. But the conflicts or strains which are acknowledged by such authors predominantly tend to concern the relation between the individual actor and the role expectations that 'society' calls upon him or her to meet. 'Role strain' derives from disjunctions between an individual's psychological traits and role demand.

Third, the conception that role is the basic constituent element of social systems is a major prop to the Parsonian view of the overriding importance of values or norms in social analysis. Role is a normative concept; hence to claim that social systems consist of roles can readily be used to affirm the primacy of the normative in social theory.

While I shall not reject the notion of role altogether, I certainly shall reject the idea that social systems can usefully be understood as consisting of roles or their conjunction; and the associated thesis that role, to requote Parsons, is 'the primary point of direct articulation between the personality of the individual and the structure of the social system'. It is fundamental to affirm that *social systems are not constituted of roles but of (reproduced) practices*; and it is practices, not roles, which (via the duality of structure) have to be regarded as the 'points of articulation' between actors and structures.

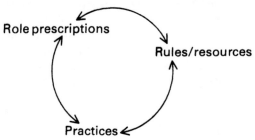

FIGURE 3.3

According to the conception of social theory I have suggested in the previous papers, social systems – but not structures – are located in time and space. There is no difficulty therefore in thinking of social systems as structured 'fields' in which (as reproduced in the temporality of interaction) actors occupy definite *positions vis-à-vis* one another. The notion of social position has been accorded nothing like the extensive discussion which that of role has received, even if most authors who have engaged in role analysis have employed it in close conjunction with role. I shall define a social position here as a social identity that carries with it a certain range (however diffusely specified) of prerogatives and obligations that an actor who is accorded that identity (or is an 'incumbent' of that position) may activate or carry out: these prerogatives and obligations constitute the role-prescriptions associated with that position. A social identity is essentially a category, or a typification, made on the basis of some definite social criterion or criteria: occupation, kin relation, age-grade, etc. Once we reject the thesis that social systems consist of either positions or roles, and recognise that roles can only be satisfactorily conceptualised in relation to practices, as indicated in Figure 3.3, there seems no reason why the notion of role should not be freed from the aforementioned weaknesses which have hampered its use in social theory. But the concept also thereby becomes a less important concept in social analysis than many of its advocates have wished to claim.

To insist that roles can only be analysed in relation to rules and resources is to accentuate the necessity of not taking role-prescriptions either as 'given' or as consensual, since role-prescriptions may incorporate contradictions, and focus conflicts, that express broad structural features of society. Role, as I have stressed above, is a normative concept, and thus connects closely to that of norm more generally: role-prescriptions are normative precepts that are organised in terms of the differentiation of social identities, and as such obviously mesh into more generalised types of normative rule. Similarly, all role-prescriptions are actualised, like any other components of social activity, through the utilisation of resources, and thus connect to structures of domination. Finally, role-prescriptions have to be studied in their interrelation with the actual practices that are the 'stuff' of social life; there may be various kinds of dislocation between what is enjoined in role-prescriptions and what actors typically do as the occupants of particular social positions.

With the above points in mind, it is relatively easy to identify in a formal way some possible sources of tension or conflict that, in the immediate nexus of the enactment of role-prescriptions, can contribute to such dislocation. None of these, of course, are to be regarded from the point of view of normative functionalism, as deviations from some assumed model of consensus; but as I have indicated in the preceding paragraph, as typically grounded in wider contradictions of the totality. Four types – not necessarily mutually exclusive – of 'role strain' seem worth distinguishing.

1. That which a good deal of the literature on role theory concentrates upon: tension between the needs or wants of actors and the role-prescriptions that are associated with social identities which they have. It is important to see however that this is neither

necessarily only psychological in character, nor 'irrational'. Such views tend to stem from the assumption of 'givenness' of roles, to which individuals 'adjust' either well or badly.

2. Tension between the elements of actors' role-sets. Merton has analysed this in some detail.[34] But we must make certain reservations about Merton's analysis. One is that he writes of disjunctions within role-sets in a functionalist vein: if his view does not accentuate consensus as much as Parsons's 'normative functionalism', he nevertheless still writes of conflict as interfering with the 'functional efficiency' of role systems.[35] The other is that he does not relate tensions within role-sets to more general features of social systems: conflicts rooted in role-set dislocations, as with those related to type 3 below, can be related to sources of system contradiction, which they express 'in miniature'.

3. Tension between the role-prescriptions of different social identities with which an individual is ascribed, adopts or is forced to assume. One may accept, with Merton, that it is worthwhile making a conceptual distinction between 'role-sets' and 'multiple roles', the former being the role-prescriptions associated with a single position, the latter concerning the intersection between different social identities.

4. Tension deriving from the contested character of role-prescriptions. Role-prescriptions, like any other normative elements, are potentially subject to diverse 'interpretations' in the context of the practical enactment of social life, and the power relations thus involved. All social positions, within social systems, are 'power positions' in the sense that they are integrated within reproduced relations of autonomy and dependence; contestation of role-prescriptions is a characteristic feature of power struggles in society.

These comments on role theory lead readily into a discussion of socialisation, since the notion of role has often figured as a major link in the sociological literature – again, especially that of functionalism – between personality development on the one hand, and institutionalised structures of society on the other. Much of this literature assumes a point of view I particularly want to criticise: that 'socialisation' concerns only the adaptation of the child to, and adoption by the child of, the roles he or she is called upon to play in society. Temporality appears here only on the level of the psychological development of the child, confronted by an already-formed society to which that child is moulded, 'successfully' or not so 'successfully'.

This temporality has to be grasped in conjunction with two of the other senses in which, as I have said previously, temporality is involved in social reproduction: as integral to social interaction, and as implied in the reproduction of the personnel of social systems.

Socialisation and the unconscious

I have argued in earlier papers that it is the task of social theory to seek to overcome traditional dualisms of subject and object in the analysis of social reproduction. Social analysis must be founded neither in the consciousness or activities of the subject, nor in the characteristics of the object (society), but in the duality of structure. But if the subject/object dualism has to be transcended in respect of the immediate nexus of interaction, it has also to be overcome in the rather different form in which it appears in theories of socialisation. That is to say, we have to avoid any account of socialisation which presumes either that the subject is determined by the social object (the individual as simply 'moulded' by society); or, by contrast, which takes subjectivity for granted, as an inherent characteristic of human beings, not in need of explication. Both approaches lack a 'theory of the subject', since the first reduces subjectivity to the determined outcome of social forces, while the second assumes that the subjective is not open to any kind of social analysis.

A theory of the subject, when posed in developmental terms, demands a theory of the unconscious. In working out the rudiments of such a theory, we can draw (critically and sparingly) upon 'Lacan's Freud'. One of the most important features of Lacan's psychoanalysis is that Lacan recognises the essential significance of the Freudian emphasis that ' "it" thinks in the space where "I" has yet to appear': that he links the emergence of 'I', and thus of a predicative object-relation, with basic features of language as Other. Lacan reads *Wo es war soll Ich werden*, not as a therapeutic injunction of psychoanalytic practice (cf., by contrast, Habermas's model of psychoanalysis as critical theory), not as implying that 'the ego must dislodge the id',[36] but as a developmental formula: 'it' precedes 'I', and the latter always remains bound to the Other.

Lacan's conceptions of the splitting and the mirror-phase bear certain affinities to the interpretation of the origins of subjectivity which has perhaps had most influence in English-speaking sociology: that of G. H. Mead. Both emphasise that a 'positioned subject' only emerges in the course of the psychological development of the individual, and hence that the reflexivity of the *cogito* is not an inherent property of human beings. But, as compared to the perspective of Lacan – and to that of psychoanalytic theory more generally – Mead's approach, and that of authors influenced by it, has major deficiences. First, Mead fails to break finally with a starting-point rooted in the subject, as is shown by the nature of the 'I' in his work. The 'I', in other words, appears as a given or unexplained component of the human psyche – even if the person only *acknowledges* himself or herself as an 'I' in relation to the formation of the social 'me'or self.

For Lacan the 'I' is conceived in imaginary relation to the body: the narcissistic 'positioning' of the child in the mirror-phase is the condition of the grasp of an 'I/me' dialectic. While both Lacan and Mead emphasise 'positionality', Lacan sees this as necessary to the very constitution of the 'I' itself, and relates it to the deictic qualities of language: the 'I' 'is nothing but the *shifter* or indicative which designates the subject of an enunciation insofar as he is speaking at the current moment'.[37] Second, Mead's 'I/me' model appears as a distinctively harmonious one: there is a certain space left for internal division and conflict within the social self, but Mead does not make much of this. The process of 'taking the role of the other' whereby the reflexive subject emerges, is portrayed as a relatively orderly and progressive one; and since the 'I' is left unanalysed, it is necessarily treated as undifferentiated. If Lacan is correct, the insertion of the infant into a subject/object relation is achieved via the mirror-phase and the castration complex, both of which involve repression; and the 'I' is already 'internally divided' through the very process of achieving that status.

I do not mean to suggest that the conception of socialisation I wish to outline here depends upon accepting the main body of Lacan's writings. I want to claim only that, in respect of interpreting the emergence of subjectivity, Lacan's Freud can be drawn upon with profit. In other respects it seems to me important to stay closer to at least some major elements of Freud's own writings than Lacan seems to do. Thus although Lacan specifically rejects the accusation that his theory is an 'intellectualisation' which ignores drive, his approach, based in a quasi-structuralist conception of language, does not in fact appear to be able adequately to incorporate the organic foundations of human motivation. At any rate, I think it important to affirm something closer to the traditional concerns of psychoanalytic theory, according to which the early period of the development of the child involves the formation of what Kardiner calls a basic security system: capacities of tension-management in relation to organic wants, that form the first and most all-encompassing accommodations the child makes to the social and material worlds.

It is still not entirely clear, in fact, given the cryptic and elusive nature of many of Lacan's formulations, how far it is possible fruitfully to detach some of his theorems from the overall scheme of his theory. But we must enter serious reservations about his interpretation of the unconscious in terms of the Saussurian formula $\frac{S}{s.}$. Lacan sees the unconscious as coterminous with the 'what cannot be said' of language: the latter being understood as the characteristics of the signifier (mediated through the whole corpus of linguistic signs). This conception however is open to criticisms I have made of other types of social theory and philosophy influenced by structuralist linguistics. One of Lacan's principal arguments is that the signifier 'insists' in the unconscious.[38] The literal form of the signifier is a structuring element of the unconscious, separated from the conscious group of signifieds, the line between them being resistant to signification. Sentences constitute the *points de capiton* which button together the two chains in signification. It cannot be denied that Lacan's application of the twin principles of metaphor and metonymy offers brilliant reworkings (or as he would prefer to say, attentive readings) of the psychoanalytic theory of the unconscious. But these do not seem to depend in an essential way upon his appropriation of structural linguistics as such. The noxious effects of the signifier/signified distinction are as apparent in Lacan's writings as in those of other structuralist authors.[39] The rebus can be seen, not as a graphic instance of the meaning-generating properties of non-meaningful forms, but as the intersection of two already-meaningful parameters. I should wish to argue, without elaborating the case, that meaning is constituted on the level of the unconscious as well as that of the conscious, whatever the dislocations that might exist between the two.

A 'stratified' model of personality, in which human wants are regarded as hierarchically connected, involving a basic security system largely inaccessible to the conscious subject, is not at all incompatible with an equivalent stress upon the significance of the reflexive monitoring of action, the latter becoming possible only following the 'positioning' of the actor in the Lacanian sense. There still are considerable gaps between psychoanalytic theory (in any guise), action theory, and more orthodox psychological accounts of socialisation. But in the post-behaviouristic phase into which academic psychology seems now to be moving, there are definite clues as to possible connections that can be forged between each. Thus if the reflexive monitoring of action only becomes possible in so far as the child becomes a 'positioned subject', there are none the less a range of competencies which precede that development, as one type of condition necessary for its accomplishment: such competencies may be plausibly supposed to be connected to contemporaneous processes in the formation of the basic security system. Human biology, not unsurprisingly, may be the immediate basis of such connections. The psychoanalytic literature has always been mainly focused upon the management of organic drives – as, in a different way, most behaviouristic theory was also. But more recent work in psychology suggests that there are 'serial orders' in learning processes that might have a definite biological base: a base of 'inbuilt' competencies rather than needs. Chomsky has argued as much in the case of the acquisition of syntactical features of language; he and others have also suggested that certain parallels may be found in the case of a variety of other skills.

Critical situations and the routine

We can learn a good deal about day-to-day life in routine settings from analysing circumstances in which those settings are radically disturbed: something of a parallel to Freud's method in psychology. I want briefly to consider a range of materials relevant to this. An appropriate point of departure can be found in an area that might initially seem unpromising: the study of 'mob behaviour' as formulated by Le Bon, Sighele and others at the turn of the century. The works of such authors are actually of interest for several reasons. They represent one of the sources of what has come to be called 'social psychology'.[40] They also form part of a conservative critique of liberal democracy that has similarities to the 'elite theory' developed by Pareto and Mosca; at the same time, however, they may be read as an early anticipation and critique of fascism. But quite apart from such considerations, these writings retain an intrinsic interest as providing exemplary analyses of a particular type of *critical situation*. By a critical situation I mean a set of circumstances which – for whatever reason – radically disrupts accustomed routines of daily life. This is not the framework, it should be pointed out, within which Le Bon and the others saw their own works. Le Bon saw mob behaviour as a sort of prototype of behaviour in collectivities in general; I interpret crowd activity rather as taking place in social conditions which depart from the routinised character of social reproduction characteristic of most settings of social life.

In *The Crowd*, Le Bon is concerned with the significance of the unconscious in mob behaviour, and it is not surprising that the book was later subjected to a critical but sympathetic appraisal by Freud.[41] According to Le Bon it is a 'truth of modern psychology' that

unconscious phenomena play an altogether preponderating part not only in organic life, but also in the operations of the intelligence .... Behind the avowed causes of our acts there undoubtedly lie secret causes that we do not avow, but behind these secret causes there are many others more secret still, of which we ourselves are ignorant. The greater part of our daily actions are the result of hidden motives which escape our observation.[42]

Mob behaviour makes this apparent, because under the stimulus of crowd action – Le Bon's chief example being the revolutionary mobs of 1789 – unconscious responses come to the fore in ways that are not found in ordinary social activities. When caught up in crowd action, individuals lose the 'critical faculties of the intellect' which they are able to display in day-to-day social life. They become highly suggestible to influences which, outside of the charged atmosphere of the mob, they would be prone to appraise in a more reasoned fashion. Le Bon compared the suggestibility of the mob to that of the hypnotic subject, the 'state of "fascination" in which the hypnotised individual finds himself in the hands of the hypnotiser';[43] it is effectively a state of loss of the conscious sector of the personality. Under the influence of the mob, individuals regress to more 'primitive' kinds of reaction: 'Isolated, a person may be a cultivated individual; in a crowd, he is a barbarian – that is, a creature acting by instinct. He possesses the spontaneity, the violence, the ferocity, and also the enthusiasm and heroism of primitive beings.'[44] In such a situation, the members of the crowd are readily exploited by leaders or demagogues: the influence of the crowd leader is a phenomenon to which Le Bon devoted a considerable part of his work.

I am not interested, for the purposes of my present discussion, in mob behaviour as such, but in tracing through the significance of several phenomena to which Le Bon drew attention: notably, suggestibility, regression and the importance of the crowd leader. I want to propose that similar responses to these can be discerned in a variety of circumstances that have little in common with one another, save that in each of them the accustomed routines of daily life are drastically disrupted. Consider the description which Bettelheim has given of the responses of prisoners in Nazi concentration camps (based partly on his own experiences).[45] According to Bettelheim, those interned in the camps underwent a number of changes in their conduct and attitudes which were more or less universal – among those who survived long enough. In the first period of their imprisonment, the internees would attempt to sustain the modes of customary behaviour associated with their previous existence, in the face of the privations and brutalities of camp life. These included physical torture, overcrowded living and sleeping conditions, various other sorts of abuse, plus a severe shortage of food. Exposed to these conditions, any endeavour to sustain pre-existing modes of conduct was rapidly broken down; the frame of reference of the 'outside' lost its salience, and prisoners became wholly preoccupied with the internal world of the camp. During this stage prisoners underwent what Bettelheim describes as a regression to child-like attitudes of dependency. Regressive behaviour included: a diminution in the time-span of phenomenal experience, a concentration upon immediate events and loss of any long-term perspectives; rapid emotional oscillation swinging from elation to depression; and a reversal of the serious and trivial, whereby apparently minor events would be attributed with more significance than ones of much of greater consequence for the individuals concerned. At a subsequent stage, something like a 're-socialisation' process occurred, but based upon identification with the very oppressors themselves, the camp guards. 'The result of all these changes', Bettelheim says, although 'by no means fully produced in all old prisoners, was a personality structure willing and able to accept SS values and behaviour as its own.'[46]

Bettelheim's account may be compared with the wide-ranging discussion of critical situations furnished by Sargant.[47] Sargant compares such diverse interruptions of routine existence as behaviour under fire on the battle-field, forced interrogation and religious conversion. While I have a number of reservations about the nature of Sargant's own intepretations of these phenomena,[48] some interesting congruities emerge with Le Bon and Bettelheim. Forced interrogation perhaps comes closest in form and outcome to the situation of the camp prisoners as portrayed by Bettelheim. Prisoners the world over are subject to forms of bodily and mental degradation which, if they rarely rival the fearful conditions of the concentration camp, approach them in greater or lesser degrees. Under severe and protracted interrogation, the reactions which occur strikingly resemble those noted by Bettelheim. In the initial stages, the individual attempts to resist the pressures imposed. If the process of interrogation is continued over a protracted period, phases of personality change take place similar to those discernible in Bettelheim's analysis. Regressive behaviour involving each of the three aspects mentioned above is a prominent feature: culminating again in identification with the aggressor, the interrogator. Sargant notes: 'One of the more horrible consequences of these ruthless interrogations, as described by victims, is that they suddenly begin to feel affection for the examiner who has been treating them so harshly . . .'[49]

The common elements involved in critical situations seem to be the following. The radical disruption of routine produces a sort of corrosive effect upon the customary behaviour of the actor, associated with the impact of anxiety or fear. This circumstance brings about heightened suggestibility, or vulnerability to the promptings of others; the correlate of such suggestibility is regressive behaviour. The outcome of these is a new process of identification – transitory in the case of the mob, more permanent in protracted critical situations – with an authority figure.

Freud has a convincing interpretation of the last of these

phenomena, and it is one which I want to interpolate in my account of the implications of the study of critical situations for routinised, everyday social reproduction. Identification, Freud says, is 'the earliest expression of an emotional tie with another person'; it is an essential part of the Oedipal stage of personality development. Identification is always ambivalent, and 'can turn into expression of tenderness as easily as into a wish for someone's removal'.[50] As the earliest form of emotional tie, identification underlies more mature capabilities of object-choice; affiliation through identification in adults is thus a regressive formation, which can be either with someone who is loved or someone who is hated. Identification with a mob demagogue, who can be initially an object of either positive or negative emotions,[51] is a process in which the crowd leader becomes a temporary surrogate for the superego or ego ideal.

This provides us with a helpful explanation of the psychological elements involved in critical situations. In such situations, *heightened anxiety* renders actors vulnerable to *regressive modes of object-affiliation* involving a strong measure of ambivalence. Such an analysis helps to understand the process of events involved in the two protracted sorts of critical situation I have analysed: internment in the concentration camps and forced interrogation. Its sociological significance also relates to phenomena close to those discussed by Le Bon: not behaviour in mobs as such, but *the psychological dynamics of social movements*, particularly in relation to the demand for a 'strong leader'.

However in the present context I am also concerned with the implications of behaviour in critical situations for understanding their contrary: the routine and the mundane. Is one such implication that unreason generally prevails over reason, that our conscious acts are dominated by impulses or feelings of which we are quite unaware? For an impressive feature of protracted critical situations is that changes occur in the personalities of those exposed to them, in spite of their conscious resolution to resist – although the length of time involved may vary widely, presumably in large degree as a result of the relative strength of an individual's determination to hold out. But a critical situation of a protracted type is precisely one that is radically removed from the habitual contexts of social reproduction; we should not be led to the conclusion that the conscious is ordinarily swamped by the unconscious. The study of critical situations in fact suggests an analysis of routinised social interaction which allows us to connect together two features of the theory of structuration: the conception of a stratification model of the agent on the one hand, and the emphasis upon actors' knowledge of the conditions of their action on the other.

The outline of this analysis runs as follows. The reflexive monitoring of action draws upon and reproduces forms of tacit and discursively available knowledge: *continuity of social reproduction involves the continual 'regrooving' of established attitudes and cognitive outlooks* holding down potential sources of anxiety in the basic security system. 'Socialisation' should be understood as an element of the continuity of social reproduction – of the inherent temporality of social process – rather than as just referring to the temporality of the personality formation of the child. (We should note, however, that personality is a *'time module'*, in which the past history of the individual lies sedimented, or stored up, ready to influence the present.) Routinisation of social relations is the mode in which the stratification of personality is sustained: that is to say, in which potentially corrosive effects of anxiety are contained. The familiar is reassuring; and *the familiar in social settings is created and recreated through human agency itself, in the duality of structure*. This should not be understood as a paean for social stability. On the contrary, I want to suggest (cf. also pp. 216–19, below) that certain schools of social theory have been prone to overestimate the level and detail of motivational commitment to the social practices which constitute a given social system. Most elements of social practices are not directly motivated. Motivational commitment more typically involves the generalised integration of habitual practices, as reflexively monitored productions of interacting agents, with the basic security system of personality. Routinisation implies *'ethnomethodological continuity'* more than reproduction of the empirical content of practices.

Socialisation: concluding remarks

Durkheim treated socialisation as one of the modes in which the constraining properties of social facts make themselves felt. The 'externality' of society *vis-à-vis* the individual, he proposed, is shown by the fact that society exists before each of its members is born, and constrains or moulds the process of their development.

But this thesis is better presented as an interplay between the two forms of social reproduction noted before. We can accept that processes of socialisation are basic to an account of the institutional organisation of social systems, so long as three important points are borne in mind, each of which tends to be obscured, or not properly confronted, in Durkheim's standpoint, and in the writings of those influenced by it.

First, socialisation is never anything like a passive imprinting by 'society' upon each 'individual'. From its very earliest experiences, the infant is an active partner in the double contingency of interaction and in a progressive 'involvement with society'. Second, socialisation does not just stop at some particular point in the life of the individual, when he or she becomes a mature member of society. That socialisation is confined to childhood, or to childhood plus adolescence, is an explicit or implicit assumption of a good number of those who have made use of the term. But socialisation should really be understood as referring to the whole life-cycle of the individual. Such an assertion does not go far enough if it simply refers to the continuity or temporality of the life-course. For this still treats 'society' as a static or finished order, rather than recognising the *mutuality of time-process*, linking the life-course to the inherent temporality of social reproduction.

Third, we cannot appropriately speak of *the* process of socialisation, except very loosely. Such a phrase implies too much standardisation or uniformity on two sides: as if there were a single and simply mapped type of 'process' which every individual undergoes, and as if there were a consensual unity into which each individual is socialised.

It is clear that much work on the psychological development of the individual is deficient as an account of socialisation, in so far as the overriding focus is upon the differentiation of personality within an undifferentiated 'society'. This is true also in some considerable degree of the theory that has long dominated child psychology in respect of cognitive development: that associated with Piaget. Certain issues have to be particularly borne in mind if we are to avoid the shortcomings of such conceptions. We have to recognise that 'becoming social' cannot be understood in 'monological' terms: as a series of competencies simply 'stored' in the learner.[52] Rather, becoming social involves, on the level of cognition, mastery of the 'dialogical' contexts of communication. Such mastery is by no means wholly discursive, but involves the accumulation of practical knowledge of the conventions drawn upon in the production and reproduction of social interaction. Moreover, it will not do just to emphasise that the child is an active participant in processes of socialisation, important as that is, and leave matters there. In understanding why, it is helpful to notice the close connection between 'socialisation' (cf. the German term often employed by Simmel, *Vergesellschaftung*) and the conception of production and reproduction of society that I have advanced in each of these papers. Socialisation only sounds a rather special, distinctive term, emphasising process and time, if employed in the way I have previously disclaimed, where society is treated as a static form, into which the individual is progressively incorporated. *The unfolding of childhood is not time elapsing just for the child*: it is time elapsing for its parental figures, and for all other members of society; the socialisation involved is not simply that of the child, but of the parents and others with whom the child is in contact, and whose conduct is influenced by the child just as the latter's is by theirs in the continuity of interaction.[53] Since the newborn human infant is so helpless, and so dependent upon others, normally its parents, it is easily forgotten that children 'create parents' as well as parents creating children. The arrival and development of a child reorders the lives of the adults who care for it and interact with it. The category 'mother' is given by the arrival of a child, but the practice or enactment of motherhood involves processes of learning that stretch back before and continue after the birth of the child. Socialisation is thus most appropriately regarded not as the 'incorporation of the child into society', but as the *succession of the generations*.

4

Contradiction, Power, Historical Materialism

In this paper, I shall develop an interpretation of a series of issues grouped around problems of contradiction and conflict in society, against the background of the elements of the theory of structuration presented in the previous papers. The method of social analysis I shall propose may be regarded as almost the obverse of functionalism; its guiding tenet is: don't look for the functions social practices fulfil, look for the contradictions they embody!

CONFLICT	Struggle between actors or collectivities expressed as definite social practices
CONTRADICTION	Disjunction of structural principles of system organisation

FIGURE 4.1

As Figure 4.1 indicates, I intend to formulate a clear conceptual separation between contradiction and conflict. We have to recognise two senses of the term 'conflict', as many writers have pointed out. One is conflict as opposition or division of interest; the other is conflict as actual struggle between actors or groups: in my terminology, conflict that occurs on the level of social practices. No particular conceptual problems are involved in elucidating the nature of conflict as active struggle. Such is not the case, however, for the concepts of interest or contradiction; I shall postpone discussion of the first of these until the following paper, concentrating here upon the notion of contradiction.

The concept of contradiction in Marx

Consideration of the concept of contradiction in the social sciences poses difficult problems, but ones whose resolution are none the less of great importance. We have to begin from the Hegel–Marx relation. It is often said that Hegel borrowed the idea of contradiction from logic, and applied it ontologically. But this is really a misconception, for Hegel wanted to show that logic and the real cannot be partitioned off from one another, as though they belong to quite distinct spheres. He did not just insert contradiction into the real, he sought to demonstrate how contradiction is at the root of logic and reality alike. Contradiction is bound up with the finitude of being, and hence with the pervasiveness of becoming. In Hegel's philosophy, therefore, 'contradictoriness' is the source of a motility ontologically inherent in the nature of all existents: the expression of the negation of the negation.

From an early stage, Marx rejected the thesis that negativity is to be found in the essence of the real. Following Feuerbach, he wanted to recover the 'positivity' of things: Hegel's identification of the source of the dissolution and transformation of the real in negativity was disavowed as unacceptable idealism.

> In conceiving the negation of the negation, from the aspect of the positive relation inherent in it, as the only true positive, and from the aspect of the negative relation inherent in it, as the only true act and the self-confirming act of all being, Hegel has merely discovered an *abstract*, *logical* and *speculative* expression of the historical process, which is not yet the *real* history of man, as a given subject....[1]

Marx therefore denied contradiction an ontological status in the constitution of things. Contradiction and negativity remain driving forces of change for Marx, but of change in the historical movement of the 'real history of man' (an emphasis that was later to be partly reversed, although in relatively crude fashion, by Engels in *Anti-Dühring* and *The Dialectics of Nature*). 'Contradictoriness' is located in the character of class society. Capitalism maximises the contradictions inherent in class relations, and at the same time prepares the stage for the transcendence of contradiction in a classless society. The 'clash of reciprocal contradictions', as Marx puts it, is the pitting of capital against labour. The proletariat is 'radical negativity', suffering from a 'total loss of humanity', the accumulated weight of contradictions; in redeeming itself, the proletariat redeems the whole of society from the contradictory nature of class society.[2]

Contradiction and negativity for Marx hence reflect not the finitude of being, as a universal ontological condition of the real, but refer instead to the finitude of class society: as a transitional, not a universal, type of human social order.[3] Contradiction plays its part in history in mobilising social transformations between the class-lessness of tribal society and the classlessness of socialism; contradiction belongs only to what Marx sometimes referred to as the 'pre-history' of man, and hence can and will be transcended.

How does Marx use 'contradiction' in his writings? It is not difficult to unearth general consistencies in his usage, although on the surface there is considerable variety. Since Marx interpolates the notion of contradiction into his account of class conflict, it is perhaps not surprising that he often tends to use 'contradiction' (*Widerspruch*), 'antagonism' (*Gegensatz*) and 'conflict' (*Konflikt*) as interchangeable terms. Perhaps the most celebrated passage in the whole of Marx's writings where the term contradiction appears is in the Preface to *A Contribution to the Critique of Political Economy*. The relevant lines are perhaps worth quoting at some length:

At a certain stage of their development, the material productive forces of society come in conflict [*Widerspruch*] with the existing relations of production.... From forms of development of the productive forces these relations turn into their fetters. Then begins an epoch of social revolution. With the change of the economic foundation the entire immense superstructure is more or less rapidly transformed.... Just as our opinion of an individual is not based on what he thinks of himself, so we cannot judge such a period of transformation by its own consciousness; on the contrary, this consciousness must be explained rather from the contradictions [*Widersprüchen*] of material life, from the existing conflict [*Konflikt*] between the social productive forces and the relations of production. No social order ever perishes before all the productive forces for which there is room in it have developed; and new, higher relations of production never appear before the material conditions of their existence have matured in the womb of the old society itself. Therefore mankind always sets itself only such tasks as it can solve. . . . In broad outlines Asiatic, ancient, feudal, and modern bourgeois modes of production can be designated as progressive epochs in the economic formation of society. The bourgeois relations of production are the last antagonistic [*antagonistische*] form of the social process of production – antagonistic not in the sense of individual antagonism, but of one arising from the social conditions of the life of the individuals; at the same time the productive forces developing in the womb of bourgeois society create the material conditions for the solution of that antagonism.[4]

The passage brings together all of the main elements of the scheme of contradictions and their resolution that Marx applied to social development, indicating both the dynamism of contradiction and his progressive view of the course of history through the sequential formation of types of society. The aphorism, 'mankind always sets itself only such tasks as it can solve' expresses this progressive view very aptly: each stage creates not just the possibility, but the means of advancement to a 'higher' order.

There are various difficulties with this scheme, even if adjudged purely within the context of Marx's own views, as developed in other works. Placing the Asiatic type as a prior stage to the forms of society that developed in Europe is something Marx himself later rejected: he came to take the view that the Asiatic mode of production and Classical society are independent developments out of tribal society. And we can ask: in what sense did mankind in the Ancient World 'only set itself such tasks as it could solve'? Marx's analysis of the disintegration of the Roman Empire suggests that it collapsed as a result precisely of its internal contradictions, which could not drive it on to a higher stage of synthesis because of certain impediments (most notably, slavery) to the further expansion of manufacture and trade.[5] Of course, it could be argued that the decline of the Roman Empire in some sense provided the necessary conditions for the creation of feudalism, which in turn provided such conditions for the rise of modern capitalism. But this sort of elliptical reasoning is not very convincing, and I shall want to propose a different standpoint below.

If we ignore the terminological diversity in Marx, it can be said that there are two main contexts in which the concept of contradiction appears in Marx's works. One, as in the quotation above, is in relation to general portrayals of historical materialism as an approach to the explanation of social change. Here Marx writes of contradictions 'of material life', or invokes what has been called the 'canonical formula' of Marxism, the contradiction between the forces and relations of production.[6] The forces/relations of production scheme appears in Marx's writings on various occasions both prior to and after the appearance of *A Contribution to the Critique of Political Economy* (1859). In *The Communist Manifesto* of 1848, for instance, Marx applies the forces/relations of production formula to feudalism and to capitalism. 'At a certain stage' in the development of the former type of society, Marx says, 'the feudal relations of property became no longer compatible with the already developed productive forces': the result was the revolutionary transformation leading to the establishment of bourgeois society. But in the latter, 'a similar movement is going on before our own eyes'. 'For many a decade past', Marx continues, 'the history of industry and commerce is but the history of the revolt of modern productive forces against modern conditions of production, against the property relations that are the conditions for the existence of the bourgeoisie and its rule.'[7] In volume one of *Capital*, Marx returns to the same theme, emphasising particularly the development of monopoly capital. 'The centralisation of the means of production and the socialisation of labour', he writes, 'at last reach a point where they become incompatible [*unverträglich*] with their capitalist integument.' There follow these famous phrases: 'The integument is burst asunder. The knell of capitalist property sounds. The expropriators are expropriated.'[8]

The forces/relations of production scheme clearly cannot be discussed apart from broad issues concerning Marx's 'materialist interpretation of history', and I shall have a good deal to say about the 'materialist conception' below. More relevant to the sections of the paper immediately following this, is the second type of context in which Marx frequently speaks of social contradiction. This is the type of context in which he is concerned to examine the specific character of the contradictions of capitalist production.

'Contradiction' appears frequently throughout the three major works of Marx's 'mature period': the *Grundrisse*, *Capital* and *Theories of Surplus Value*. Various aspects of the capitalist system are said to be contradictory. They include the following:

1. The relation of capital and wage-labour, as a class relation. However, although the English translations often translate this as contradiction, when referring to this relation Marx normally uses the term *Gegensatz*, not *Widerspruch*.
2. The connection between use-value and exchange-value, between the 'specific natural properties' and the 'universal social properties' of commodities.
3. The circumstances involved in the generation of surplus-value, especially as involving the tendency of the profit-rate to fall.
4. The nature of the labour-process, as expressed in the alienation of the worker set by the side of the wealth created by capitalism.[9]

The implication is that capitalism multiplies contradictions, as compared to prior types of productive system. But does Marx recognise that there is one source or type of contradiction in capitalism that underlies the others? Is there a *primary contradiction* involved in the capitalist mode of production and, if so, what is it? Most Marxists have assumed that there is, and I think they are right to have done so: both as regards the exegesis of Marx, and as regards the structural analysis of modern capitalism. But interpreters of Marx have not always been agreed about how the primary contradiction of capitalism is to be characterised. In a recent discussion of contradiction, for example, Young has argued that 'strictly speaking', the primary contradiction of capitalism is not between forces and relations of production, but lies wholly within 'capitalist productive relations'.[10] According to Young, this contradiction is to be found in the process of exchange: it is a contradiction between the sale and purchase of commodities in the process of circulation, rooted in category 2 of the classification I offered above.

But this is implausible, because it does not connect in a direct way to a major feature of Marx's standpoint – and one which I shall want to defend. This is that social contradiction manifests an immanent form of social order, stimulated in its development by an existing one. The primary contradiction in capitalism surely has to be that which presages a new type of social and economic system, socialism. There is, I think, only one candidate for the job: the contradiction between *private appropriation* and *socialised production*. I shall attempt to explicate this more fully later. The main sense of it, however, can be indicated by any number of quotations from Marx's later works, such as the following:

> The division of labour results in concentration, co-ordination, co-operation, anatagonism of private interests and class interests, competition, the centralisation of capital, monopolies and joint stock companies – so many contradictory forms of unity which in turn engenders all these contradictions. In the same way private exchange creates world trade, private independence gives rise to complete dependence on the so-called world market, and the fragmented acts of exchange make a system of banks and credit necessary.... [We can find] embedded in society as it is today the material conditions of production and the commercial relationships of the classless society.[11]

Two later views

In much of the Marxist literature since Marx, 'contradictory' is used liberally, but in an unexamined way: thus compounding the somewhat cavalier use of terminology already found in Marx. Not much would be gained by attempting a survey of uses of the term by subsequent Marxist authors, and I shall refer here only to two recent discussions which attempt a direct analysis of the concept of contradiction in social theory – discussions that contrast both with each other and with the views I wish to develop.

The first is to be found in a well-known article by Godelier, elaborating a standpoint influenced by Lévi-Strauss and Althusser.[12] According to Godelier we can find two primary senses in which Marx speaks of the contradictions in capitalist society. One is that in which Marx holds that capital and wage-labour, as two classes, stand in a contradictory relation to one another. This is contradiction within the capitalist mode of production, or as Godelier puts it, 'the internal contradictions of a structure'.[13] The contradiction between capital and wage-labour expresses the distinctive character of capitalism, as compared to other types of productive system. It is there, Godelier says, from the very beginnings of the capitalist mode of production, and in this respect as well as others can be distinguished from the second way in which Marx uses 'contradiction'. This second sense is that in which Marx speaks of the emergent antinomy between private appropriation and socialised production with the growing maturity of capitalism. This is not, in Godelier's terms, a contradiction within a structure, but rather a contradiction between two structures: the one characteristic of capitalism, and the other foreshadowing the emergence of socialism. The contradiction between private appropriation and socialised production only comes into being at a relatively late stage in the development of capitalism, because in its early phases capitalist relations of production are 'functional' for the forces of production. According to Godelier, the second sort of contradiction, as contrasted to the first, is 'unintentional' and 'without teleology';[14] it exposes the functional limitations of capitalism, limits beyond which it cannot expand without introducing new relations of production, based upon different principles.

The specific interest of Godelier's account, in my opinion, is not that it shows the importance of differentiating between two senses or types of contradiction, as he says; but that it indicates that we should distinguish conflict from contradiction (even if Marx did not do so explicitly: but then he did not explicitly distinguish two types of contradiction either).[15] There is no point in using the notion of contradiction so diffusely that it is more or less equivalent to conflict. I shall therefore say that the relation between capital and wage-labour, as a class relation between capitalists and workers, *is one of inherent conflict, in the sense of opposition of interest,* and of more or less continuous active struggle.

To say, as I have done previously, that conflict as struggle operates on the level of social practices seems similar to one of the points Godelier wishes to make. But Godelier's formulation of the point is not at all satisfactory: it displays several of the prime features of functionalist argument that I am concerned to reject in this book. Godelier emphasises so strongly, in the manner of Althusser, that Hegel's conceptions of contradiction and negativity are irrelevant to those developed by Marx, that he is forced to reject the idea that contradiction in Marx has any resemblance to contradiction in logic. Consequently, he understands contradiction as functional incompatibility, contrasting it with integration as the functional correspondence of social items. The equation between contradiction and functional incongruity is one that is not infrequently made in the functionalist literature of American sociology,[16] but it is certainly one I wish to disavow. Godelier says that his second sort of contradiction, 'contradiction between structures', is 'non-teleological', but actually it is not, as his text clearly shows. The teleology of 'contradiction between structures' is that of functional need: the need of the structure or system, unacknowledged by social actors themselves. Godelier's formulation in fact bears a striking resemblance to the distinction between manifest and latent functions which has been so prominent in the functionalist literature. (For further considerations on functionalist theories of social change, see pp. 210–14, below.) What he calls the 'intentional behavioural rationality of the members of a society' is separated from the 'unintentional rationality of the hierarchical structure of the social relations characterising that society', the latter expressing the functional necessity governing change from one structure to another.[17]

A discussion of contradiction by Elster provides a useful and interesting complement to the standpoint set out by Godelier.[18] Elster tries carefully to distinguish conflict from contradiction, and at the same time relates social contradiction closely to logical contradiction – although not in a way that owes anything to Hegel.[19] Elster's analysis is complicated and ambitious, and I shall refer only to certain parts of it. He relates contradiction to two kinds of situation, one of which concerns what he calls 'the fallacy of composition', the other of which he refers to as 'suboptimality'; but since the second of these is admitted to be less important than the first, I shall ignore it. By the fallacy of composition, Elster means the thesis, or the assumption, that what one actor can do, in a given set of circumstances, it must be possible for an indefinite number of actors to do simultaneously. For instance, it is a mistake to suppose that, just because any one individual investor can draw money out from a bank at any particular time, all investors can do so. Elster discusses the fallacy of composition in conjunction with 'counterfinality', which is the main basis of his interpretation of contradiction. Counterfinality refers to the unintended consequences that ensue when all members of a group act upon premises that involve the fallacy of composition. Such a situation, he proposes, meets the requirements specified for contradiction in logic, while preserving the rationality of each individual actor: for there is nothing wrong with the grounds of each person's action, taken separately.[20] Although Elster provides a variety of examples of counterfinality as contradiction, it is perhaps most appropriate here to quote one held to conform to contradiction in Marx: that associated with the falling rate of profit in capitalism. In Elster's words, 'Marx explained the fall in rate of profit as the result of measures (labour-saving devices) taken to counteract the falling rate of profit.'[21]

The importance of Elster's work, I think, is quite different to that of Godelier. Whatever the limitations of the latter's account, it is anchored in substantive problems: the dynamic processes involved in capitalist development as described by Marx. Elster, on the other hand, is more concerned with a formal analysis of the concept of contradiction (among other concepts) and the examples he provides, detailed as they are, are more incidental to his discussion than in Godelier's case; other examples could have been chosen. The significance of Elster's analysis is the forceful case he makes for the claim that conflict and contradiction should not be conceptually merged, and that contradiction in social theory need not be distanced too far from logical contradiction.

However, I have a number of reservations about Elster's position. Elster links social contradiction, via counterfinality, to the unintended consequences of the behaviour of individual actors (although he is careful to limit such consequences to those which come about instead of what was intended, excluding those which ensue in addition to what was intended). I do not have any objection to the claim that the examples of contradictions with which Elster illustrates his arguments *are* worthwhile calling contradictions; rather what is at fault with Elster's standpoint is the mode of approach he takes in analysing those examples, which treats contradiction only as an aggregate outcome of individual acts. Consider the case mentioned previously: Marx on the falling rate of profit. Elster makes this conform to his notion of counterfinality as contradiction by taking it, as it were, only 'from one side': a decline in the rate of profit is the overall outcome of numbers of actors taking measures to increase their rate of profit. But this is *not*, as Elster holds, how 'Marx explained the fall in the rate of profit'. Taken 'from the other side', the tendency of the profit-rate to decline provides the circumstances (or one of the circumstances) in which individual capitalists are prompted to take measures to generate increased surplus value. The contradiction is a *structural feature*, in other words, of the system of capitalist production; counterfinality as evinced in the activities of capitalist entrepreneurs is an expression of, and to be explained in terms of, *system contradiction* (as I hope I have made clear in the previous paper, 'explained' here does not mean 'reduced to', but implies reference to the duality of structure).

Godelier's exposition may be deficient, but it does attempt to provide a notion of contradiction that connects to the immanent tendencies of structural change in society. Elster's contradictions are all between intended (or desired) outcomes and unintended (or undesired) ones: this finds no place for the 'positive side of the negative' that is a main feature of Marx's interpretation of social change – and a feature which I think it important to sustain. Elster defines out of court, as having anything to do with contradiction at any rate, Godelier's second sense of contradiction in capitalism: between private appropriation and socialised production. This, Elster says rather rashly, is 'a favourite phrase of vulgar Marxism', which actually has no place in Marx's own writings. Such surely is not the case, even if Engels was more fond of speaking in a blunt way of 'the contradiction between capitalistic appropriation and socialised production'[22] than Marx was. As I have said previously, there are many passages in Marx's writings which document that he held the same view, and I certainly want to accept this as not just one among others, but as the paramount instance of the contradictory nature of capitalist production.

Contradiction and conflict

The concept of contradiction in social theory, then, should relate to the structural components of social systems, but at the same time should be differentiated from any version of 'functional incompatibility'. I shall define social contradiction as an *opposition or disjunction of structural principles* of social systems, where those principles operate in *terms of each other* but at the same time *contravene one another.*[23] I want to propose that contradictions arise in the midst of, and as a result of, the structuration of modes of system reproduction. By a structural principle, or principle of system organisation, I mean an institutionalised set of interconnections which govern system reproduction; interconnections which may operate at any or all the three levels of system integration distinguished previously: homeostasis, feed-back or reflexive self-regulation.

To explain what is implied by saying that structural principles may operate in terms of one another and at the same time contravene one another, it is best to turn to what is involved in treating the disjunction between private appropriation and socialised production as contradictory. (In some ways, the adjective 'contradictory' is preferable to the noun form, 'contradiction', since the latter tends to imply static relations of a fixed nature, whereas social contradictions are always in movement or process.) Private appropriation is a shorthand term for the cycle of investment–production–profit–investment, dominated by private capital, that is involved in the reproduction of the capital/wage-labour relation. I do not agree with Godelier's view, or with his interpretation of Marx, when he says that the contradiction between private appropriation and socialised production is not there at the beginning of capitalism, or is not inherent in the capitalist mode of production. On the contrary, capitalist production is *intrinsically contradictory* in this sense, although the consequences of its contradictory character become accentuated in so far as the development of capitalism follows the trajectory Marx outlines. Marx's argument can best be expressed, I think, by saying that, in the relatively early stages of the emergence of modern capitalism, the inherent contradiction which the formation of capitalist production itself represents *within feudalism* greatly overshadows the contradictory nature of the capitalist mode of production as such. Capitalism is intrinsically contradictory because the very operation of the capitalist mode of production (private appropriation) *presumes* a structural principle which negates it (socialised production). From its earliest days, capitalist production, as involving the accumulation of privately-owned capital within an investment–production–profit–investment cycle, presupposes and tends to further the existence of structural elements that contravene it. The focal point of these contradicting elements is the 'anarchy' of capitalist accumulation versus socialised control of productive processes. Such contradictoriness is expressed, as Marx says in the quotation on p. 137, as 'contradictory forms of unity'. The modes of such negation are complex; the contradictory relation of private appropriation and socialised production is a mobile one, altering its form as changes occur within the overall character of the capitalist system.

I do not wish to question – and I accept as a basic theorem – the Marxian position that contradiction underlies the possibility of progressive movement in history. I do not intend to try to make 'progressive' a morally neutral term here, either. But I do propose to interject also a concept of *system degeneration*: in other words, if we accept in full the contingency of history, we have to accept the possibility that *contradiction can underlie or stimulate retrograde movements of historical change.*

MODERN CAPITALISM

PRIMARY CONTRADICTION	Private appropriation/ socialised production
MAJOR SECONDARY CONTRADICTION	Hegemony of nation-state/internationalisation of capital
TYPE OF SYSTEM DEGENERATION	Right totalitarianism (fascism)

FIGURE 4.2

Since Marx used the term contradiction in quite a diffuse way, he did not explicitly make a further distinction I wish to make. I introduced this earlier: it is a distinction between primary and secondary principles of organisation, and thus between *primary* and *secondary* contradictions.[24] By primary contradictions I mean those which can be identified as fundamentally and inextricably involved in the system reproduction of a society or a type of society – not on a functional basis, but because they enter into the very structuring of what that system *is*. By secondary contradictions I mean those which are brought about through the existence of primary contradictions, and which are in some sense a result of them. The primary contradiction of capitalism, for example, the disjunction between private appropriation and socialised production, can be connected to other contradictory elements within the system that are derivative of it (for example, urban renewal/decay cycles). Secondary contradictions are not 'attempts of the system to cope with primary contradictions'. As I have often repeated, in the view developed here, systems do not attempt or cope with anything; such predicates simply do not apply to systems or collectivities.

I shall not attempt to explicate Figure 4.2 here. In the volume to follow this one, I shall analyse in some detail the contradictory character of state socialist societies (which in any case operate in a world economic context still dominated by capitalist economic mechanisms). I shall want to say that the state socialist societies manifest a generic type of system degeneration, namely *left totalitarianism* (Stalinism).

It is worth emphasising that the social integration/social conflict and system integration/system contradiction distinctions are not just opposites, or the 'poles' of two dimensions. The conceptualisation I intend is a more dialectical one than this. Contradiction only occurs *through* system integration, since the very notion of contradiction, as I have formulated it, involves that of system integration.

I want to suggest the view that, *ceteris paribus*, conflict and contradiction have a tendency to coincide, but that there are various sets of circumstances that can serve to distance the one from the other. Here the analysis of contradiction and conflict converges with that of domination: any or all of these types of circumstance can become incorporated as features of structures of domination. I shall distinguish three such sets of circumstances, which may be called the *opacity* of action, the *dispersion of contradictions*, and *direct repression*. By opacity I refer to a low degree of penetration by actors of the conditions of their action and its involvement in the reproduction of social systems. According to the theory of structuration, there is no circumstance in which the conditions of action can become wholly opaque to agents, since action is constituted via the accountability of practices; actors are always knowledgeable about the structural framework within which their conduct is carried on, because they draw upon that framework in producing their action at the same time as they reconstitute it through that action. But the penetration that this 'knowledgeability' allows is typically limited in terms of the boundaries of action identified in the previous paper: the situated character of action; the degree to which tacit knowledge can be articulated in discourse; unconscious sources of motivation; and unintended consequences of action as incorporated within system reproduction. I shall not discuss here the modes in which these may be opaque, since this presumes an extended treatment of ideology, which I shall undertake in the following paper.

In speaking of the dispersion of contradictions I mean to indicate that the tendency of contradiction to involve conflict is weakened to the degree to which contradictions are kept separate from one another. Conversely, the more there is a fusion or 'overlap' of contradictions, the greater the likelihood of conflict, and the greater the likelihood that such conflict will be intense. Clearly the dispersal of contradictions is related to the opacity of action, since the greater such dispersal the less the tendency for any particular elements of 'contradictoriness' to become a mobilising source of conflict.

Of direct repression, little needs to be said here. However it should be acknowledged that some of the major traditions in social science are prone to underestimate how far force and violence (or its threat) can be succesfully employed to forestall the emergence of conflict as overt struggle.

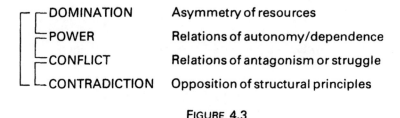

DOMINATION	Asymmetry of resources
POWER	Relations of autonomy/dependence
CONFLICT	Relations of antagonism or struggle
CONTRADICTION	Opposition of structural principles

FIGURE 4.3

In Figure 4.3 , I bring together in an abstract way ideas set out in this and the previous papers. Both domination and contradiction are structural concepts, but they are not on a par. Domination is reproduced in and through contradiction, and may be studied in terms of its consequences for connections between contradiction and conflict. Contradiction and conflict are directly linked, although there is an area of contingency between them. Contradiction is however connected to power only via domination, as the form in which resources are structured within the reproduction of social interaction. Domination and power are closely tied, but the connections between domination and conflict are mediated through power relations.

Power, control, subordination

In this section I want to discuss what I shall call the *dialectic of control* in social systems. This is one of the central areas in which the theorem that social actors know, and must know, a great deal about the circumstances of their action, can be most readily related to domination and power (see also pp. 208–9, below). Although the problems at issue have a broad scope, I shall approach them in a particular context: the critique of Max Weber's conception of bureaucracy.[25] Weber's analysis of bureaucracy is so well known as to need virtually no description here. According to the ideal-type, bureaucracy is distinguished by: its rational-legal order of legitimation; hierarchy of offices in a pyramid of authority; the existence of written rules; vocational specialisation of salaried, full-time officials; and, highly relevant to other themes of Weber's historical analysis, the separation of officials from ownership of their means of administration.

I am not interested here in discussion of the logical nature of ideal-types, and shall only be concerned to comment upon certain aspects of Weber's treatment of bureaucratic organisation.[26] The two elements of Weber's conception that I want to single out for particular attention are those of the hierarchy of offices, and the significance of bureaucratic rules. According to Weber's view, in bureaucracies both authority and power – in his senses of those terms – become 'drained off' towards the top, such that the advance of bureaucratisation more or less inevitably means a progressive decline in autonomy of action of those in the lower echelons. This was the stimulus to Michels's even more firmly drawn 'iron law' of oligarchy within organisations. Such a loss of autonomy of action, in Weber's writings, is embodied within a distinctly sombre world-view: the expansion of an industrial civilisation breeds 'specialists without spirit, sensualists without heart'. We do not have to look far for other, more recent, authors, more radical in intent than Weber was, who have developed views that have definite parallels with his. Whatever his differences with Weber,[27] Marcuse's one-dimensional society looks somewhat like Weber's bureaucracy writ large: a society organised in a tight hierarchy, closed and conformist.[28] In a rather different context, Braverman's analysis of the division of labour within the industrial enterprise suggests that the draining-off upwards of control of the labour-task from the worker is a progressive (and also seemingly irresistible) process in the technological development of modern capitalism.[29] I do not question the importance of these writings, nor the pressing nature of the issues to which their authors point. But it is one of their notable features that the trends diagnosed are made to appear so entrenched and difficult to reverse, especially by those whom they affect most, that the expressed hopes for radical transformation appear as mere pious wishes. It might well be suggested that Weber's pessimism accords better with the implications of his analysis than do the views expressed by authors whose interpretations of the 'steel-hard cage' of the modern division of labour resemble his, but who anticipate not just a general break-out from the cage, but a dissolving of its bars altogether.

However, neither the societies of Western capitalism, nor those of the state socialism of the Eastern bloc, are in fact one-dimensional, nor is there any need to accept certain major features of Weber's analysis that might seem to reinforce such a standpoint.

1. On the level of the philosophy of history (which, in spite of his denials often emerges in his writings)[30] Weber drew a generalised, although largely implicit, contrast between the autonomy of action enjoyed by actors in traditional communities, and the 'steel-hard' organisation of developed bureaucratic systems. But it is surely a mistake to counterpose bureaucracy and autonomy of action in this way. Some forms of small-scale, traditional collectivity have hardly allowed a great deal of autonomy for their members, or the more subordinate of them: consider, for example, the position of women in patriarchal family systems.

2. We have good reason to suppose that, in modern bureaucratic systems, there are far more 'openings' for those in formally subordinate positions to acquire or regain control over their organisational tasks than Weber recognised. Weber treated the advance of bureaucratisation as increasingly producing a rigid hierarchy of power inside an organisation. But, as Crozier has effectively pointed out, the relations between offices in organisations typically provide spaces of potential control that are unavailable in smaller, more traditional collectivities.[31] The more tightly-knit and inflexible the formal relations of authority within an organisation, in fact, the more the possible openings for circumventing them. Weber tended to write as though the formal authority relations within bureaucracies are consensually accepted through all levels of the organisation. But dominant symbol-systems are usually accepted – with any degree of commitment – predominantly by those in the higher authority positions (cf. pp. 71–2, above). Successful struggle

for the maintenance of elements of control by subordinates is much more prevalent than Weber seemed to hold: as is the sheer day-to-day resistance or 'distancing' from oppressive tasks.[32] Distancing is not *ipso facto* control, but it may be an important factor in permitting the type of penetration of the authorised view of things – an unhappy consciousness – which stimulates practical attempts at an extension of control.

Weber was no doubt right to accentuate the importance of the existence of written rules within bureaucratic organisations. But rules do not follow or interpret themselves, and often tend to provide much more of a focus for conflict than Weber acknowledged. The written rules, like the formal authority relations they nominally co-ordinate, are frequently honoured in the breach. 'Working to rule' is more than just a slogan brandished in capital–labour conflicts. But even if it were only this, it is a clear enough illustration of a deliberately semi-ironic distancing by subordinate groups from the injunctions they are supposed to observe, which are bent back against those who seem to profit most by their implementation.

To mistake pragmatic/ironic/humorous, distanced participation in the routines of alienated labour for normative consensus, was one of the great errors of the orthodox academic sociology of the 1950s and 1960s (cf. pp. 235–8, below). The error was not unrelated to the *derogation of the lay actor* of which I have spoken before on the level of the more general theory of agency: a derogation which, however, has certainly not been confined to non-Marxist social science. Three factors have led sociological observers to imagine that those who work in deadeningly monotonous and repetitive occupations are more often than not 'adjusted' to what they do. One is that the level of discursive penetration in such circumstances is only grasped via what participants offer 'seriously' about them; or in terms the observer is 'looking for', or is prepared to find acceptable. The aggressive banter of the shop-floor is likely to give more insight, by its *form*, as well its manifest content, into how labour is experienced and understood, than any number of questionnaire responses, or even lengthy interviews. A second reason is that observation is often confined only to discourse, however that may be construed; but oppositional styles are also expressed in practical consciousness. A third reason, however, is simply the lack of any apparently available alternatives. The point needs to be strongly stressed, and connects directly to problems of ideology. I mean by 'available alternatives' not the possibility of lateral mobility between occupations of a similar character, but conceptions of 'how things could be otherwise'.[33] We might note at this point the tie between human agency as such – which counterfactually implies the possibility of doing otherwise – and alienated labour. The 'doing otherwise' in circumstances which starkly confine that possibility, may take forms which are not immediately identifiable as opposition in any obvious sense.[34]

The dialectic of control operates even in highly repressive forms of collectivity or organisation. For it is my argument that the dialectic of control is built into the very nature of agency, or more correctly put, the relations of autonomy and dependence which agents reproduce in the context of the enactment of definite practices. *An agent who does not participate in the dialectic of control, in a minimal fashion, ceases to be an agent.* As I have emphasised before, all power relations, or relations of autonomy and dependence, are reciprocal: however wide the asymmetrical distribution of resources involved, all power relations manifest autonomy and dependence 'in both directions'. A person kept thoroughly confined and supervised, as an individual in a strait-jacket, perhaps has lost all capability of action, and is not a participant in a reciprocal power-relation. But in all other cases – that is, in all cases in which human agency is exercised within a relationship of any kind – power relations are two-way. This accounts for the intimate tie between agency and suicide.[35] Self-destruction is a (virtually) always-open option, the ultimate refusal that finally and absolutely cancels the oppressive power of others; hence suicidal acts themselves can be understood as concerned with the exercise of power.[36]

I do not want to make the dialectic of control into a metaphysical principle, a modern version of the master–slave dialectic. The dialectic of control is simply an intrinsic feature of regularised relations of power within social systems. As such, however, it is necessarily relevant to the analysis of class conflict in modern capitalism. I shall not attempt to provide such an analysis here. But we may regard the early origins of the labour movement as almost the type case of the operation of the dialectic of control. The 'free' labour contract introduced with the advent of capitalism, as Marx showed in his critique of classical political economy, served to consolidate the power of employers over workers. But the workers succeeded in turning the labour contract into a resource of their own, through the collective withdrawal of labour: and from this the labour movement was born.

The materialist interpretation of history

The theory of contradiction in Marx is developed in the context of an interpretation of historical change, a 'materialist interpretation of history'. In this section I shall consider some (although only some) of the issues posed by Marx's materialism.

A diversity of versions of Marx's materialist conception of history can be found both in the works of those favourable to, and those critical of, Marx. This is perhaps not particularly surprising since the various descriptions and glosses of the materialist conception which Marx provided are by no means all unambiguous or mutually consistent. I shall be less interested here in what Marx might have been concerned to say, than with analysing how far any of the views which have supposedly been based on Marx's writings can be regarded as potentially valid.

We can distinguish the following explications (no doubt more could be found) of the materialist interpretation of history, all of which have at least some minimal plausibility in segments of Marx's writings. It may be regarded as:

1. A *methodological prescription*, or a type of approach to historical analysis. Marx developed his views in specific opposition to forms of idealist philosophy and historiography, especially that of Hegel and his followers. 'In direct contrast to German philosophy which descends from heaven to earth, here we ascend from earth to heaven. That is to say, we do not set out from what men say, imagine, conceive, nor from what has been said, thought, or conceived of men, in order to arrive at men in the flesh. We begin with real, active men ...'[37] The materialist conception, Marx often commented, substitutes concrete historical research into the actual conditions of human social life, for abstract dogmas that hypostatise historical trends.

2. A *conception of human Praxis*, emphasising that human beings are neither to be treated as passive objects, nor as wholly free

subjects. The materialist conception of history, in this context, is opposed both to idealism and to 'passive' or 'mechanical' materialism. The most famous and most brilliantly succinct exposition of this is given in the theses on Feuerbach, where Marx argues that the main shortcoming of previous forms of materialism (and many subsequent types also, one might add!) is that the relations between human actors, and between human actors and the material world, are treated as ones of passive contemplation, not as active, practical relations. The study of human life, Marx emphasises, is the study of definite social practices, geared into human needs. The interaction of human beings with nature is one of active appropriation: 'The whole of history is a preparation for "man" to become an object of sense perception, and for the development of human needs (the needs of man as such).'[38]

3. A perspective closely linked to 2, but in some part distinguishable from it, which emphasises *the significance of labour in the development of human society*. Labour appears in Marx in a twofold sense, not always clearly differentiated. One is that which owes a good deal to Hegel, in which labour refers to the interplay of human activity and material nature: an interplay that is at the root of the 'historical' character of human culture when contrasted to the 'fixed' or instinctive life of the animals. Labour here shades into *Praxis*, as the generic production and reproduction of human social life. But labour is also used by Marx to denote the labour process or work process, that is, the more narrowly prescribed sphere of economic activity. To regard the analysis of labour in the first sense as providing the key to the historical understanding of human society, is clearly different from attempting to explain history in terms of the primacy of the second. The latter verges on a fourth sense of the materialist interpretation, as:

4. A *theory of social change*, asserting in some sense the primacy of economic factors in determining social development. There are of course various ways in which Marx's conception, thus understood, can be framed, depending upon how the 'economy' or the 'economic' on the one hand, and 'determine' on the other, are conceived. As is well known, it is not at all difficult to find in Marx statements that come close to some form of economic or even technological determinism; especially the much-debated passage from *The Poverty of Philosophy*: 'Social relations are intimately connected with the forces of production. In acquiring new forces of

production, men change their mode of production, their way of earning their living; they change all their social relations. The hand mill will give you a society with the feudal lord, the steam mill a society with the industrial capitalist.'[39] As is equally well known, towards the end of their careers both Marx and Engels were anxious to play down interpretations of their ideas that gave undue emphasis to the influence of the economic infrastructure, stressing the interdependence of infrastructure and superstructure (most especially in Engels's famous designation of the determining role of the economy 'in the last instance'). This has stimulated some commentators to treat their views as implying:

5.   A *functional theory of the relations between infrastructure and superstructure* stressing, again in opposition to idealism, the need to connect political and ideological institutions to economic institutions as elements of a totality. According to this view, if we reject any version of 4 as tenable, we are left with a standpoint that emphasises the functional interdependence of the different spheres of human social activity. A functionalist interpretation can still salvage the 'special' character of economic activity by treating the latter as the first and most fundamental functional prerequisite of the existence of society. There is at least some sort of possible justification for this tactic in Marx:

> We must begin by stating the first presupposition of all human existence, and therefore of all history, namely that men must be in a position to live in order to be able to 'make history' . . . The first historical act is, therefore, the production of material life itself. This is indeed a historical act, a fundamental condition of all history, which today, as thousands of years ago, must be accomplished every day and every hour merely in order to sustain human life.[40]

6.   A *reductionist theory of consciousness,* which treats the content of human consciousness as in some way determined by 'material factors'. There are various renderings of such a view. But the basic thesis, advanced with differing degrees of emphasis, is that 'ideas' have little or no autonomy in relation to 'material' or 'economic reality' in the determination of social development; ideas 'reflect' material conditions of social life. The sort of passage in Marx that

might be considered to lend itself to such a reading is: 'Consciousness can never be anything else than conscious existence, and the existence of men is their actual life process ... We begin with real, active men, and from their real life process show the development of the ideological reflexes and echoes of this life process.'[41]

7. A *theory of the centrality of class divisions*, according to which class relations largely determine or govern the alignments of other institutions, such that class conflict is the fundamental motor of social change (in class societies, at any rate). The *Communist Manifesto*, of course, announces that 'The history of all hitherto existing society is the history of class struggles'.[42] Underlying this is the thesis that property relations, as co-ordinated within modes of production, provide the basis of both classifying types of society (as in *The German Ideology* and later in the *Grundrisse*), and of explaining major processes of social change.

Clearly these are not all mutually exclusive, although some of them are. I shall not discuss here 1, 2; the first part of 3; or 5 and 6, for different reasons: the first three because they express a position I accept, and indeed have tried to expound at some length in the previous papers; the second two because they represent views which – as also follows from my other discussions – are unacceptable. I shall argue that both of the remaining interpretations, 4 and 7, have important ingredients of validity, although their identification presupposes both considering more precisely how they should be formulated, and how they relate to one another.

In the above classification, I have not quoted (although I have done so in an earlier section of this paper) the most famous passage in which Marx set out his approach: his Preface to *A Contribution to the Critique of Political Economy*. This contains a number of different ideas stated at a high level of generality, but I wish to pick out and consider the following assertions:

At a certain stage of their development, the material forces of production in society come into conflict with the existing relations of production or – what is but a legal expression of the same thing – with the property relations within which they had been at work before. From forms of development of the forces of production these relations turn into their fetters. Then occurs a period of social revolution. With the change of the economic foundation the entire immense superstructure is more or less rapidly transformed . . . [43]

In assessing the significance of this passage, in the light of problems raised under 4 and 7, two basic questions have to be asked. Can the forces/relations of production scheme in fact be applied as broadly as Marx suggests, as something like a general framework for the explanation of radical social transformation? How does the forces/relations of production scheme relate to class divisions, and to class conflict?

I shall analyse the second of these questions in the concluding section of the paper. The first question can be usefully reformulated, I think, as the following: does the evolution of the forces of production characteristically occur on the level of the forces of production? By this I mean, how far are developments in the productive forces, in different periods of history or types of society, the result of relatively 'autonomous' processes of economic change? I shall discuss in the following section Althusser's response to this question. The view I want to advocate, however, is different from his. Althusser seeks to avoid 'economistic' accounts of social development – those which involve a version of 7 – by distinguishing between the 'determinant' and the 'dominant' in social formations. He is thus able to recognise that, prior to capitalism, the economy is not dominant. It remains determinant 'in the last instance'. But the conception of the 'last instance' as Althusser formulates it, as I shall suggest below, does not seem defensible, and appears to be little more than a concession to orthodoxy. It seems more reasonable to be bold enough to drop the 'last instance' altogether and to suggest that Marx gave so much of his effort to studying capitalism that he underestimated its distinctiveness, as compared to other historical forms of society. That is to say, we may suggest that *it is only with the advent of capitalism* that the evolution of the forces of production characteristically occurs on the level of the forces of production. For capitalism (as indicated by the very fact that the name can be applied both to a type of production system and to an overall type of society) *turns the exploitation of nature into a propelling force of social change.* The development of capitalism sets under way an impetus to continuous technical innovation and expansion of the productive forces: this is 'autonomous' in the sense that the expanded reproduction of capital is promoted by the very operation of capitalist production itself.

Althusser on structural causality

Althusser's writings represent a strong reaction both against 'technicist' or 'economistic' interpretations of Marx on the one hand, and against 'historicist' interpretations on the other: the latter category including particularly versions of Marx strongly influenced by Hegel.[44] Hence the 'totality', in Althusser's usage, is intended to be quite distinct from that employed by authors such as Lukács in his earlier writings. The totality is a unity of 'objective levels' that operate relatively autonomously from one another as constitutive elements of a social formation. These levels are not symmetrical in terms of their influence within a social formation: we can speak of a 'structure in dominance'. The economic infrastructure is one of these levels, but it does not 'determine' the other levels in the formation in the ways in which that term has often been understood. The economic infrastructure only determines, and then 'in the last instance', which elements are dominant in a social formation.

> The economic dialectic is never active in *the pure state*; in History, these instances, the superstructures, etc. are never seen to step respectfully aside when their work is done, or when the Time comes, as his pure phenomena, to scatter before His Majesty the Economy as he strides along the royal road to the Dialectic. From the first moment to the last, the lonely hour of the 'last instance' never comes.[45]

Thus, according to Althusser, the contradiction between forces and relations of production cannot in and of itself bring about a situation of radical social transformation. As the most basic contradiction in any social formation, it expresses itself through the asymmetry of the other levels within the totality. He explains this in terms of his concepts of overdetermination and structural causality. Each of these are relevant to how Althusser seeks to escape the charge of having replaced a Marxist theory of infrastructure/superstructure with a 'pluralist' view or one which relapses into the category I have distinguished as 5 above. According to Althusser, contradictions are never simple, but are overdetermined: the structure in dominance is present in each of the contradictions constituting the whole. The forces/relations of production contradiction is expressed in the uneven relations of the levels of the totality; but these in turn 'reverberate' upon one another to multiply contradictions, which then can 'play back' through the forces/relations of production contradiction, and so on. In so far as these contradictions are dispersed, or displaced, there is not an impetus to revolutionary change; if they become fused, on the other hand, a 'rupture' with the pre-existing constitution of the social formation may be brought about. Uneven development is thus made not just incidental to a social formation, but integral to it: Althusser in fact justifies his application of the notion of overdetermination by generalisation of Lenin's analysis of Russia as the weakest link in the chain of capitalist countries.

The idea of overdetermination, in Althusser's opinion, cannot be explicated in terms of traditional views of causality. He distinguishes two such views, each of which he contrasts with his own. One is a 'mechanical' conception, associated particularly with Descartes but presumably including the Humean view also, in which causality is treated as a 'transitive' relation between causes and effects seen as events or classes of events. The other Althusser traces to Leibnitz, but regards as developed especially by Hegel: this involves a concept of 'expressive' causality. Whereas the former has no way of conceptualising the effects of a whole upon its parts, the concept of expressive causality involves exactly that: it represents the thesis that each of the elements of a totality are expressions or moments of the 'essence' of the whole: 'the inner principle of the essence being present at each point in the whole'.[46] Both of these views Althusser associates with Marxist approaches he rejects: the first with economistic versions of Marx, the second with historicist ones. Althusser's own category of 'structural causality' resembles the latter rather than the former, in so far as it too is concerned with the reciprocal influence of part and whole; but in a structured totality, according to him, we cannot think in terms of essences.

Structural or metonymic causality, Althusser claims, is a concept that can be discovered in Marx and in Freud. Hence the borrowing of the term 'overdetermination' from the latter is not an alien importation into social theory; both Marx and Freud were seeking to resolve a similar issue: how a structure and its effects determine one another. Structural causality Althusser takes to denote the existence of a structure through its effects:

> This implies therefore that the effects are not outside the structure, are not a pre-existing object, element or space in which the structure arrives to *imprint its mark*: on the contrary, it implies that the structure is immanent in its effects, a cause immanent in its effects in the Spinozist sense of the term, that *the whole existence of the structure consists of its effects*, in short that the structure, which is merely a specific combination of its particular elements, is nothing outside its effects.[47]

This brief exposition of Althusser's views cannot be left without a few comments about that author's discussion of the relevance of metonymic causality to human agency. If we understand the social totality as a structure, according to Althusser, and thus as 'self-determining' or, as he puts it, 'determining its elements', it follows that human actors are never more than occupants of positions within the structure: they are, in his now notorious terms, 'supports' or 'bearers' of the structure. The '*relations* of production (and political and ideological social relations) are irreducible to any anthropological inter-subjectivity – since they only combine agents and objects in a specific structure of the distribution of relations, places and functions, occupied and "supported" by objects and agents of production.'[48] The category of subject, or more accurately, the subject/object differentiation, Althusser claims, is constituted only in ideology. This is one main sense in which the notion of superstructure is retained in Althusser's theory: ideology integrates the 'individual' in 'society' by transforming the 'supports' of the real movers of history – structural features of social formations – into subjects with definite forms of consciousness and needs.

I shall not consider Althusser's view of ideology for the present, but I shall attempt such a discussion in the context of a comprehensive treatment of ideology in the following paper. I shall concentrate here on: the notion of overdetermination, as Althusser employs it; the conception of determination 'in the last instance' by the forces/relations of production scheme; the notion of metonymic causality; and finally I shall revert briefly to questions of structure and agency.

In assessing Althusser's use of 'overdetermination', it is worthwhile tracing the process of reasoning whereby Althusser connects the notion with the Leninist idea of the weakest link. Russia was a country ripe for revolution because there were concentrated in it a number of major contradictions, deriving from the conjunction of advanced sectors of capitalist development with a backward, semi-feudal order. This example, Althusser argues, demonstrates with particular clarity that the forces/relations-of-production contradiction does not directly initiate social change; there must be an accumulation of other contradictions which 'fuse into a ruptural unity'. The 'revolutionary break', in other words, Althusser says, is overdetermined. If this is so in this apparently unusual set of circumstances, he goes on to add, why should we suppose that it is confined to them? In fact, in the situation in revolutionary Russia we see a special case of what is generic to social formations in overdetermined contradiction.

Now the idea of analysing social change in terms of a fusion of contradictions, as I have argued earlier, is an important one. The introduction of the notion of overdetermination into social theory can also be defended: but only with two major reservations.

1. As Laplanche and Pontalis point out, 'overdetermination' in Freud has two distinct meanings. One is that a given psychological formation expresses a plurality of unconscious elements, expressed in divergent sequences of meaning, each of which is coherent at different levels of interpretation. The other is that a psychological formation results from the convergence of several types of causes, none of which is sufficient alone to account for it.[49] Only the second of these, which is not actually Freud's most characteristic usage, seems relevant to overdetermination as Althusser employs it.
2. Use of the concept of 'overdetermination' in social analysis presupposes an adequate account of the 'determination' of social change – of causation and agency. But these are the most defective parts of Althusser's whole theoretical scheme.

There is undoubtedly merit in Althusser's critiques of both 'economism' and of Hegelian versions of the totality. So far as the former goes, he tries to break with interpretations of Marx that regard political or ideological elements as having little influence upon the development of society, or seek reductively to explain them away. As regards the latter, he quite rightly seeks to emphasise the differentiation of 'levels' or 'regions' that compose the whole, stressing particularly the tensions that exist between them – even if this conception is by no means as distant from Hegelian or Hegel-influenced versions of the totality as he seems to believe. Moreover, the thesis that the forces/relations of production contradiction is only determinate in the (non-temporal) 'last instance' allows a welcome recognition of the importance of non-economic institutions in the organisation of society. But a considerable price is paid for this: for the idea of the 'last instance' surely remains obscure in Althusser, and wavers oddly between being a metaphysical dogma on the one hand, and an interpretation that comes uncomfortably close to a sort of pluralist functionalism on the other.[50] As a defence of the infrastructure/superstructure distinction, or of the role of economic factors in social change, it is both too strong and too weak. It is too strong in so far as it is asserted as some sort of unequivocal principle (although it is at the same time obscure, since it is not clear in what sense the last instance is 'ultimately' determinant). It is too weak in so far as the character of the economy is largely unspecified – or at least, how the forces/relations of production contradiction actually exerts its determinant influence.[51] Althusser sometimes compares the influence of the economy to the unconscious in psychoanalysis: it cannot be directly observed, and only exists as refracted through other structures. But this neither clarifies anything about the nature of economic determination, nor justifies the thesis that economic relations determine which levels are dominant in a social formation.

These difficulties stem in some part from limitations in Althusser's conception of metonymic causality. In assessing this we have to mention Althusser's debt to structuralism. Althusser is often regarded as a structuralist, in spite of frequent denials.[52] The question need not delay us long, since it is largely a matter of terminology. Althusser's theory is not a 'structuralist' one if that term is defined with any degree of precision – any more, to take a parallel from another context, than Popper is a 'positivist' in the philosophy of science.[53] Althusser is particularly critical of some of the cardinal doctrines of Lévi-Strauss. On the other hand, there is no doubt at all that, like Popper and positivism, Althusser shares certain of the general perspectives adopted by other authors – including Lévi-Strauss – who are normally grouped as 'structuralists'. These include a predilection for the notion of structure itself, a stringently critical attitude towards 'humanism', and a certain conception of the social whole. It is the third of these that is especially important here. As I have indicated earlier in this book, in his account of linguistics Saussure employed a conception of the totality that diverges from notions of the whole that have been most prominent in the social sciences. The dialectic of presence/absence which Saussure formulated, adopted into the social sciences, provides an idea of major importance, when appropriately developed. One of its main characteristics is the notion that the totality only exists in its moments – or, as Althusser says, in its effects. There is no doubt that such a conception can be found in Marx, although in spite of what Althusser claims, there is just as little doubt that he owed it primarily to Hegel. What Althusser does is to construe this conception of the totality in terms of causality, by speaking of the 'structure existing in its effects'. But this is not a helpful move. The presence/absence dialectic is not a causal relation as ordinarily conceived, nor is there much point in trying to make it into one: indeed it is a counter-productive move in so far as it excludes 'transitive' causality, as Althusser calls it. Althusser's theory conforms to the leading perspectives of structuralism in lacking a distinction between structure and system: if we adopt such a distinction, I have tried to show in a previous paper, we can acknowledge the fundamental importance of the presence/absence dialectic without sacrificing the analysis of 'transitive' causality as involved in social reproduction.

Althusser's discussions of subjectivity also bear a strong imprint of structuralist emphases, although the space he allows to the self-understanding of the human actor is even less than that characteristic of structuralist authors. Neither the treatment of agents as 'supports' of the relations constituting social formations, nor the thesis that subjectivity is formed wholly in ideology will withstand much scrutiny. Althusser's conception of structure, in which the only moving force is overdetermined contradiction, treated as metonymic causality, has no mode of grasping the duality of structure and agency.

Contradiction and class domination

To conclude this paper, I want to sketch in an approach to the connection of contradiction with class domination: setting out very cursorily the essential features of a more extended account that I shall seek to provide in the volume subsequent to this one.

In reacting against Hegel, Marx associated the notions of contradiction and negativity primarily with class conflict. I want to argue here that Marx was right (although it was not an idea for which he claimed originality) to suppose that the emergence of class domination injects a new dynamic into history. But it was a mistake, I want to propose, to link contradiction and negativity purely to class domination rather than seeing class domination as one mode in which human society expresses a contradictory form.

I want to suggest the following, as a fundamental theorem: in all forms of society, human beings exist in *contradictory relation to nature*. Human beings exist in contradictory relation to nature because they are in and of nature, as corporeal beings existing in material environments; and yet at the same time they are set off against nature, as having a 'second nature' of their own, irreducible to physical objects or events. This contradiction, which is perhaps at the heart of all religions, has its universal expression in the finitude of *Dasein* as the negation of the apparent infinity of time – space in which each human life makes its fleeting appearance. It is contradictory in a genuine sense, for the negation of nature by 'second nature', the 'contradictory unity' that is man's distinctiveness from nature, sustains the accommodations reached with it, and the modes of control to which nature is made subject. But the relation between *Dasein* and the continuity of Being is always mediated: by society, or the institutions in terms of which, in the duality of structure, social reproduction is carried on. The existential contradiction of human existence thus becomes translated into structural contradiction, which is really its only medium.

The institutional mediation of contradiction, I want to propose, takes a different form, if we adopt Lévi-Strauss's designations, in 'cold' societies as compared to 'hot' ones – the second category being mobilised by the dynamic impetus of class divisions. In cold societies, the contradictory relation of man and nature is expressed *through its internal incorporation*. This, I take it, is one of the main themes which Lévi-Strauss wishes to emphasise: nature is not separated from the categories of human thought and action, but forms an integral part of their constitution. *Christophorus Christum, sed Christus sustulit orbem: Constiterit pedibus dic ubi Christophorus?* Contradiction is mediated in the very form of institutions: especially in those of kinship and myth. Only with the appearance of class division *is contradiction mediated through sectional group formation.* This is not the tautology it might appear to be.

It is not a tautology, because conditions other than the appearance of classes are involved in the origin of class-divided societies. I use the term *class-divided society* as distinct from that of *class society.* A class-divided society is a society in which there are classes, a class relation always being inherently a conflict relation in the sense of opposition of interest; but it is not a society in which class analysis provides the key to unlocking all the most significant features of the institutional order. The only type of society which is a class society in this sense, is that in which I have earlier suggested the forces/relations of production scheme applies: capitalism. Marx's forces/relations of production scheme may be read as asserting the universal primacy of allocation over authorisation, both in the constitution of society and in the dynamics of social change (in all forms of society divided into classes). But I want to suggest that in fact something like the reverse is the case: in class-divided societies, as contrasted to class society, *authorisation has primacy over allocation.* To repeat the argument made earlier: only in capitalism, because of the specific character of the capitalist mode of production, setting into motion an accumulation process ultimately dominated by private capital, is the mechanism of economic activity the prime mover.

All class-divided and class societies are *administered societies*: the significance of this was never fully acknowledged by Marx, writing at the time of the greatest triumphs of entrepreneurial capitalism, in a country where state direction of economic enterprise was probably as minimal as it has ever been anywhere within the modern capitalist order. An administered society is one in which centralised control of 'knowledge' or 'information' is a medium of domination. The significance of this might have been more apparent had Marx given consideration to the class-divided civilisations of the Near East, which emerged in the Third Millennium B.C. In these civilisations, administrative control of human beings, directed to the exploitation of nature, was applied with a ruthlessness that has no parallel until modern times.[54] The structural characteristics of class-divided and class societies, I propose, are basically governed by *the character of the connections between authorisation and allocation*: especially by the connections between *authority* and *property*. These conjoin in different ways not only in relation to one another, but in relation to the exploitation of nature.

The early civilisations and modern capitalism share in common an 'externalised' or instrumental relation to nature. An *exploitative attitude to nature* in both is associated with *social exploitation*, directly geared into it. I regard this as a point of fundamental importance. In feudalism, the extraction of a surplus product, through the *levée*, tithe, etc., was *not as such part of the immediate productive process*. A bonded peasant may have to allocate part of his product to his local *seigneur*, but while this exploitative relation is at the basis of class domination, it is not an integral part of production as such. The same was not the case in the early civilisations, and the same is not the case in contemporary capitalism: in each the exploitative class relation is made part of the mechanism of production, and in each the society/nature relation is predominantly one of instrumental control. In the early civilisations, however, authorisation rather than allocation was the primary medium whereby both the exploitation of nature and the exploitation of human beings was organised: neither technical advance in the tools of production, nor control of property, were of primary importance in this. What was decisive was the mobilisation of 'human machines', in an authoritarian division of labour. Modern capitalism conjoins the exploitation of nature and of human labour in a different way: a way that has to be seen as a distinctive outcome of the disintegration of feudal society in Europe. Capitalism developed in the urban communes, in the context of a newly-emergent class system that existed both within, yet outside, the institutional framework of feudal society. The early capitalists did not have at their disposal the means of co-ordinating masses of human beings into 'human machines'; their innovation was the co-ordination of *the immediate productive enterprise*, as a division of labour linking men and machine.

Capitalism is a class society, by contrast to class-divided societies, because in capitalist enterprise property becomes both the organising principle of production at the same time as it is the source of class division. Only in capitalism are the sources of contradiction and class conflict identical. Ownership of private property is both the means of appropriating a surplus product, as in class-divided societies, and simultaneously the means whereby the economic system is mobilised. This is why Marx's stress upon the process whereby labour power itself becomes a commodity is so important; for it is in the labour contract that contradiction and class conflict, in the capitalist mode of production, coincide.

5

Ideology and Consciousness

Ideology: Comte and Marx

The history of the concept of ideology has often been analysed.[1] None the less, there is some point in commenting upon this history here, since I shall argue that it is indispensable to an evaluation of how 'ideology' should be understood in the social sciences. I shall concentrate only upon certain phases in the evolution of the notion: its usage by Marx, still the inevitable point of departure for any contemporary discussion of ideology; Mannheim's version of the 'sociology of knowledge'; and the more recent accounts of ideology suggested by Habermas and Althusser.

Most histories of ideology begin with Destutt de Tracy, since that author is usually accredited with being the first to have used the term in print; but some (including Mannheim) see an early antici- pation of it in Bacon's conception of the *idola*. Association with the 'idols', impediments to valid knowledge, would lend a pejorative tone to 'ideology'. Destutt de Tracy himself however used the term in a positive way in his *Éléments d'idéologie*, published soon after the turn of the nineteenth century, to sanction a new 'science of ideas'. But Destutt drew heavily upon the writings of Condillac, who had in turn asserted the need to expand Bacon's critique of the 'idols' as a basis for the reform of consciousness: 'prejudices' were to be transformed by reason.

As is well known, Napoleon's polemic against the 'ideologists' helped to establish the term 'ideology' in a depreciative sense, which since then has remained predominant. But the repudiation of ideology subsequently assumed two divergent forms, manifest in the contrasts between the perspectives of Comte and Marx.[2]

Comte's criticisms of the ideologists centred upon the radical character of their attack upon tradition and metaphysics. However in substituting 'positivism' for their 'radical negativism' he continued their emphases, while making them part of a view which stressed the necessity of tempering change with 'order'. Since he envisaged sociology as concerned with synthesising progress and order, Comte saw the main practical aim of the new science of society as that of completing the transcendence of metaphysics while forging new bonds of social unity. In the tradition of thought developed by Comte, and appropriated in substantial degree by Durkheim, the concept of ideology does not appear as central. Comte retained the ideologists' programme of studying the natural evolution of the human mind, but rejected the form in which this had been expressed by Destutt, which was individualistic in character: individuals and their ideas, he believed, are all that are real.[3] Breaking with the latter notion, Comte also dropped the term ideology.

The matter was quite otherwise, of course, for Marx, whose thought does have direct intellectual ties back to the ideologists, but whose incorporation of the term into his own writings was vitally influenced by Hegel and the 'Feuerbachian inversion'. Feuerbach attempted to escape Hegel's idealism and his 'mystical theology' not only by substituting 'materialism' for 'idealism', but by restoring the principles of study of the French Enlightenment. Marx however came to see Bauer and others among his early associates (and later, Feuerbach himself), as 'ideologists' themselves. Marx's position involved both a rejection of Hegel, and a recovery of certain features of Hegel's philosophy that had largely evaporated in Feuerbach's 'inversion'. In Hegel, human beings appear as the creators of their own history, but in conditions only partly disclosed to them in terms of their own consciousness: conditions that can only be understood retrospectively. In rejecting the latter claim, and in holding that social analysis (as opposed to philosophy) can discern and help to actualise immanent tendencies in contemporary social development, Marx introduced a radically new perspective into social theory. Henceforth the diagnosis of ideology became a mode of penetrating beyond the consciousness of human actors, and of uncovering the 'real foundations' of their activity, this being harnessed to the end of social transformation. What was in Comte the juxtaposing of science and metaphysics became in Marx to some degree a juxtaposition of science and ideology. The empirical, scientific study of society would make possible the dispelling of the distortions of consciousness exemplified in ideology: *but only in so far as the critique of ideology could be realised in actual social intervention*, since the 'critique of consciousness, by consciousness' is just what Marx castigated the 'German ideologists' for.

The first chapter of *The German Ideology* is in fact the only part of Marx's writings where the notion of ideology is discussed at any length. One of the notable aspects of the discussion in that source is the imagery used on various of the occasions where Marx referred to ideology: imagery that is not confined, however, to this relatively early work, but appears occasionally also in Marx's later writings. It is the imagery of the *camera obscura*, of the world turned upside down, or of reflections or echoes:[4]

Consciousness can never be anything else than conscious existence, and the existence of men is their actual life-process. If in all ideology men and their circumstances appear upside down as in a *camera obscura*, this phenomenon arises just as much from their historical life-process as the inversion of objects on the retina does from their physical life-process.[5]

If this owed a good deal to Feuerbach, it was nevertheless offered by Marx in criticism of that philosopher, because the inference Marx draws from it is not simply that things have to be set right side up again: we have to disclose, through empirical historical study, the circumstances which have led to the formation of different kinds of ideology.

There is another context in which ideology appears in *The German Ideology*, one which initially might not seem particularly close to the first. This is where Marx asserts that ideologies express or justify the interests of dominant classes:

The ideas of the ruling class are in every epoch the ruling ideas: i.e., the class which is the ruling *material* force of society, is at the same time its ruling *intellectual* force. The class which has the means of material production at its disposal, has control at the same time over the means of mental production, so that thereby, generally speaking, the ideas of those who lack the means of mental production are subject to it . . . For instance, in an age and

in a country where royal power, aristocracy and bourgeoisie are
contending for mastery and where, therefore, mastery is shared,
the doctrine of the separation of powers proves to be the dominant idea and is expressed as an 'eternal law'.[6]

The connection between the two, however, is supplied precisely
by the demystifying of ideology that the *camera obscura* allusion
suggests: history must not be written 'upside down' – as it is by
'ideologists' – from within the sway of such dominant ideas.[7]
Historians or social analysts who have failed to examine the
'material' basis of ideology in any particular epoch have fallen
prey to the 'illusions of that epoch'. Hegelian philosophy, according
to Marx, is a prime example of such a tendency.

Marx establishes here a link between two usages of 'ideology'
which constantly reappear in the subsequent literature. It is important to recognise certain core differences between them. The first
tends to operate around a polarity of science/ideology, the second
around a polarity of sectional interests/ideology. The term 'false
consciousness' (introduced by Engels rather than Marx) is ambiguous between these, depending upon how 'false' is interpreted. If it is
understood as contrasted to 'valid' or 'true' propositions, the phrase
stands closer to the first conception; if however what is 'false' is
actors' comprehension of their own interests or motives, it is closer
to the second. Much the same applies to the infrastructure/super-
structure distinction. If this differentiation is related to the first
sense of ideology, the issues that arise concern the social determination of ideas – and lead into the kind of problems upon which
Lukács concentrated, and which Mannheim discussed within the
rubric of the 'sociology of knowledge'. Where, on the other hand,
the distinction between infrastructure and superstructure is interpreted mainly in the context of the second connotation of ideology,
it leads more towards the sociological issue of 'hegemonic culture'
rather than, as in the former case, broaching epistemological issues
directly.

Mannheim and the sociology of knowledge

Mannheim's concern with the 'sociology of knowledge' did not arise
directly as a result of a 'dialogue with Marx'. It seems to have been
in some part stimulated by Lukács's *History and Class Conscious-*

ness (the influence of Lukács over Mannheim is a matter of some controversy). But Mannheim's work was steeped in the traditions of German historicism from which Dilthey, Weber and Lukács himself drew – traditions which had, in their Hegelian version, influenced Marx's own writings. It is of some interest to see how Mannheim traced out what he called the 'transition' from ideology to the sociology of knowledge. 'Marxism', he argued, 'merely discovered a clue to understanding and a mode of thought, in the gradual rounding out of which the whole nineteenth century participated.' This 'clue to understanding' is that the analysis of the views of one's opponents as ideological allows those views to be deflated. But such a tactic cannot be monopolised by Marxism; the critics of Marxism are able to turn it back against its source, treating Marxism itself as an ideology. When the situation has been reached in which everyone can analyse the claims of their adversaries as ideology, we are forced 'to recognise that our axioms, our ontology, and our epistemology have been profoundly transformed'.[8] Hence discussion of ideology must rejoin the tradition of thought which helped to generate it: for German historicism has always been preoccupied with the developing, 'produced' character of knowledge as situated in history.

The process whereby use of the term 'ideology' becomes generalised is, in Mannheim's terms, a movement from the 'particular' to the 'total' conception of ideology. The first of these concepts Mannheim applied to situations where one party is sceptical of the ideas advanced by another because those ideas are designed to conceal interests that the other has but will not admit to: concealment that may be calculated or largely unwitting. The total conception refers to the overall ideology of a group, class or historical period. The particular and total concepts of ideology are linked by the fact that each involves going beyond or 'below' the manifest content of beliefs or ideas: both views of ideology treat ideas as in some sense a product of the social milieu of those who profess them. The particular conception, however, involves regarding only part of an antagonist's declarations as ideological, whereas the total version places in question the whole conceptual apparatus of the other. The former, Mannheim says, concerns only the individual and operates on a psychological level; the latter concerns the organisation of groups. And it is the total conception which has assumed predominance in contemporary times: in politics, in social theory and in philosophy, where it gives rise to characteristic problems of *relativism*.

As long as the total conception of ideology is only applied to an opponent's ideas, Mannheim reasoned, there is still one further step to be taken: that of acknowledging that one's own world-view can be legitimately subjected to ideological analysis. When this step has been taken, the theory of ideology develops into the sociology of knowledge. 'It becomes the task of the sociological history of thought to analyse without regard for party biases all the factors in the actually existing social situation which may influence thought. This sociologically oriented history of ideas is destined to provide modern men with a revised view of the whole historical process.'[9] The problem of 'what constitutes reliable knowledge' then admits of two possible solutions. One, which Mannheim of course rejected, is actually to adopt some kind of relativistic viewpoint; the other, which he accepted, is to opt for 'relationism' rather than relativism. Relationism involves accepting, and studying, the influence of social or historical contexts upon the formulation of ideas, but recognising that we can and have to discriminate between valid and erroneous claims to knowledge. Mannheim differentiated two branches of the sociology of knowledge. As an account of what he labelled the 'social determination of knowledge', the sociology of knowledge may be conceived of simply as the empirical analysis of the manner in which forms of social life influence the production of ideas. This *may* shade into epistemological inquiry, the second type of concern of the sociology of knowledge; but Mannheim considered that these two forms of investigation can be kept quite separate.

In view of the constant tendency among commentators on Mannheim's work to suppose that he regarded the 'socially free-floating intellectuals' as providing an epistemologically privileged standpoint, which escapes the potential collapse of 'relationism' into relativism, it is worth while indicating what the main thrust of his views was on the position of intellectuals. Intellectuals, according to Mannheim, are not guaranteed a privileged access to truth, or a mode of escaping the social determination of ideas. But their education, Mannheim held, which allows them in some part to transcend class standpoints (as perhaps one might suppose Marx managed to do), gives them more chance to discover valid knowledge about total ideologies. Whatever we may think of

Mannheim's claims, they are not, as they stand, necessarily paradoxical.[10] The core of Mannheim's view is expressed in his critique of positivism, which he saw as having the following characteristics:

> Every kind of knowledge which only certain specific historical-social groups could acquire was distrusted. Only that kind of knowledge was wanted which was free from all the influences of the subjects' *Weltanschauung*. What was not noticed was that the world of the purely quantifiable and analysable was itself only discoverable on the basis of a definite *Weltanschauung*. Similarly, it was not noticed that a *Weltanschauung* is not of necessity a source of error, but often gives access to spheres of knowledge otherwise closed.[11]

I shall not be concerned to comment here on Mannheim's conception of the sociology of knowledge except in so far as this is relevant to problems of ideology. As I have mentioned previously, it would be misleading to regard Mannheim's treatment of ideology as developed on the basis of a critique of Marx, even if Mannheim himself sometimes liked to accentuate the connection.[12] Marx shared with Mannheim a background in German historicism, but was never particularly occupied with problems of relativism.[13] Such problems, on the other hand, were Mannheim's starting-point, and both his social analysis and his political theory have to be understood in terms of them. On the level of social analysis, Mannheim argued that historicism is an intellectual current that expresses the major feature of modern culture: everything is in a process of change or becoming.[14] This was the backdrop to his sketch of the movement from the particular to the general conception of ideology, noted above. On the level of politics, Mannheim sought to achieve a synthesis that would reconcile or transcend the particular ideologies of the political arena. This was the basis of his view of the key role to be played by intellectuals.

As Merton has stressed,[15] although Mannheim denied that his approach to the sociology of knowledge was at all strongly influenced by neo-Kantianism, the latter made a decisive imprint upon the cast of his thought. Indeed, it can be plausibly argued that it is the commingling of notions derived from neo-Kantianism with others influenced by Hegel and Marx, that is at origin of the vacillating and ambiguous character of a good deal of Mannheim's work. For the neo-Kantian philosophers, two issues in the philosophy of history posed themselves in particularly acute fashion: one was that of relativism, and the other that of the relation between the natural and social sciences. Authors such as Rickert and Max Weber sought to resolve the former of these issues through the separation of two modes of approaching 'reality' (whether natural or social): the mode of orientation towards a 'subject-matter', governed by 'value-relevance', and the mode of examining or studying that subject-matter once constituted. All knowledge is relative, but only in respect of the values that determine which aspects of a potentially infinite reality are 'spotlighted' and hence made available for study. A subject-matter having been constituted, there are intersubjective rules available that allow the formation of valid knowledge and the discarding of erroneous hypotheses. There are insuperable difficulties, in my opinion, involved with such a standpoint. But it seems actually stronger than Mannheim's 'relationism', which in fact resembles it fairly closely. The concept of value-relevance, as differentiated from the validation of claims to knowledge, provides at least some basis for reconciling history and the possibility of abstract 'knowledge' in a plausible way. Since Mannheim does not sustain a concept of value-relevance, while still separating relationism from relativism, his thesis that the sociology of knowledge is relationalist rather than relativistic comes down to little more than an unsubstantiated assertion.

In Mannheim's writings, the combination of elements derived from Hegel and Marx with a neo-Kantian view has particular consequences for the supposed movement from the particular to the total conception of ideology. What is stated to be a transition from a limited version of ideology to a more comprehensive one is in Mannheim in some part a transition from one philosophical standpoint to another. Marx's treatment of ideology, fragmented and undeveloped as it may have been, was not an attempt to 'contextualise', and thereby relativise, consciousness. The two main senses in which, I have indicated above, Marx used 'ideology', were each directed towards criticising the 'ideologists', as he saw them: those who wrote history as if it were 'upside down' – and who understood events only from the point of view of dominant classes. Each sense has immediate relevance to idealist interpretations of history, but there is little difficulty involved in adjusting them to take as their target that set of ideas with which Marx was preoccupied in the latter part of his career: classical political economy. Political economy is not idealism, but tries instead to do away with history altogether, treating 'individuals freely entering into exchange' as a starting-point of social analysis, rather than a condition that is a result of historical change in the past and open to change in the future. In this way, if political economy does not act as a *camera obscura*, it nevertheless turns history 'back to front', thus being ideological in a manner akin to idealism.

Marx did not consider himself vulnerable to the charge that his own writings were ideological, but not because he failed to see that they were produced in a social context. The 'contextuality' of ideas was not the basis of his identification of modes of thought as 'ideological' – at least, not as a generalised thesis. Modes of thought, for Marx, are ideological, in so far as they do not portray things as they are, and where this misrepresentation serves certain sectional interests. He never wrote anything at length about what criteria or forms of validation have to be used to demonstrate 'how things really are': the most likely view seems to be that he simply held that application of the procedures of science allows us to penetrate ideological façades. But there is more than a hint of an alternative view (or perhaps, depending upon how it is construed, a complementary one): that theory has to be validated in practice. These provide two poles towards which Marxist analyses may gravitate. Lukács's perspective was oriented towards the second alternative, and was a mediator between Marx and Mannheim's translation of the study of ideology into the sociology of knowledge. But while he was influenced by Lukács's approach (which also owed a good deal to Max Weber), Mannheim of course repudiated both Lukács's conception of the role of the party, and the latter's notion of truth. Hence Mannheim's discussions of 'truth' and of 'knowledge' waver between various different stances, not satisfactorily elucidated in respect of one another.

Mannheim never seems to have made up his mind about what counts as a valid claim to knowledge, or at least where the boundary lies between knowledge and mere partisan belief. The types of thought that he actually employs to illustrate problems of the sociology of knowledge are mainly political ideas, or philosophies of history, rather than 'science'.[16] According to Mannheim, social perspectives penetrate 'most of the domains of knowledge'. But some domains they do not: 'formal knowledge' is not conditioned by social circumstances. Sometimes by 'formal knowledge' Mannheim appears to mean only that knowledge which might be held to be analytic (logic and mathematics). However on other occasions this category appears to extend to knowledge of a broader kind developed in natural science and in sociology ('formal sociological thinking and other sorts of purely formalising knowledge'[17]). Sometimes, by contrast to each of these positions, and in the manner of the *Geisteswissenschaften* tradition, Mannheim implies that there is a radical difference between the natural and the social sciences in that the latter are penetrated by historical situations, whereas the former are not. Similar ambiguities appear in respect of the notion of truth. In some instances, Mannheim seems to suggest, or take for granted, that there is one (unelucidated) conception of truth which applies throughout all areas of human knowledge. Elsewhere, however, he takes to task those who 'take their criteria and model of truth from other fields of knowledge', and who 'fail to realise that every level of reality may possibly have its own form of knowledge'.[18] The notion of truth associated with such 'levels' is apparently concerned in some way with practice (Mannheim's favourable attitude towards pragmatism in the latter stages of his career is well known), and is more 'restricted' than traditional concepts of truth: but just what each of these elements involves remains quite obscure.

We cannot dismiss Mannheim's ideas about the tasks of intellectuals in the contemporary age merely by rejecting the idea that intellectuals can occupy an epistemological 'point zero': a notion which, as I have suggested above, he did not propose. Mannheim's view is open to criticism precisely in respect of the perspective of his discussion, which is a political one. Intellectuals are held to be both capable of, and willing to, rise above the partisan struggles of political life, thus being able to arbitrate between conflicting protagonists. I shall not consider such an issue here, but there surely are few today who would be as optimistic as Mannheim was about the conciliatory skills or inclinations of the intelligentsia.[19]

Habermas: ideology as distorted communication

To move from Mannheim to a more contemporary conception of ideology, as found in the writings of Habermas, is not altogether to leave the traditions of thought within which Mannheim worked, since the intellectual sources that have concerned Habermas include most of those which Mannheim also drew upon. But Habermas has not himself been influenced by Mannheim, and his approach to problems of ideology does not share much in common with that of Mannheim: the work of the latter author, indeed, has had considerably more impact in the English-speaking world than in Germany.

There are two strands in Habermas's writing relevant to the characterisation of ideology – and to its critique. One is more substantive, the other more abstract. The first is part of Habermas's discussion of the development of modern society and politics; the second locates ideology on the level of methodological analysis. In each case, however, *the notion of ideology is linked intrinsically to the critique of ideology*. The concept of ideology, Habermas argues, did not just come into being with the rise of bourgeois society; it is actually only relevant to the conditions of public debate forged by that society. These conditions involve the creation of a 'public sphere', in which issues of concern to the community can (in principle) be openly debated, and decisions arrived at that are based upon reason rather than upon tradition or the fiat of the powerful.[20] The development of the concept of ideology, according to Habermas, is 'coeval with the critique of ideology',[21] since identifying thought as ideological presupposes uncovering modes in which ideas are governed by forces other than conscious, rational processes. Habermas does not contrast ideology directly with science, since he wishes to make the case that, in the contemporary world, science and technology become bound up with ideology. Processes of secularisation, Habermas argues, dissolve traditional forms of legitimation and at the same time release the content of tradition to be reorganised in a formally rational way (in Weber's sense). New modes of legitimation

emerge from the critique of the dogmatism of traditional interpretations of the world and claim a scientific character. Yet they retain legitimating functions, thereby keeping power relations inaccessible to analysis and to public consciousness. It is in this way that ideologies in the restricted sense first come into being. They replace traditional legitimations of power by appearing in the mantle of modern science and by deriving their justification from the critique of ideology.[22]

In the contemporary era, Habermas argues, as a result of the fusion of science and technology and the undermining of bourgeois ideas of 'fair exchange', the dominant ideology becomes one of 'technocratic consciousness'. The fulfilment of technical imperatives becomes the main legitimating ethos of politics. Habermas's assessment of the problem of ideology in modern society thus in one way appears almost the contrary of Mannheim's. Mannheim was worried above all by the 'babble of tongues', by the clash of multiple ideologies; Habermas, like Marcuse, sees the pre-eminent trend to be the stilling of such clamour in favour of a pervasive reduction of norms to technical decisions. But Habermas and Mannheim do share an underlying similarity of orientation: each counterposes the study of ideology to the possibility of attaining consensus untainted by ideological distortions. For Habermas, this is not to be analysed in terms of a 'non-evaluative' conception of ideology, but via the counterfactual positing of a situation in which communication is 'unrestricted' or 'free from domination'.

Habermas's approach to how such a situation may be conceptualised can perhaps best be understood against the background of his critique of Gadamer's claim for the 'universality of hermeneutics'.[23] The debate between Gadamer and Habermas recalls issues raised by the Enlightenment philosophers: the same kind of issues which originally stimulated the formulation of the notion of ideology itself. Gadamer identifies hermeneutics with the fruitfulness of tradition, in explicit contrast to the Enlightment critique of 'prejudice'. Tradition is the necessary source of all human understanding and knowledge, and 'preconceptions' thus their necessary basis.[24] Habermas rejects Gadamer's standpoint precisely in so far as it provides no overall perspective for the critique of tradition as ideology, or as 'systematically distorted communication'. The critique of ideology, for Habermas, hence involves uncovering the sources of distorted communication, a process which can be illuminated through developing a parallel between psychoanalysis and the social sciences. The object of analytic therapy is to overcome barriers to dialogue between patient and analyst: to free the patient from repressions which inhibit the patient's rational understanding of his or her own conduct and thereby the capability of communicating with others. The repressions which distort communication are equivalent to the social sources of ideology. Hermeneutics, according to Gadamer, can be regarded as concerned with the creation of dialogue from the encounter of traditions. But in Habermas's eyes such a conception fails to provide any means of grasping the involvement of traditions with forms of domination that produce imbalances in possible modes of dialogue.

It might seem that Habermas's view threatens to relapse into a relativism not too distant from that which so preoccupied Mannheim: if the frames of meaning embodied in tradition are at the origin of all human understanding, how can we locate a position 'outside' such frames of meaning from which they can be criticised as ideological? Habermas's response to this question involves his conception of an 'ideal speech situation' immanent in all communication, in terms of which distortions of communication can be diagnosed. All communication in social interaction, according to Habermas, implicitly involves four types of 'validity claim': that what is communicated is mutually intelligible; that its propositional content is true; that each contributor has the right to speak or act as he does; and that each speaks or acts sincerely. In so far as any given circumstances of social interaction do not in fact sustain these validity claims, communication is distorted.[25]

Habermas's conception of ideology is so closely involved with these general themes of his writings that it would be quite impossible to discuss it adequately here. Much the same comment applies to Althusser's theory of ideology, which I shall consider in the following section. In each case therefore I shall offer only some brief comments relevant to the approach to ideology I propose to develop in the concluding parts of the paper.

1. Habermas uses 'ideology' in two ways. What he calls the 'restricted' sense of the term refers to ideas of a definite type: those which introduced the concept of ideology itself within political discourse, and which require defence by 'reason', as contrasted to traditional or customary modes of legitimation.[26] Ideology in this sense comes into being at a particular period of history, being justified 'internally' as attacking prejudice. In its more general connotation in Habermas's writings, ideology is regarded not as a type of idea system as such, but as *an aspect or a dimension of symbols involved in communication*: any type of symbol system is ideological in so far as it operates within conditions of distorted communication. It seems evident enough that the restricted sense is a sub-type of the more general one, but I do not think that it is

entirely clear what the nature of the relations between them is. The first sense apparently concedes some positive significance to ideology, as involved with the expansion of discourse in social evolution. In its second sense, ideology appears as wholly negative. We cannot regard 'ideology' both as a type of symbol system, distinct from other types, and at the same time as a set of characteristics which can apply in principle to all forms of symbol systems.

2. Habermas also uses the term 'interest' in two ways, a practice that is at best terminologically misleading. In *Knowledge and Human Interests*, Habermas uses 'interests' in what he terms a 'quasi-transcendental' sense, to refer to the 'interest-bound' character of different forms of knowledge. But in other parts of his writings, he refers to 'interest' in a more conventional sense, to mean the specific interests of definite actors or groups. Once again it is not wholly apparent what connections are presumed to exist between these two senses of interest. I shall suggest below that the concept of ideology should be understood as having reference to interests, but in the second of these terms rather than the first.

3. In analysing ideology as distorted communication, Habermas suggests that the critique of ideology can be compared to the translation of the unconscious into the conscious. This view seems to equate repression *en bloc* with distortions of communication. But this seems unsatisfactory in more than one way. (a) We may point out that repression seems a necessary part of personality development, and a means to the achievement of self-identity (Lacan), not just a barrier to self-understanding. (b) The actual *content* of unconscious elements of personality matters to the theory of ideology. It is not just the 'fact' of repression, but *what* is repressed, that is relevant to ideology-critique. Habermas tends to ignore this, because he looks to psychoanalysis as a model for ideology-critique in social analysis, rather than as a substantive theory.

4. The psychoanalytic model does not help to clarify how ideology might be related to social domination or power.[27] Psychoanalytic theory, in Habermas's interpretation of it, is directed towards freeing the patient from influences that 'dominate' him or her, and subordinating those influences to conscious control, thereby expanding the person's autonomy of action. But it is difficult to see that 'domination' in this sense has much similarity to that involved in the power relations between collectivities.

Althusser's theory of ideology

Althusser's conception of ideology contrasts considerably with that employed by Habermas. Ideology for Althusser is neither specifically a creation of bourgeois society, nor is it distorted communication: rather it is *a functionally necessary feature of the existence of every type of society.* Ideology, according to Althusser, 'is indispensable in every society, in order to shape men, to transform them and enable them to respond to the exigencies of existence'.[28] Althusser distinguishes 'ideology' as such, or 'ideology in general', from empirically existing ideologies, found in particular social formations. While ideologies change in conjunction with processes of societal development, there can be no 'end of ideology', even with the transcendence of capitalism by socialism. Althusser not infrequently compares ideology and the unconscious, but with different implications to those drawn by Habermas: 'ideology', he argues, 'is eternal, just like the unconscious'.[29]

Althusser's main concern is to combat those interpretations of ideology which treat the latter – as is suggested by various of Marx's comments – as a 'reflection' of the real. But Althusser is equally concerned to reject the alternative conception of ideology as some sort of expression of the interests of dominant groups or classes. Each of these locates ideology within a subject – object relation and is, for Althusser, linked to 'empiricism'. The study of ideology is not an avenue to obtaining a veridical representation of social reality; ideology has instead to be treated as a part of that reality, as integral to the constitution of social life. The mistake of many previous theories is to presume that ideology is merely a passive, 'imaginary' representation of political and economic conditions. The imaginary in ideology, Althusser holds, is not to be found in ideological representations themselves, but in the relations to the real that are sustained through ideology. Ideology is, in Althusser's phrase, the 'social cement', the indispensable source of social cohesion: through ideology, human beings live as 'conscious subjects' within the totality of social relations. Ideology is not the conscious creation of human subjects; it is only through and in ideology that conscious subjects exist. The imaginary in Althusser's sense does not refer to ideas or beliefs as such, but to the practical organisation of day-to-day conduct as experienced by social agents. 'Ideology', as Karsz has remarked, 'is not an imaginary realm but the realm where the imaginary realises itself.'[30]

These considerations are important to Althusser's view of the relation between science and ideology. Science and ideology are linked in terms of their connection to the real: science is not a means of dissolving the misrepresentations of ideology, but a different form of enterprise to the latter. Science, like any other type of human activity, only exists through ideology; but science breaks with ideology in instituting its own autonomous level of discourse, producing new knowledge which can then react back upon ideology.

As an element of concrete social formations, ideologies are 'regions' whose form is determined by their articulation within the social whole, and which thus express modes of class domination (in class societies). Ideologies are directly embroiled in political and economic struggles: in any given type of society a dominant ideology provides the overall frame of meaning within which ideological contestations occur. Such an ideology cannot validly be criticised as 'false', since that category does not apply to ideological forms. It can only be assessed functionally: by making clear how the real and imaginary interweave in ideological practice. This can be illustrated by the example of the liberal ideology of individualism:

> In the ideology of *freedom*, the bourgeoisie lives in a direct fashion its relation to its conditions of existence: that is to say, its real relation (the law of the liberal capitalist economy), *but incorporated* in an imaginary relation (all men are free, including free workers). Its ideology consists in this word-play about freedom, which betrays just as much the bourgeois will to mystify those it exploits (free!) in order to keep them in harness, by bondage to freedom, as the need of the bourgeoisie to *live* its class domination as the freedom of the exploited.[31]

Althusser's approach to ideology cannot be evaluated without reference to his theory of science and the *coupure épistémologique*. The *coupure* marks the differentiation between a scientific and an ideological problematic, where the latter is constituted in the form of a 'theoretical ideology': that is to say, ideology as discursively formulated (for example, as political economy, or as 'bourgeois social science'); 'theoretical ideologies' still remain tied to the practical contexts of the ideologies from which they derive. At first sight this position seems to escape the issues of relativism which Mannheim made central to the analysis of ideology. Actually it does not do so at all – or it only does so through dogmatic assertion. A science is formed when it constructs its 'theoretical object', but as many critics have remarked, Althusser supplies no plausible criteria to which recourse can be made when there are disputes over what is 'scientific' and what is not. The two examples which Althusser usually refers to as 'sciences' in the realm of social analysis, Marxism and psychoanalysis, have been taken by others (for example, Popper) to be prime examples of types of intellectual enterprise whose scientific status is particularly suspect. The characteristics of a science most often mentioned by Althusser, its systematic and relational character, have no relevance to assessing such controversies.[32] Although Althusser seeks to escape the polarity of ideology as 'false', and science as 'valid', his standpoint in fact rests upon a peculiarly ungrounded version of such a differentiation. Marxism (in Althusser's understanding of it) is a science, and political economy, etc. are not, since they remain rooted in 'practical ideology'. Others, however, declare exactly the opposite: and we are back in the struggle of Mannheim's 'particular ideologies'.

Thus it can be argued that Althusser's view does not depart as far from the themes established by Mannheim as might appear at first sight. For Mannheim also wished to escape from the presumption that ideology is simply 'false': hence his contrast between the particular and total conceptions of ideology. The total conception of ideology, like Althusser's 'ideology in general', is the necessary condition of existence of human society, and the medium of individual consciousness. We might recall Mannheim's statement that 'strictly speaking it is incorrect to say that the single individual thinks. Rather it is more correct to say that he participates in thinking further what other men have thought before him . . . on the one hand he finds a ready-made situation and on the other he finds in that situation preformed patterns of thought and conduct.'[33] Mannheim also emphasised that it is mistaken to treat total ideologies as merely 'systems of ideas' or 'thought-systems': they are incorporated within, and make possible, the everyday practical conduct of social actors.

Ideology: some basic questions

The concept of ideology had its origins in the Enlightenment critique of tradition and prejudice: rational, grounded knowledge was to replace the mystifications of pre-existing modes of thought. In Comte's appropriation of this perspective, the term ideology itself was abandoned: not just because of his wish to distance his views from the individualism of Destutt, but because there was no significant place for it in his system. *Sociology, as Comte formulated it, replaced ideology in its original sense*, as the triumph of the positive method, or science, in the field of human social conduct. The survival of the notion of ideology in the social sciences is due to Marx's incorporation of it in the twofold usage I have identified earlier. Although Marx gave a particular twist to the concept in his criticisms of the 'German ideologists', he sustained the emphasis upon the replacement of mystification by 'real, positive science'. But he made a crucial addition to this, linking ideology to the sectional interests of dominant groups in society. The critique of ideology henceforth could no longer be left solely to the 'inevitable' victory of science over traditional prejudices, but would have to be harnessed to the practical overcoming of class domination. The conjoining of the science/ideology contrast to that of sectional interest/ideology is responsible for the fruitfulness of the Marxian approach – and, at the same time, the main source of the vagaries experienced by the concept of ideology since then. Concerned as he was above all with attacking specific 'ideologies', in the shape of idealist philosophies of history, and later, political economy, Marx gave little attention to working out the possible general implications of his treatment of ideology.

Each of the three authors whose views I have discussed briefly above have taken different routes onward from Marx, while of course also adding perspectives of their own. But each have had to contend with a phenomenon which did not significantly impinge upon Marx, since Marxism did not become of major political importance during his lifetime: *the interpretation of Marxism itself as an ideology*. For latent within Marx's writings was the problem: how can Marxism escape the strictures which it directs at other systems of ideas, namely that they are rooted in definite interests and are thereby ideological? The problem becomes particularly acute when seen against the backdrop of German historicism, as it was by

Lukács and Mannheim. Ideology then merges with issues of the historical determination of knowledge or of truth. Of the two, Lukács was the most consistent, in attempting to reconcile historicism with the defence of a version of truth via the privileged position of the Party as the 'vanguard of history'. But Lukács had little to say about the objectivity of natural science and its possible divergence from the historically determined character of the 'human sciences', one of the characteristic preoccupations of German historicism. Mannheim took over aspects of the postulated division between natural and social science, but in an ambiguous and inconsistent fashion.

Mannheim presented his distinction between particular and total ideologies as though this were largely a movement from a 're-stricted' version of ideology to an all-encompassing one. It is important to see a differentiation which this conceals, but which has been chronically involved with discussions of ideology since Marx: between ideology *as referring to discourse* on the one hand, and ideology *as referring to the involvement of beliefs within 'modes of lived existence'* – the practical enactment of life in society – on the other. Such a differentiation is again implied, although not explicitly developed, in the science/ideology and sectional interest/ideology polarities found in Marx. The first tends to treat ideology on the level of discourse, as a barrier to the production of valid knowledge; the second involves regarding ideology as incorporated within the practical conduct of social life. These are not seen by Marx as wholly separate since, as I have pointed out, the writings of 'ideologists' in the first sense form part of 'ideology' in the second sense. The distinction between ideology as discourse and ideology as lived experience appears again in the writings of Habermas and Althusser. Each of these authors, in fact, explicitly acknowledges its importance. Habermas's account, however, perhaps tends to concentrate more upon ideology as discourse; whereas Althusser's major contribution is to focus upon ideology as an inherent feature of the conduct of social life.

Three basic questions suggest themselves from the foregoing: how should we approach the relation between ideology and science, both natural and social? What connections should be made between the science/ideology polarity and that of sectional interest/ideology? Should ideology be understood as relating to discourse, to practical social conduct, or to both? To this we can add two others. In the Enlightenment view of ideology, reason was to dispel the errors and the shortcomings of tradition and habit: in so far as this became a confrontation between ideology and science, an implication that might be drawn from it is that science, or 'validly grounded knowledge', occupies a different sphere from ideology, as two types of belief system, or two types of 'claims to knowledge'. Such a conception of ideology persists strongly in Althusser's writings, in the contrast between science and both 'practical' and 'theoretical' ideologies. Ideology here excludes science, even if it is the basis from which science derives, while on the other hand it becomes impossible to treat science as itself ideological. In Habermas's approach, ideology (in one of the versions that appear in his works) concerns aspects of symbol-systems, including science, rather than referring to a type of system. Thus one further question that can be posed is: should ideology be regarded as a type of idea – or belief-system – divergent from science in some sense, or should we only speak of *ideological aspects of symbol-systems*?

A fifth question is not too difficult to unearth from the literature discussed previously: can there be an 'end of ideology'? The issue, of course, has been much debated, in various guises. In Marx's own writings, the end of class domination appears to signal the end of ideology, and most Marxists have agreed – although Althusser is an exception. But the phrase 'end of ideology' has been normally associated with critics of Marxism. According to such critics, Marxism is a prominent ideology, but one in decline: the end of ideology represents the end of Marxism (as well as of right-wing radical beliefs) as a significant political force.

The concept of ideology

In broaching the issue of the relation of science and ideology, it would be as well once more to begin from the Enlightenment and its impact on Comte. Reason was to replace prejudice: for Comte, as for many others, the ascent of reason was equivalent to the dominance of science.[34] Science was to repeat, in our understanding of human society, the demystifications it had seemingly accomplished in respect of the world of nature.[35] The same viewpoint was accentuated by Marx, but it was made more complex and subtle by its fusion with themes drawn from Hegel and classical German philosophy. In Comte, and more uncertainly in Marx, the capability of science to 'correct' pre-existing beliefs embodied in tradition or habit assimilated two elements, two senses in which 'prejudice' can be understood: as 'preconception' and as 'unreason'.

From there it was but a short step to radicalising the science/ideology opposition, and attempting to *define* ideology as 'non-science': as necessarily involving either 'invalid' claims to knowledge, or as distinct from science (natural and social) in some other clearly ascertainable way. No one who has taken this position has been able to defend it satisfactorily. The main reason for this is clear. To attempt to conceptualise ideology in such a way places too great a burden upon its proponents to separate science or 'valid knowledge' in a distinct and unchallengeable manner from the excuses or pretensions of ideology. Those who have adopted such an approach to ideology have naturally often been more pre-occupied with the ideological pretensions of 'pseudo-sciences', false pretenders to the throne of science, rather than with religion, etc. (Although it has proved much more difficult to reach plausible philosophical criteria to separate science from religion than any progressive thinker of the late eighteenth or early nineteenth centuries would have credited.) Althusser and Popper have produced the most articulate defences in recent years of the view that science can be quite rigorously separated from other types of symbol-system. But as I have remarked before, what are prime instances of sciences for Althusser, Marxism and psychoanalysis, are for Popper the leading examples of 'pseudo-sciences'. Neither Althusser's version of 'demarcation criteria', nor that of Popper, hold much water.[36]

Mannheim must take a good deal of responsibility for the pervasiveness of the view that problems of ideology are necessarily bound up with epistemology. His version of the science/ideology opposition hinged mainly upon the notion that ideology is 'contextual' in a fashion that science (or 'formal knowledge') is not. I have tried to indicate how he was led in this direction by merging Marx's concerns in ideology–critique with traditions of historicism and hermeneutics. Mannheim took up what he saw as the implications of Marx's discussion of ideology in terms of the contextuality of symbol-systems. The problem of ideology, for Mannheim, was coterminous with the problem of how relativism could be avoided, both on the level of epistemology and on that of the struggle of ideological standpoints in the political sphere. Thus Mannheim interpreted Marx's critique of ideology primarily as undercutting the validity or justifiability of ideas by showing them to be associated with certain social or historical conditions. In Mannheim's thought, of the two aspects of the Marxian legacy in the theory of ideology, the differentiation of science/ideology and of sectional interests/ideology, the first opposition is definitely the most prominent. Thus the study of ideology merges without abrupt transition into the sociology of knowledge: the only difference between the two is that the sociology of knowledge recognises that all types of world-view are conditioned by the context of their production.

But the difficulties Mannheim encountered in separating ideology from science via the contextual character of knowledge are every bit as intractable as those faced by others who have sought to define ideology by contrast to science. Mannheim was unable to provide any clear criteria that could distinguish relationism from relativism, and his characterisations of 'formal knowledge', which somehow escapes the contextual determination to which other ideas are subject, are less than plausible.

These considerations suggest that we should in fact discard the legacy of the prejudices of the Enlightenment critique of prejudice: the view that ideology is to be conceptualised in terms of a science/ideology opposition. I do not want to deny the importance, or underestimate the difficulty, of epistemological questions concerning the 'contextuality' or 'circularity' of knowledge. I do not want to say that the analysis of ideology can escape epistemological issues altogether. I do want to argue – to anticipate my answer to the fourth question posed above – that if we free ourselves from the conception that ideology is a definite type of symbol-system, separate from science, we can claim that the analysis of ideology faces no *special* epistemological difficulties as compared to other areas of social analysis. The approach to ideology I shall suggest certainly implies accepting that social science can deliver objectively valid knowledge. But it involves rejecting the line of argumentation according to which the relation between such 'valid knowledge' and 'invalid knowledge claims' is the defining feature of what ideology *is*.

We can break with the whole orientation just referred to *by treating the sectional interests/ideology polarity as basic to the theory of ideology*, rather than the opposition of ideology and science. This is the connotation of Habermas's work, which in this respect is closer to Marx than that of Althusser is. For to locate the theory of ideology primarily in terms of the sectional interests/ideology differentiation *is to insist that the chief usefulness of the concept of ideology concerns the critique of domination.* This was certainly Marx's principal concern, both in his earlier and his later critiques of ideology. In criticising the 'German ideologists', Marx appropriated the opposition of ideology to science in the *camera obscura* metaphor, but reconnected this to ideology as domination in terms of the contributions of ideologists to the 'illusion of the epoch'. In attempting an extended critique of political economy, in *Capital*, Marx was not preoccupied with condemning political economy as 'non-science', but with relating its inadequacies to its filtering-out of the facts of class domination.

As I have mentioned, repudiating the conception that the basic traits of ideology are to be identified by contrast to science involves taking a definite stance towards the fourth question mentioned above: the question of whether or not ideology should be regarded as a type of symbol-system. The view that it should be so regarded normally involves an explicit opposition of ideology to science, as in Althusser. A variant, however, is that which appears in one of the usages of Habermas, indicated previously, where ideology is treated as a specific form of idea-system characteristic of modern politics: the contrast here is with religion as a traditional type of system of legitimation. Ideology is also quite commonly used as equivalent to what Mannheim called 'utopia', as modes of belief which mobilise political activity directed against the *status quo*.[37] While this differs from the former concept in that it tends to associate religious and modern political movements quite closely, ideology still appears here as a type of idea-system (usually again implicitly or otherwise contrasted with science). In the approach I wish to suggest however there is, strictly speaking, no such thing as *an* ideology: there are only ideological aspects of symbol-systems. The thesis, or the assumption, that ideologies are types of symbol-system is usually based upon the ideology/science division, which I have already discarded. But I also reject the notion of ideology as limited to the forum of modern politics: any type of idea-system may be ideological. There can be no particular objection to continuing to speak of 'ideology', or even of 'an ideology', so long as it is understood that this is somewhat elliptical: *to treat a symbol-system as an ideology is to study it as ideological.*

Ideology, interests

All this, of course, does not show how ideology is to be related to interests or to domination. We can hope to clarify the issues involved, however, by determining a response to the other questions posed previously. I shall try to do this by also drawing upon notions which have been introduced in other papers. To analyse the ideological aspects of symbolic orders, I shall argue, is to examine *how structures of signification are mobilised to legitimate the sectional interests of hegemonic groups.*

The concept of interest has been as contentious as any in social theory, and gives rise to a number of difficult problems. I make no claim to deal with these in the detail they deserve, but wish rather to make a number of observations about how questions of interests might be approached in the light of the perspective I have tried to establish in this book. I have posed five basic queries which a theory of ideology has to answer; let me also use the same numerical division in discussing interests. Following Barry, we may consider three types of definition which have sometimes been offered of 'interest';[38] having looked at these, I shall briefly consider in what sense we may speak of 'objective interests', and of 'collective' or 'group interests'.

One argument makes interests identical with wants, such that to say that a given course of action is in someone's interests is synonymous with saying that the actor wants to carry out that course of action. But this will not do, because it excludes the possibility of there being circumstances in which what an actor wants to do is not in his interests; and there seems no reason to deny that such circumstances can exist. A second usage of interest seeks to elucidate the idea by substituting 'justifiable claim' for 'want' in such an equation.[39] But this meets with a similar objection to the first: justification of claims seems usefully separable from acting in accordance with interests. A third formulation is a utilitarian one: a course of action could be held to be in a person's interests if it is more pleasurable than any alternative course of action. The objections that can be made against any such conception are several, and converge with traditional dilemmas of utilitarian calculi. If pleasure is understood in anything like an ordinary sense, it is certainly false; for the undertaking of an action which causes an individual pain can without difficulty be said on occasion to be in his or her interests.

I shall argue that interests are closely related to wants, even if it is a mistake to identify the concept of interest with that of want. To attribute interests to an actor or actors logically implies the imputation of wants to them also. Wants (or 'wanting') are the 'basis' of interests: to say that A has an interest in a given course of action, occurrence or state of affairs, is to say that the course of action, etc. facilitates the possibility of A achieving his or her wants.[40] To be aware of one's interests, therefore, is more than to be aware of a want or wants; it is to know how one can set about trying to realise them.

If interests are logically connected with wants, and wants can only be attributes of subjects (which is a position I have consistently argued for: social systems have no wants or needs), can we speak meaningfully of 'objective interests'? We can, for interests would only be 'subjective' (in a certain sense anyway) if interests were *equated* with wants. Interests presume wants, but the concept of interest concerns not the wants as such, but the possible modes of their realisation in given sets of circumstances; and these can be determined as 'objectively' as anything else in social analysis. The notion of objective interests is frequently linked to that of 'collective interests': the thesis that interests are structural properties of collectivities, which have nothing to do with actors' own wants. If groups do not have wants or needs, do they have interests? The answer must be that they do not. None the less actors have interests *by virtue of their membership of particular groups, communities, classes, etc.* This is why it is so important not to treat wants and interests as equivalent concepts: interests imply potential courses of action, in contingent social and material circumstances. A person shares certain interests in common with others (given also the presumption of common wants), for example, by virtue of being a member of the working class; there are conflicts of interest between capitalists and workers which are integral to capitalist production.

Now in my opinion, a fully elaborated theory of ideology requires a philosophical anthropology. *We must not simply identify wants with 'empirical wants'* (what people actually want in a given time and place), since the latter are conditioned and confined by the nature of the society of which an individual is a member. The questions raised by this are complex, and very important to the nature of critical theory in sociology; I shall not, however, confront them in this context. Significant though they are, the thread of the present discussion can be readily maintained without seeking to resolve them. For there is one sectional interest, or 'arena of sectional interests', of dominant groups which is peculiarly universal: an interest in maintaining the existing order of domination, or major features of it, since such an order of domination *ipso facto* involves an asymmetrical distribution of resources that can be drawn upon to satisfy wants.

Discourse and lived experience

We can formulate a scheme for analysing ideological aspects of discourse and more 'deeply engrained' symbolic orders by employing distinctions suggested in previous papers. As represented in Figures 5.1 and 5.2, ideological analysis can be undertaken at two levels, which correspond methodologically to the differentiation of strategic action and institutional analysis. To study ideology as strategic action is to concentrate upon the top left-hand corner in Figures 5.1 and 5.2 (which have to be thought of as superimposed). In its most 'conscious' and 'superficial' form, as discourse, ideology here involves the use of artifice or direct manipulation of communication by those in dominant classes or groups in furthering their sectional interests. The sorts of political strategy to which

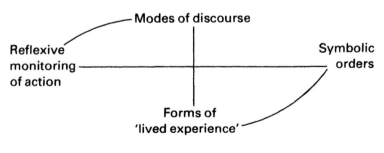

FIGURE 5.1

Machiavelli has given his name are the type case. This is often ideology of the most easily penetrated sort, however, by those who are the object of political manipulation – however subtle and clever the prince may be.

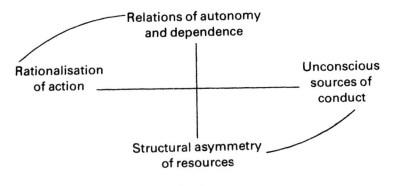

Relations of autonomy
and dependence

Rationalisation
of action

Unconscious
sources of
conduct

Structural asymmetry
of resources

FIGURE 5.2

The existence of *front* and *back* regions, in the spatial settings of interaction, which I shall discuss in the next chapter in relation to time–space presence and absence (pp. 207–9), is especially relevant to the more manipulative and discursive aspects of ideology. The maintenance of differentiations between the 'publicly displayed' aspects of social activities, and those that are kept hidden, is a major element both of the ideological use of symbol-systems by dominant classes or groups, and of the response of those in subordinate classes or positions. All the more discursive types of ideological phenomena have 'display settings', often of a partly ritualised kind, which readily lend themselves to front/back divisions.

The ideological analysis of modes of discourse (in which I include the formalised discourses of the intellectual disciplines) obviously cannot be confined within the methodological *epoché* of strategic conduct. To examine ideology *institutionally* is to show how symbolic orders sustain forms of domination in the everyday context of 'lived experience'. The institutional analysis of the ideological aspects of symbol-systems is represented in the lower right-hand corner of the Figures 5.1 and 5.2. To study ideology from this aspect is to seek to identify the most basic structural elements which connect signification and legitimation in such a way as to favour dominant interests. The most 'buried' forms of ideology would be at the outer arc on the diagram, connecting unconscious sources of conduct with structural asymmetries of resources. Ideological elements here are likely to be deeply sedimented in both a *psychological* and an *historical* sense. Consider, for example, the repressions sustaining 'privacy' and 'self-discipline' in day-to-day life. Such repressions might be quite immediately connected with the prevalence of back/front differentiations in post-feudal society. As Elias has shown, the 'civilising process' proceeded through the increasing confinement or 'hiding behind the scenes' of that which is distasteful.[41] The resulting 'order' and 'discipline' of daily life, including but not limited to the routines of industrial labour, might be regarded as among the most profoundly embedded ideological features of contemporary society.

Several of the main points made by Geertz, in one of the most illuminating discussions of ideology to be found in the literature,[42] are compatible with the standpoint I am suggesting. But Geertz follows common usage in regarding ideology as equivalent to what I have called a symbol-system. What he treats as the characteristics of 'ideology' – metaphor and metonymy, generating multivalent levels of meaning – I regard as features of symbol-systems in general. To discuss these as ideology, as in Barthes's famous analysis of the picture of the black soldier on the cover of *Paris-Match*, is to show how they sustain an existing order of domination. I consider in the following paper how the multivalence of symbol-systems links to the influence of tradition, and to social factors which create divergent 'interpretations' of texts and other symbolic forms. But it is perhaps important to mention this here, in the light of the strong tendency among those who have written about ideology to define the concept in terms of 'emotive' or 'arousing' symbols that have a mobilising force upon action – and which 'go beyond science'. This is one way in which ideology has been conceptualised in terms of a science/ideology opposition: and one which has been popular among proponents of the 'end of ideology thesis'. In denying the usefulness of grasping the notion of ideology via the science/ideology opposition, I mean to deny that the concept of ideology can be defined in terms of the epistemological status of the ideas or beliefs to which it refers, that is, in terms of their 'scientificity'. I do not want to say, of course, that there are no differences between science and other modes of discourse or symbol-systems, in respect of their potential ideological incorporation within social systems.

Ideology, domination

It is obviously not enough to leave matters at this high ·level of abstraction: we have to try to indicate some of the major ways in which ideology actually operates in society. In doing so we are looking for the modes in which *domination is concealed as domination*, on the level of institutional analysis: and for the ways in which power is harnessed to conceal sectional interests on the level of strategic conduct. These do not imply different types of ideological elements, but two levels of ideological analysis, connected via the duality of structure. I shall suggest that the principal ideological forms are the following:

1. *The representation of sectional interests as universal ones.* This is *one* sense which can be given to Marx's theorem that 'the ideas of the ruling class are in every epoch the ruling ideas'. In modern politics – in which, in Habermas's sense, 'ideology is coeval with the critique of ideology' – the need to sustain legitimacy through the claim to represent the interests of the community as a whole becomes a central feature of political discourse. But it may be regarded as a basic characteristic of the incorporation of symbol-systems within a society more generally, that claims to legitimacy rest upon implicit or explicit appeal to universal interests.

The paramount context for the critique of ideology in modern politics in capitalist society remains the analysis of class domination. The most important ideological struggles still turn upon concealment versus disclosure of class domination as at the origin of the capital accumulation process. Many Marxists however (not so much Marx himself) have been prone to dismiss too lightly sectional 'bourgeois freedoms' that have turned out – in some substantial part as a very result of the struggles of labour movements – to be capable of a certain universalisation within the framework of capitalist society. 'Freedom of contract', for example, is still today in substantial degree an ideological prop to the power of capital. On the other hand, as I have pointed out in the previous paper, freedom of contract has also been at the same time an important element facilitating a real extension of the rights of workers, through its connection to the collective wielding of power on the part of labour. No one today, in the historical aftermath of Nazism and Stalinism, can any longer associate 'capitalism' *en bloc* with unfreedom, or socialism with the necessary creation or extension of liberties.

The twin processes of the growth of the liberal-democratic state (where in fact established), and the heavy concentration of capital, are phenomena which in large part post-date Marx. The expansion of the 'democratic' half of the liberal-democratic couplet provides another significant instance of the universalising potential contained in originally sectional political ideals. As Macpherson has plausibly argued, liberal democracy in the West is an 'historical compound' of the liberal state and the democratic franchise.[43] The liberal state involved above all equality before the law and the right to form political associations. These two principles, however, which originally largely served the sectional interests of the entrepreneurial class, helped to make possible the achievement of the mass franchise – which until late in the nineteenth century was mostly perceived by the dominant class as a danger to the liberal state.

2. *The denial or transmutation of contradictions.* I have suggested in another paper that the translation of system contradiction into social conflict depends upon various factors, including the degree of penetration that actors have of the structural conditions of their action. It is normally in the interests of dominant groups if the existence of contradictions is denied or their real locus is obscured.

In capitalist society, this applies particularly to the primary contradiction between private appropriation and socialised production. I should want to argue that one of the main features of political ideology which serves to disguise the location of this contradiction concerns the domain that is allocated to the 'political', as distinguished from the 'economic'. The political is supposed ideologically to concern only the incorporation of the citizen in political society, as regulated primarily by the franchise. Conflict that occurs outside this sphere, particularly economic conflict, is declared to be 'non-political'. The authority systems of industrial enterprise are protected from the potentially explosive convergence of contradiction and class conflict in so far as industrial conflict is 'kept out of politics' – or 'politics is kept out of the workplace'. As I have tried to show elsewhere, this is the element of validity in the thesis of the so-called 'institutionalisation of class conflict'.[44]

3. *The naturalisation of the present: reification.* The interests of dominant groups are bound up with the preservation of the *status quo*. Forms of signification which 'naturalise' the existing state of affairs, inhibiting recognition of the mutable, historical character of human society thus act to sustain such interests. In so far as reification is understood as referring to circumstances in which social relations appear to have the fixed and immutable character of natural laws, it can be regarded as the principal mode in which the naturalisation of the present is effected.

Although I have no particular sympathy with most of the views expressed in *History and Class Consciousness*, Lukács's discussion of reification in that work must still be regarded as a basic source for any analysis of the problem. To this a major qualification has to be added: the epistemological stance that underlies Lukács's treatment of reification, involving the anticipated reconciliation of subject and object, is quite unacceptable.[45]

Lukács relates reification, as an ideological phenomenon, to the commodity form, taking as his starting-point Marx's concept of commodity fetishism. I think he is right to propose that 'commodity fetishism is a *specific* problem of our age, the age of modern capitalism' – although one must also say today, in contradistinction to Lukács, that this judgement must be extended to include state socialism. Lukács makes it clear that reification is a phenomenon which thoroughly permeates the taken-for-granted assumptions of lived experience, as well as one that is a pervasive characteristic of intellectual discourse:

> Just as the capitalist system continuously produces and reproduces itself economically on higher and higher levels, the structure of reification progressively sinks more fatefully and more definitively into the consciousness of man ... Just as the economic theory of capitalism remains stuck in its self-created immediacy, the same thing happens to bourgeois attempts to comprehend the ideological phenomenon of reification. Even thinkers who have no desire to deny or obscure its existence and who are more or less clear in their own minds about its humanly destructive consequences remain on the surface and make no

attempt to advance beyond its objectively most derivative forms, the forms furthest from the real life-process of capitalism, i.e. the most external and vacuous forms, to the basic phenomenon of reification itself.[46]

The question of reification is of course immediately relevant to ideological features of the social sciences themselves. The association between naturalistic sociology and the reified mode is necessarily a close one. But a similar, although less direct association, can readily exist between reification and hermeneutic philosophies: that is, those which deny that causal laws operate in human social activity. To fail to analyse causal regularities in definite forms of human society may be equivalent in its ideological connotations to treating such generalisations as laws of the same logical character as those found in the natural sciences. Now the social sciences are often enough used ideologically in a directly manipulative fashion: one of the most significant and far-reaching applications of this sort is the application of systems analysis as a medium of the social control of human beings. But it would be a mistake to suppose that the ideological influence of the social sciences can be simply understood in these terms. The reifying character of naturalistic versions of sociology – those which have dominated what in a later paper I shall call the 'orthodox consensus' – expresses deeply-formed elements of the content of lived experience, which it helps reinforce. Bauman has expressed this very well. Naturalistic sociology

> is fed by the pre-predicative experience of the life-process as essentially unfree, and of freedom as a fear-generating state, and it aptly supplies apposite cognitive and emotional outlets to both intuitions . . . It assists the individual in his spontaneous effort of disposing of the excessive, and, therefore, anxiety-ridden freedom of choice, by either positing this freedom as illusion or advising him that such freedom is supported by reason which has been delimited and defined beforehand by society whose power of judgement he cannot challenge.[47]

Concluding comment: the end of ideology

Of the questions posed earlier, there remains that of the 'end of ideology'. The notion of an end of ideology goes back again to the first origins of the term: to the programme of the early ideologists who sought to replace prejudice by science, or by rational knowledge. Ideology originally referred to the dissolution of irrational or unfounded types of belief, to the end of unreason – a perspective which later became identified with the dissolution of ideology itself. In Marx, the end of ideology can be envisaged from the point of view of each of the two strands that I have distinguished: so long as ideology-as-domination is equated with class domination, such that the transcendence of classes *ipso facto* entails the disappearance of ideology. Among the later theorists of the end of ideology, who have sought to turn the perjorative connotation of the term 'ideology' back against Marxism, the dissolution of ideology has been understood mainly within the framework of a science/ideology differentiation. 'Ideology', according to one such author, is a 'set of beliefs, infused with passion which seeks to transform the whole of a way of life . . . a secular religion.'[48] Ideology is any system of belief which proclaims the need for radical change, reactionary or progressive, in the existing order of things. It has often been remarked (by C. Wright Mills, among others) that, as used in this context, the proclamation of the end of ideology was itself ideology. Certainly there is no difficulty in accepting the logic of such an assessment in terms of the use of ideology that I have suggested in this paper, for the effect of the 'end of ideology thesis', it can be argued, was to help to legitimate pre-existing relations of domination.[49] The point is an important one, for it offers the possibility of generalisation: *any type of political discourse, including Marxism, which anticipates an end to ideology, carries thereby the potentiality of becoming itself ideological.*

6

Time, Space, Social Change

In developing the account of agency and structure suggested earlier, I have proposed that the conception of structuration introduces temporality as integral to social theory; and that such a conception involves breaking with the synchrony/diachrony or static/dynamic divisions that have featured so prominently in both structuralism and functionalism. It would be untrue of course to say that those writing within these traditions of thought have not been concerned with time. But the general tendency, especially within functionalist thought, has been to identify time with the diachronic or dynamic; synchronic analysis represents a 'timeless snapshot' of society. The result is that *time is identified with social change*.

The identification of time and change has as its obverse the assimilation of 'timelessness' and social stability: the notion, explicitly or implicitly associated with most varieties of functionalism in social theory, that static analysis allows us to determine the sources of stability, while dynamic analysis is needed to understand the sources of change in social systems. This was, in a way, incorporated methodologically into the functionalist anthropology of Radcliffe-Brown and Malinowski and those influenced by them. Since we are ignorant of the past of many small-scale, isolated societies, we cannot study them dynamically, we cannot specify the changes they have gone through. But we can, by studying them in the present, disclose what holds them together; we can indicate the sources of their stability by showing the factors which lend them their cohesion. That such an equation of the static and the stable is untenable is demonstrated by two ways in which time obstinately intrudes into this mode of approach. First, on the practical level, there simply is no way in which a 'static' analysis can actually be carried out: the study of social activity involves the elapse of time, just as that activity itself does. In the face of this, the functionalist anthropologists have effectively developed their own version of Lévi-Strauss's 'reversible time', as if this cancels out the intrusion of temporality. Thus it is recommended as a research principle that the anthropologist should not spend less than a year studying a society, since thereby it is possible to gain material upon the whole of the annual cycle of social life.[1] However if time is acknowledged on the level of the practical exigencies of research, through being viewed as 'reversible time', it remains foreign to the theoretical scheme in terms of which that research is organised and explicated. Second, even on the level of theory the assimilation of the static and the stable surreptitiously incorporates an element of time. To speak of social stability *cannot* involve abstracting from time, since 'stability' means continuity over time. A stable social order is one in which there is a close similarity between how things are now and how they used to be in the past.[2]

In structuralist thought, much more attention has been given to the relations between temporality, history and the synchrony/diachrony division than within functionalism.[3] In some part, this is no doubt because of the interchanges between Lévi-Strauss and Sartre. Lévi-Strauss's views on these matters owe a good deal to Jakobson, although the former elaborates considerably upon Jakobson's position, even if not in a detailed and comprehensive fashion. In his discussion of Sartre, Lévi-Strauss makes certain points that are worth sustaining – although not exactly in the form in which Lévi-Strauss presents them. One concerns the reservations he makes about history as a 'code'. Another is his identification of certain fundamental contrasts – contrasts which concern problems of time and history – between small, relatively 'unchanging' societies, and the more developed ones: between cold and hot societies.

Now in a sense Lévi-Strauss is right when he speaks of history as a type of code, and Sartre is also right when he insists that it is not just a code like any other. For history, as an interpretation or analysis of the past, involves the application of a conceptual apparatus of some sort; while history as temporality, or the occurrence of events in time, is an inevitable feature of all social forms. What is at issue is not just time, nor history, but also *historicity*: consciousness of 'progressive movement' as a feature of the social life of certain societies, above all those of the post-feudal West, in which that consciousness is organised actively to promote social change. Lévi-Strauss is surely justified in emphasising the importance of the emergence of historicity, and the various conceptions of history associated with it, in the modern world; and to contrast this with the 'reversible time' of traditional cultures. But 'reversible time' is a misnomer.[4] It is not really time as such that Lévi-Strauss is referring to, but social change: or rather its relative absence in the sorts of society to which his research is devoted. Here again, then, we see an equation of time with social change, albeit in different form to that characteristic of functionalism. Time elapses in a sequential way in all societies, but in those in which tradition is pre-eminent, processes of social reproduction are interwoven with different forms of awareness of past, present and future than in the contemporary industrialised world.

Tradition is the 'purest' and most innocent mode of social reproduction: tradition, in its most elemental guise, may be thought of, as one writer puts it, 'as an indefinite series of repetitions of an action, which on each occasion is performed on the assumption that it has been performed before; its performance is authorised – though the nature of the authorisation may vary widely – by the knowledge, or the assumption of previous performance'.[5] The sloughing-off of tradition in a certain sense begins with its understanding *as* tradition: tradition has its greatest sway when it is understood simply as how things were, are (and should be) done. The encapsulation of certain practices as 'tradition', however, undermines tradition by placing it alongside other modes of legitimating established practices. The advent of literacy, especially mass literacy, is a major influence modifying tradition. When literacy is confined to a small elite, it is not necessarily directly corrosive of tradition, since its monopoly by the few can be used to sanction doctrines held to be inherent in 'classical scriptures'. But we may concur with the author quoted above in his claim that 'a literate tradition is never a pure tradition, since the authority of written words is not dependent on usage and presumption only. As durable material objects they cut across processes of transmission and create new patterns of social time; they speak directly to remote generations . . .'[6]

When tradition is not 'pure social reproduction', when it is no longer dependent on 'usage and presumption only', the way is cleared for the intrusion of 'interpretation'. Thus although writing and the text have become the preoccupations of some of the more abstract forms of structuralism (Barthes, Derrida), the emergence of writing actually tends to be connected, in a profound sense, to hermeneutics and to historiography; further, it can be argued, each of these is associated with the rise of a concern for problems of ideology, in both intellectual disciplines and in practical political activity. 'Hermeneutical concerns', in the sense of the confrontation of conflicting interpretations of written materials, have emerged in all the major world religions. But it is a mark of the encroachment of historicity in the post-feudal West that it is only there that hermeneutics and historiography became closely meshed. The conjunction was effected as a crucial part of the Enlightenment critique of tradition: for the Enlightenment philosophers did not remain at the level of the interpretation of the past, but questioned the very principle of tradition itself, the authority which the past exercises over the present.[7]

It is not too fanciful to suppose that the development of writing underlies the first emergence of the 'linear time consciousness' which later, in the West, became the basis of historicity as a feature of social life. Writing permits the contact with 'remote generations' mentioned above, but in addition its very linearity as a material form perhaps encourages the consciousness of the elapsing of time as a sequential process, leading 'from' one point 'away' to another point in a progressive manner. It is probably reasonable to say that, as with tradition, 'time' is not distinguished as a separate 'dimension' in traditional cultures in terms of time consciousness itself: the temporality of social life is expressed in the meshing of present with past that tradition promotes, in which the cyclical character of social activity is predominant. As time becomes acknowledged as a distinguishable phenomenon in its own right, and as inherently quantifiable, it also of course becomes regarded as a scarce and an exploitable resource.[8] Marx rightly pin-pointed this as a distinctive feature of the formation of modern capitalism. What makes possible the transmutation of labour-power into a commodity is its quantification in terms of labour-time, and the creation of the clearly defined 'working day'.

Time–space relations

I have said earlier that it is a basic mistake to identify time and social change, and we can now pursue this further by looking more closely at temporal aspects of the constitution of social systems. In the context of doing so, I want to lodge a further claim, which is that most forms of social theory have failed to take seriously enough *not only the temporality of social conduct but also its spatial attributes*. At first sight, nothing seems more banal and uninstructive than to assert that social activity occurs in time and in space. But neither time nor space have been incorporated into the centre of social theory; rather, they are ordinarily treated more as 'environments' in which social conduct is enacted. In regard of time, this is primarily because of the influence of synchrony/diachrony differentiations: the assimilation of time and change has the consequence that time can be treated as a sort of 'boundary' to stable social orders, or at any rate as a phenomenon of secondary importance.[9] The suppression of space in social theory derives from different origins, probably in some part from the anxiety of sociological authors to remove from their works any hint of geographical determinism. The importation of the term 'ecology' into the social sciences has done little to help matters, since this tends both to encourage the confusion of the spatial with other characteristics of the physical world that might influence social life, and to reinforce the tendency to treat spatial characteristics as in the 'environment' of social activity, rather than as integral to its occurrence.

In a previous paper, I have argued that social systems may be treated as systems of interaction, and have discussed some of the characteristics of systemness. But it is important at this point to consider some features of interaction passed over fairly cursorily there. Most schools of social theory, but especially functionalism, have failed to situate interaction in time, because they have operated within a synchronic/diachronic division.[10] A synchronic image of a social system writes out social reproduction, or at least takes it for granted: the other side of the assimilation of time and change, as I have noted above, is the equation of the a-temporal or the static with stability. When social analysts writing in this vein speak of systems of interaction as 'patterns' they have in mind, often in a fairly vague way, a sort of 'snapshot' of relations of social interaction. The flaw in this is exactly the same as that involved in the presumption of 'static stability': such a snapshot would not in fact reveal a pattern at all, because *any patterns of interaction that exist are situated in time*; only when examined over time do they form 'patterns' at all. This is most clear, perhaps, in the case of individuals in face-to-face encounters. Whatever else the concern of ethno-methodological writers with 'turn-taking' in conversations might or might not have illuminated, it points up something important: the seriality of the activities of the participants.[11] It is not just a trivial and obvious feature of conversational talk that only one person usually speaks at a time; or at least, it has not been obvious to most social analysts. If ethnomethodological examinations of turn-taking appear trivial, it is because their authors have not pursued their implications by connecting them in a broad way to temporality and social reproduction. The ethnomethodological study of conversation has, however, made a significant contribution in stressing that the 'managing' of talk by social actors routinely employs the location of a conversation in time as a mode of organising that conversation.[12]

The distinction commonly made between 'micro-' and 'macro-sociological' studies does not really help to elucidate some of the key differences between face-to-face interaction and other types of interactive relation in terms of which social systems are constituted. The term *face-to-face*, however, does convey a sense of the importance of the positioning of the body in space in social interaction. The face is of course normally the focus of attention in social encounters, and as the most expressive part of the body is chronically monitored by actors in checking upon the sincerity of the discourse and acts of others. Not all interaction which takes place in the presence of others, where sensibility of that presence influences that interaction, is 'face-to-face': some instances of crowd behaviour may be an exception to this. But most such examples are quite marginal: it is striking how far, even in large-scale assemblies, the term 'face-to-face' still applies in a significant way. In assemblies, lectures, concerts, etc., the positioning of the audience is nearly always such that the members of the audience collectively face the performers.

In face-to-face interaction, the presence of others is a major source of information utilised in the production of social encounters. The micro- versus macro-sociological distinction puts an emphasis upon contrasting small groups with larger collectivities or communities; but a more profound difference is between *face-to-face interaction and interaction with others who are physically absent* (and often temporally absent also). The extension of social systems in space and in time is an evident feature of the overall development of human society. The extension of interaction in time, as has already been suggested above, is opened out in a fundamental way by the development of writing. Tradition in non-literate cultures incorporates the sum of the cultural products of past generations; but the emergence of the text makes possible communication with the past in a much more direct way, and in a fashion which bears certain similarities to interaction with physically present individuals.[13] The access to the past that is opened up by the material existence of texts is however a distanciated interaction, if we contrast it to the presence of others in face-to-face interaction. The development of writing greatly extends the scope of distanciated interaction in space as well as in time. In cultures which do not have writing, contact both within the cultural group as well as with other groups is perforce always of a face-to-face kind. Of course in these circumstances actors themselves can act as mediators between others. But writing alters the nature of the transactions that can be carried out: the letter by-passes its carrier, and 'speaks' directly to its recipient. It should be noticed that the extension of interaction in space expressed in the transmitting of a letter from a sender to a recipient also involves the temporal absence of the sender, *vis-à-vis* the moment of communication when the letter is opened and read. The temporal gap between an exchange of letters is obviously much greater than that in the 'turn-taking' of conversations; on the other hand, of course, one of the main features of modern technologies of communication is that they no longer allow distance in space to govern temporal distance in mediated interaction. The telephone recaptures the immediacy of face-to-face interaction across spatial distance, at the cost of the restriction of the sensory context of communication; television and video communication restore considerably more, by returning distanciated interaction to a face-to-face form. If some of McCluhan's claims as to the significance of television and video are extreme, they none the less raise some salient questions about transmutations that might be occurring in structures of signification in the contemporary world.[14]

Time, space and repetition are closely intertwined. All known methods of assessing or calculating time involve repetition: the cyclic movement of the sun, the hands on a watch, the vibration of quartz crystals, etc.; all involve motion in space.[15] It is difficult to speak of time without reference to spatial metaphors – although if

Whorf is right this may be in some part derivative of particular characteristics of the Indo-European languages. My argument in previous paragraphs attests to the closeness of the connections between time, space and repetition in social life. The cyclical character of repetition or social reproduction in societies governed by tradition is geared indirectly to the experience and mapping of time. But the experience of time probably never entirely sheds its cyclical guise, even when 'linear time consciousness' comes to predominate. Just as calendars and clocks interpolate cycles into the sequential movement of time, so daily, weekly and annual periods of time continue to maintain cyclical aspects in the organisation of social activities within contemporary societies. The same is true of the life-span of the individual, which we still continue aptly to call the 'life-cycle'.

The extension of social life in time and space has already been mentioned, as an overall characteristic of social development: time-scales of social activity are altered by the transmutation of communication over distance (cf. Heidegger's 'de-severance' – making the farness vanish). The interconnection of time and space can be explored in terms of the participation of social actors in cycles of social activity as well as at the level of the transformation of society itself.[16] Time–geography deals with the time–space 'choreography' of individuals' existence over given time periods: the day, week, year or the whole life-time. A person's daily routine of activities, for example, can be charted as a path through time–space. Thus the social transition involved in leaving home to go to work is also a movement through space. Social interaction from this point of view can be understood as the 'coupling' of paths in social encounters, or what Hägerstrand calls 'activity bundles'. 'Activity bundles' occur at definite 'stations' – buildings or other territorial units – where the paths of two or more individuals coincide; these encounters dissolve as actors move off in space and time to participate in other activity bundles. The interest of this conception of social activity as 'a weaving dance through time–space'[17] does not depend upon Hägerstrand's particular formulation of it, to which various objections can be made; its general importance is that it emphasises the co-ordination of movement in time and space in social activity, as the coupling of a multiplicity of paths or trajectories. The same conception can be applied to much broader problems of social change, to which I shall turn later: change in society can also be understood in terms of time–space paths. *Social development characteristically involves spatial as well as temporal movement*: the most significant form of which, in our times, concerns the world-wide expansion of Western industrial capitalism.

Spatial presence and absence

The fact that the concept of social structure ordinarily applied in the social sciences – as like the anatomy of a body or the girders of a building – has been so pervaded by spatial imagery, may be another reason, together with the fear of lapsing into geographical determinism, why the importance of space itself has rarely been sufficiently emphasised in social theory. The significance of spatial elements for social analysis can be illustrated in numerous ways, but we can keep a thread of continuity with previous chapters by first of all referring to class theory.

In class society, spatial division is a major feature of class differentiation. In a fairly crude, but nevertheless sociologically significant, sense, classes tend to be regionally concentrated. One can easily instance the contrasts between the north and south of England, or west and east in Scotland, to make the point. Such spatial differentiations always have to be regarded as time–space formations in terms of social theory. Thus one of the important features of the spatial differentiation of class is the sedimentation of divergent regional 'class cultures' *over time*: class cultures which today, of course, are partly dissolved by new modes of transcending time–space distances.

The most consequential connections of class and space, however, are both more far-flung and more immediately confined. On the one hand, the class-character of capitalism incorporates international systems of centre and periphery; on the other, class domination is strongly influenced and reproduced by patterns of rural/urban difference, and by the differentiation of neighbourhoods within cities.[18] Neighbourhood segregation, in capitalist society, is not predominantly a managed process: rather, it is the result of class struggle in housing markets.[19] The social management of space is none the less in definite ways a feature of all societies. Virtually all collectives have a *locale* of operation, spatially distinct from that associated with others. 'Locale' is in some respects a preferable term to that of 'place', more commonly employed in social geography: for it carries something of the connotation of space used as a *setting* for interaction. A setting is not just a spatial parameter, and physical environment, in which interaction 'occurs': it is these elements mobilised as part of the interaction. Features of the setting of interaction, including its spatial and physical aspects, as I have indicated earlier (pp. 84–5) are routinely drawn upon by social actors in the sustaining of communication – a phenomenon of no small importance for semantic theory.

If the notion of locale is combined with the influence of physical presence/absence (this being understood as potentially both temporal and spatial), we can characterise the *small community* as one in which there is only short distance in time–space separations. That is to say, the setting is such that all interaction has only a small 'gap' to carry over in crossing time and space. It is not just physical presence in immediate interaction which matters in 'small-scale' interaction: it is the temporal and spatial *availability* of others in a locale.

No one has analysed such phenomena more perceptively than Goffman, who in all his writings has brought out the significance of space and place – or what in his first work he called 'regions'.[20] A region, in Goffman's sense, is part of what I have called a locale, which places bounds upon one or other of the major features of presence. Regions differ in terms of how they are confined or demarcated, as well as in terms of which features of presence they might 'let through'. A thick glass screen in a broadcasting studio can be used to isolate a room aurally but not visually. Regions are usually defined, he points out, in terms of time–space relations: the separation of 'living space' from 'sleeping space' in homes is also differentiation in times of use.

Goffman's contrast between *front and back regions* in which social performances are carried on is one of great interest – and one which has been unjustifiably ignored in the literature of social theory (Goffman's own works excepted). The spatial and social separation of back and front regions, as distinguished by Goffman – whereby various potentially compromising features of interaction are kept absent or hidden – can be connected in an illuminating way to practical consciousness and the operation of normative sanctions. The sustaining of a spatial discrimination between front and back is a prominent feature of the use of locale within the reflexive monitoring of action in discursive and practical consciousness.

On various occasions in this book I have sought to criticise Parsons's theorems about the relation he presumes between the 'internalisation of values' and normative constraints. One of my concerns has been to emphasise the importance of modes of normative conformity and deviance other than those given prominence by Parsons – without relapsing into the sort of futile confrontation between 'consensus' and 'conflict theory' which for a time held sway in discussions of such issues. One such mode of conformity is that of 'pragmatic acceptance' (grudging, semi-cynical, distanced through humour) of normative prescriptions as 'facts' of the circumstances of action. The front/back region contrast helps to demonstrate how such pragmatic acceptance is sustained through *control of the setting*.

The normative significance of the difference between front and back regions of interaction is well analysed by Goffman. Performances in front regions typically involve efforts to create and sustain the appearance of conformity to normative standards to which the actors in question may be indifferent, or even positively hostile, when meeting in the back. The existence of front/back discriminations normally indicates substantial *discursive penetration* of the institutional forms within which interaction is carried on. It is easy to relate this again to issues of class theory and the legitimation of structures of domination. Workers on the shop-floor work in a setting, for instance, in which it is often possible to turn spatial separation from management supervision into a practical back region, which becomes fully frontal [*sic*] only when management or other supervisors are immediately present. An example quoted by Goffman, describing the attitudes of workers in a shipyard, is a good illustration:

> It was amusing to watch the sudden transformation whenever word got around that the foreman was on the hull or in the shop or that a front-office superintendent was coming by. Quartermen and leadermen would rush to their groups of workers and stir them to obvious activity. 'Don't let him catch you sitting down', was the universal admonition, and where no work existed a pipe was busily bent and threaded, or a bolt which was already firmly in place was subjected to further and unnecessary tightening.[21]

It is important to see, as the author of the quotation in fact points out, that both sides in such a situation are usually aware, to greater or lesser degree, of what is occurring. Such recognition on the part of management is an acknowledgement of the limits of its power, and hence such spatial–social interchanges are highly important in the dialectic of control in organisations.

The shop-floor is usually physically demarcated as a spatial setting from the 'office'.[22] But of course similar kinds of opportunities for the translation of spatial separations into regions, in Goffman's sense, occur throughout the locales in which organisations operate. Weber's characterisation of modern bureaucracies as involving hierarchies of offices applies to the differentiation of physical space as well as to the differentiation of authority. Spatial separation of offices permits various sorts of back-region activities which involve control of information moving 'upwards', and thus serve to limit the power of those in the higher echelons.[23] But of course the controlled use of front/back differentiations is not confined to those in formally subordinate positions in organisational locales. The capability of controlling settings is one of the major prerogatives of power itself: the board-room, for instance, may be characteristically a front region in which activities displayed for public gaze conceal more significant manipulations that are withheld from view.

Space and presence in small communities, or in collectivities involving only time–space separations of short distance, are primarily expressed through the physical characteristics and perceptual abilities of the human organism. The media of availability of presence in locales of large-scale collectivities are necessarily different, and often involve, of course, only certain features of presence-availability and the nation-state. The slum areas of a city, for letter, telephone, etc. The front/back region opposition seems to hold mainly on the level of social integration, where the setting of locales is controlled directly in the reflexive monitoring of face-to-face interaction. But something of a similar effect can occur in less calculated fashion in cities, which in contemporary societies are the major intermediate locales between those of short-term presence-availability and the nation-state. The slum areas of a city, for example, may be 'hidden away' from the time–space paths which others who use the city, but do not live in those areas, follow.

The rise of the modern nation-state, with its clearly defined territorial boundaries, exemplifies the significance of control of space as a resource generating power differentials. Much has been written about this; the control of time as a resource in structures of domination has been far less studied. One of the themes of *Capital*, as I have mentioned before, is that the economic order of capitalism depends upon the exact control of time: labour-time becomes a key feature of the exploitative system of class domination. Time remains today at the centre of capital–labour disputes, as the employers' weapon of time-and-motion studies, and the workers' riposte of go-slows, readily attest. The control of time as a resource employed in structures of domination, however, may be historically more significant than even Marx believed. The invention of the calendar seems to have been closely associated with the emergence of writing, and both in turn were bound up with the exploitation of 'human machines' in the early Near East. In the origins of modern capitalism, Mumford has suggested, the clock rather than the steam engine should be regarded as the prototype of the era of mechanised production. The applying of quantitative methods to the analysis of nature, he claims, was first of all manifested in the quantification of time. Power-machines had existed well before the invention of clocks: in the latter we find 'a new kind of power-machine, in which the source of power and its transmission were of such a nature as to ensure the even flow of energy throughout the works and to make possible regular production and a standardised product'.[24]

Stability and change: Merton and Evans-Pritchard

I have already argued (p. 114) that, in the replacement of the synchrony/diachrony opposition with a conception of structuration, the possibility of change is recognised as inherent in every circumstance of social reproduction. But it is clearly insufficient to leave matters there: the implications of this must be spelled out. Those who have employed a division between the synchronic and the diachronic have often also insisted that every analysis of social stability must also *ipso facto* be an account of change. But the point remains at the level of a truism unless it is demonstrated how this is in fact to be accomplished. Discarding the distinction of synchrony and diachrony is actually the condition of making it more than just a banality.

In advocating a programme for functionalism in the social

sciences, R. K. Merton made a now famous distinction between 'manifest' and 'latent functions', arguing that it is the task of social analysis to go beyond the former to uncover the latter. Although the distinction is not wholly unambiguous,[25] Merton sought to contrast the purposes, or perhaps the reasons, that actors have for their conduct, with the functions which unbeknownst to them that conduct fulfils. In an interpretation of a social item in terms of its latent functions, *society's reasons or society's needs are disclosed as discrepant from (and by strong implication, more important than) the purposes or reasons of the actors engaging in the activity in question.* In the theory of structuration I have outlined in the previous papers, by contrast, societies or social systems have no reasons or needs whatsoever: the decisive error in functionalism is to regard the identification of the (unintended or unanticipated) consequences of action as an explanation of the existence (and the persistence) of that action. The fact that a given social item or social practice plays a part in the reproduction of a wider social system, where this is unintended by, and unknown to, the actors who engage in that practice, or to any others, *cannot explain why it plays the part it does*: why it persists as a recurrent social practice.[26]

We can in a sense actually reverse the distinction Merton made. Although it is indispensable to social theory to study the involvement of unintended consequences of conduct in the reproduction of social systems, the only kind of 'functions' (or 'teleological outcomes') that are of explanatory significance in analysing either the stability of, or change in, society *are what Merton labelled manifest functions*. In other words, it is only when members of society themselves actively attempt to harness projected outcomes to perceived 'social needs', through the application of knowledge about the effects of conduct in reproducing social systems, that teleological explanation of social reproduction has any part to play in social analysis.

Let us look a little more closely at Merton's discussion of latent functions, taking up one of the illustrations he offers: the Hopi rain dance. The distinction between manifest and latent functions, Merton proposes, 'aids the sociological interpretation of many social practices which persist even though their manifest purpose is clearly not achieved'. One traditional tactic in respect of such phenomena, Merton argues, is to declare them to be mere 'superstitions' or 'irrational survivals'. When a given mode of social conduct does not achieve its 'ostensible purpose, there is an inclination to attribute its occurrence to lack of intelligence, sheer ignorance, survivals, or so-called inertia'. The Hopi rain ceremonials are thought by those who take part in them to produce rain; if they do not achieve this aim, and the Hopi still continue with them, it is because they are superstitious, ignorant or irrational. Merton disputes that such 'name-calling' explains anything about the persistence of the rain dance. But analysis in terms of its latent functions may do so:

> Were one to confine himself to the problem of whether a manifest (purposed) function occurs, it becomes a problem, not for the sociologist, but for the meteorologist. And to be sure, our meteorologists agree that the rain ceremonial does not produce rain; but this is hardly the point. It is merely to say that the ceremony does not have this technological use; that this purpose of the ceremony and its actual consequences do not coincide . . . [But] ceremonials may fulfil the latent function of reinforcing the group identity by providing a periodic occasion on which the scattered members of a group assemble to engage in a common activity. As Durkheim among others long since indicated, such ceremonials are a means by which collective expression is afforded the sentiments which, in a further analysis, are found to be a basic source of group unity. Through the systematic application of the concept of latent function, therefore, *apparently* irrational behaviour may *at times* be found to be positively functional for the group.[27]

Various things are worth noting in this. First, it does not require a very close perusal of the passage to show that the identification of the 'latent function' of the Hopi ceremonial actually explains nothing at all about its persistence (the qualification that latent functions may not always be discovered can be disregarded as not relevant to the points under discussion here). The thesis that the assembling of the group to engage in ceremonial helps to foster the unity of the community by giving expression to sentiments which help cohere it, identifies *an unintended consequence* of the ceremonial activity; it does not in any way explain why the activity persists. Or, more accurately, it only does given a postulate of 'society's reasons', which not only transcend those of its members, but call into play a definite social response: society not only has needs to be satisfied, but somehow manages to stimulate or sustain functionally appropriate modes of meeting those needs. The only way out of making these (latent!) assumptions is to fall back upon some sort of principle of adaptational survival: that is, that every society of this type that has survived must perforce have developed some kind of assemblies like the rain dance. But even if this were in a general way an acceptable type of argument,[28] it must be observed that again it does not explain *how it is, how it happens*, that the rain dance persists. For why should the Hopi go on carrying out an 'irrational' form of activity? Merton is surely right in saying that to label such activity mere 'superstition' or 'survival' represents a pretty poor explanation of it.

Second, Merton merges two separate issues, and the plausibility of his analysis depends upon this merging: these issues are the significance of the *unintended consequences of actions*, and the *rationality of belief and action*. Merton specifically links the diagnosis of latent functions (which I have tried to show is, or implies a reification: 'society's reasons') with the investigation of what he calls 'seemingly irrational social patterns'. His discussion, posed in terms of manifest and latent functions, actually bears a striking similarity to Evans-Pritchard's equally renowned study of oracles and witchcraft among the Azande, which however is posed in terms of the rational analysis of belief.[29] In respect of the Hopi rain rituals Merton asks, like Evans-Pritchard: why do people go on participating in certain social activities when we know the beliefs connected with them to be false? There are interesting and significant differences between the ways in which Merton and Evans-Pritchard establish and attempt to answer this question. While Merton poses the question as a sociologist, concerned to delve below the manifest purposes or reasons that the Hopi might have for carrying out the ceremonials, Evans-Pritchard interprets the issue more from the point of view of a 'Western observer', interested in the relation between belief and action in an alien cultural setting. And while Merton tries to formulate an answer in terms of the unintended consequences of the activity – to discover 'society's reasons' where those of the participant actors are deficient, Evans-Pritchard looks for an answer in terms precisely of actors' reasons: by seeking to demonstrate, in effect, that they are not so 'irrational' after all.

Now the debate over the rationality of belief involves extremely difficult problems: but fortunately these are for the most part not relevant to the present context. Both Merton and Evans-Pritchard make a good case for rejecting such gross interpretations as those of 'superstition' or 'survival'. But – although he points to the importance of examining the unintended consequences of action – Merton's argument is decisively inferior to Evans-Pritchard's. For Merton does not in fact show why the rain ceremonial persists. Evans-Pritchard does show what is wrong with talking of Zande sorcery in terms such as 'superstition' or 'irrational survival': namely that the Azande do have good reasons for acting as they do, in the context of their traditionally-established beliefs. The sociological significance of Evans-Pritchard's analysis has been rather overshadowed by the broader philosophical controversies to which it has given rise. His account provides a much better basis for understanding how stable social reproduction occurs than Merton's diagnosis of the latent functions of ceremonial. We have, as I have said above, to reverse Merton's standpoint: the tracing of regularities in the unintended consequences of action has to be preceded by investigation of how the practices in question themselves are reproduced, which must be conducted in terms closer to those of Evans-Pritchard than those of Merton. To say this, it may be worth re-emphasising, is not to deny the importance of unintended consequences in social reproduction: it is rather to hold that it is an illegitimate move which, by translating such consequences into 'functions', claims to have explained the persistence or stability of given social practices. It is worth remarking that Merton's discussion of the Hopi ceremonial, even if it is fairly brief, gives no attention at all to any material relating to the *context of participation* in the ritual. He speaks of the 'purpose' of the rain dance, that purpose being to produce rain: this is then dismissed as irrational, because the beliefs upon which it is based are false. But, apart from the aforementioned relevance of Evans-Pritchard's arguments to this, we should point out that the reasons/purposes which the Hopi themselves have for continued participation in the ceremonial are not necessarily identical with its 'public charter', or what goes on in the front region. Scepticism is not foreign to traditional cultures. We cannot even assume that social analysts were the first to discern the effects of ceremonial upon group integration. On the contrary, it seems more likely that religious leaders, and perhaps even lay participants, have often been aware of the phenomenon, and have sought to cultivate it.

Social change and the theory of structuration

There is little point in looking for an overall theory of stability and change in social systems, since the conditions of social reproduction vary so widely between different types of society. I shall concentrate upon problems in the analysis of social change in the advanced, industrialised societies in the following section; at this point I want only to indicate some general considerations whereby these problems can be connected to the conceptions of structure and agency I have previously formulated, and which derive from the critical remarks I have made about Merton's differentiation of manifest and latent functions.

It is important to see that Merton's account is wanting not just because of difficulties with the notion of latent functions, but because he gives so little attention to 'manifest functions'. He says little at all, in fact, about what manifest functions are, apparently identifying them with the purposes of a given social item or form of social practice. In his concern to 'go behind the backs' of those who engage in the activities that are under study, Merton pays hardly any heed to analysing how the persistence of social practices is related to what I have referred to as the rationalisation of conduct. This is why, when compared to Merton's discussion, Evans-Pritchard's work is illuminating. Evans-Pritchard's account can be regarded as a demonstration of the necessity of grasping the rationalisation of conduct *in situ* in explaining the continuity of institutional forms. But while Evans-Pritchard's work complements that of Merton in this sense, what the former does not do (nor was it his aim) is to examine the unintended consequences of participation in the practices he examines for other aspects of the broader society of which they form part.

The foregoing suggests that, in interpreting the relations between social reproduction, stability and change in social systems, we have to connect two modes of analysis. First we have to show how, in the context of the rationalisation of action, definite practices are reproduced: how actors' penetration of the institutions which they reproduce in and through their practices, makes possible the very reproduction of these practices. This necessarily involves applying the theorem I have stressed in previous papers: that all social actors know a great deal about what they are doing in processes of interaction; and yet at the same time there is a great deal which they do not know about the conditions and consequences of their activities, but which none the less influences their course. Second, we have to investigate the effects of the 'escape' of activity from the intentions of its initiators upon the reproduction of practices, through processes which relate the practices in question to other features of broader social systems of which they are part. These can be profitably investigated in terms of the three levels of systemness outlined in earlier pages: the third of these, reflexive self-regulation, reconnects in a direct way to the rationalisation of conduct in practices, since here conduct is guided by an awareness of the operation of feed-back principles. This, as I have implied above, is the most accurate sense that can be given to Merton's 'manifest function': for here the intentional character of conduct, or its reflexive monitoring, incorporates awareness of the consequences of conduct for system reproduction. It is worth pointing out that much hinges upon *who possesses such awareness*, something not brought out in Merton's discussion, which does not take up the issue of to *whom* 'manifest functions' are manifest. If in the case of religious ceremonials professional leaders are more likely to be cognisant of the 'latent (to others) functions' of their ritual than lay participants are, it is not difficult to see that this is likely to reinforce their power over those participants.

Reproduction and routinisation

Since I have discussed the three levels of system reproduction in some detail in an earlier paper, I shall concentrate at this point upon the proximate reproduction of practices. I have argued that the rationalisation of conduct is a universal feature of human social interaction. The rationalisation of conduct always operates in the context of the duality of structure, through which the recursive ordering of social life is achieved. The true locus of the 'problem of order' is the problem of how the duality of structure operates in social life: of how *continuity of form* is achieved in the day-to-day conduct of social activity. 'Continuity' is actually a more useful term by which to examine the relation between stability and change in society than words like 'persistence' are: for continuities exist through the most radical and profound phases of social transformation (except perhaps for the limiting case of the wholesale physical extermination of the members of a society). It is only through such continuities that notions like 'revolution' have meaning and application, both for those who engage in processes of revolutionary change and for historical or sociological observers who seek to characterise or interpret them. The current importance of discontinuist conceptions in social science and philosophy should not be allowed to obliterate the continuities that make discontinuity possible. In some part the contemporary popularity of discontinuist notions represents a welcome reaction against 'progressive evolutionism' in various spheres; but, in certain versions at least, discontinuist conceptions still operate against the backdrop of a static viewpoint, to which they are counterposed as a critique. If we properly grasp the temporal character of all social activity, we are able to see that neither the couple stability/change, nor that of continuity/discontinuity express mutually exclusive polarities. Social systems only exist through their continuous structuration in the course of time: there is no room, as I have said before, for the term de-structuration in social analysis.

The 'problem of order' is seen by Parsons – and by most of his adversaries – largely as a problem of *compliance*: of how individuals come to adhere to the normative demands of the social groups of which they are members. But to rephrase the 'problem of order' as continuity through discontinuity prises open more basic issues in social theory; and, I shall argue, offers a different view of the relation between motivation and norms to that developed by Parsons.

The views of Parsons and Althusser, treated as different forms of 'objectivism', have been criticised by Bourdieu from a standpoint in some respects similar to that which I want to suggest here. What I have called the duality of structure, Bourdieu writes of in the following way. We have to understand, he says, that 'objective structures are themselves the product of historical practices and are constantly reproduced and transformed by historical practices whose productive principle is itself the product of the structures which it consequently tends to reproduce'.[30] To express this mouthful more briefly: social life is inherently recursive. In place of the Parsonian connection of value-standards with motivation, Bourdieu introduces his notion of the *habitus*. By the latter concept Bourdieu appears to mean habits which are shared by a group or community of actors.

Now pointing to the significance of habit suggests something that is potentially significant, and which is in a certain sense almost contrary to the type of standpoint adopted by Parsons. 'Habit' or 'convention' imply activities or aspects of activities that are *relatively unmotivated*. Whereas the Parsonian approach to the 'problem of order' is based on the assumption that the most central features of social activity in a community or society are also the most strongly motivated (via the internalisation of values as motivational components of personality), I want to suggest that the reverse is rather the case. That is to say, many of the most deeply sedimented elements of social conduct are cognitively (not necessarily consciously, in the sense of 'discursive availability') established, rather than founded on definite 'motives' prompting action; *their continuity is assured through social reproduction itself*. The latter phrase itself sounds tautological, but it is not so if appropriately explicated.

The mutual intelligibility of acts and of discourse, achieved in and through language, is perhaps the most basic condition of sustained interaction. The reproduction of language, however, as condition and result of the production of speech acts or other forms of communication, *is not a motivated phenomenon*. The argument here has to be clearly understood. The speaking of a language, and therefore its reproduction, is not of course unrelated to the wants of its speaker, and is in some part a medium of their realisation. Everyone who speaks a language thus has interests in the reproduction of that language; but the securing of such reproduction is not generally a motivating force among those language-speakers. (It may become so in the case of a community, for example, who are concerned to keep alive a language threatened by extinction.)

Now if this standpoint be accepted, the routine occupies a very important place in the reproduction of practices. Routine action is action which is strongly saturated by the 'taken for granted': in which ethno-methods, however much they involve a labour of reflexive attention, used to generate interaction over time, are latently accepted by the parties to that interaction. The relation between the routine and motivation conforms to that which I have outlined in the analysis of critical situations. According to the stratification model of the agent advanced previously, actors' wants remain rooted in a basic security system, largely unconscious and established in the first years of life. The initial formation of the basic security system may be regarded as involving modes of tension management, in the course of which the child becomes 'projected outwards' into the social world, and the foundations of ego-identity created. It seems plausible to suggest that these deep-lying modes of tension management (principally reduction and control of anxiety) are most effective when an individual experiences what Laing calls ontological security. *When they are most effective, they are least obtrusive* in influencing the reflexive monitoring of conduct on the part of the actor. Ontological security can be taken to depend upon the implicit faith actors have in the conventions (codes of significa- tion and forms of normative regulation) via which, in the duality of structure, the reproduction of social life is effected. In most circum- stances of social life, the sense of ontological security is routinely grounded in mutual knowledge employed such that interaction is 'unproblematic', or can be largely 'taken for granted'.

It is not difficult to see why there should be a close relation between the sustaining of ontological security and the routinised character of social life. Where routine prevails, the rationalisation of conduct readily conjoins the basic security system of the actor to the conventions that exist and are drawn upon in interaction as mutual knowledge. This is why, in routinised social circumstances, actors are rarely able, nor do they feel the need, in response to the inquiries they make of one another in the course of social activity, to supply reasons for behaviour that conforms to convention.

If routine is such an important feature in the continuity of social reproduction, we can approach an account of the sources and nature of social change in the industrialised societies through attempting to indicate the conditions under which the routinised character of social interaction is sustained or dislocated. Routine is strongest when it is sanctioned, or sanctified, by tradition: when 'reversible time' is invoked in connecting past and present in social reproduc- tion. Although the term 'traditional society' may often be used in an umbrella-like way to cover any kind of society short of those which have become substantially industrialised, the hold of tradition is clearly likely to be firmest in the smaller, more isolated types of society: in those types of society which have today virtually disap- peared from the world. (The term 'traditional society' can be doubly misleading in so far as the influence of tradition never wholly evaporates, even in the most mobile or fluid of contemporary societies.)

Change is not of course lacking even in those societies confined most implacably within the grip of tradition. But only two broad sorts of change seem to occur within such societies. One sort could be called *incremental*: change that occurs as an unintended outcome of social reproduction itself. Perhaps the prototypical instance of this is change in language. Every instance of the use of language is a potential modification of that language at the same time as it acts to reproduce it. The example of language also shows that incremental change occurs in all forms of society. For although the rate of mutation in languages in the West since the eighteenth century is unprecedented,[31] and includes the proliferation of deliberately constructed neologisms, most linguistic change takes place only slowly in so far as it affects the overall organisation of the language. Apart from secretional change, all other sources of change in cold societies dominated by tradition can be presumed to emanate from the external impact of influences that act to produce de-routinisation: the effects of sharp ecological transmutations, of natural disasters, or the establishing of relations of dependence or conflict with societies of differing cultural composition. Such is not the case with larger societies in which ethnic or other forms of sectional domination have already come into being. It would be a mistake however to suppose that this simply introduces new internal sources of potential de-routinisation, through the influence of ethnic or class conflicts, although such is certainly the case; for it also tends to be coincident with the breakdown of easily drawn distinctions between what is 'internal' to a society and what is 'external' to it – even if it is as necessary as it ever was to draw such distinctions (as I shall argue below).

I have so far used the term 'de-routinisation' without clarifying its meaning, which it is necessary to do in order to discuss problems of social change in relation to the industrialised societies. By 'de-routinisation' I refer to any influence that acts to counter the grip of the taken-for-granted character of day-to-day interaction. Routine is closely linked to tradition in the sense that tradition 'underwrites' the continuity of practices in the elapsing of time. Any influences which corrode or place in question traditional practices carry with them the likelihood of accelerating change. But we can separate – analytically at any rate – three sorts of circumstances in which an existing set of traditional practices may become undermined; these can be placed in ascending order in terms of their potential for stimulating social change. First of all, there are those types of circumstances mentioned above, that act externally upon cold societies. Neither the impact of natural events nor collision with other societies (if they are of the same type) places broad aspects of tradition in question: rather, certain traditional practices are replaced by others. This is not the undermining of traditional modes of belief and conduct as such, but the replacement of certain traditional practices by other traditional practices. Such is not the case with the second type of social circumstances that can be distinguished, which is where there emerge divergent 'interpretations' of established norms: I have already indicated the significance of literacy in this. The clash of diverging interpretations of tradition already in some part places in question the hold of tradition itself, but only by replacing 'tradition' with 'traditions': however this is evidently a basic element in the emergence of social movements that have major transformative potential.

The third type of circumstance, which is really specific to the modern West, involves the disavowal of tradition as such as a form of legitimation, and is correspondingly the most profound potential source of de-routinisation. This is not just a matter of disenchantment in the Weberian sense, however much such disenchantment might contribute to dissolving the dominance of tradition. Its most acute expression is found in the ascendancy of historicity as a mode of historical consciousness: the active mobilisation of social forms in the pursuit of their own transformation. Whatever the precise nature of the relation involved, there is no doubt that the triumph of historicity in this sense accompanies the rise of modern capitalism.[32] The age of modern capitalism is the age that marks the dominance of two distinctive kinds of collectivity: the 'legal-rational' *organisation* and the *secular social movement.* If we reserve a special technical sense for 'organisation', it can be used to refer to collectivities which are either set up as a result of, or whose form is strongly influenced by, conscious social innovation. Weber's concept of 'routinisation', as closely linked to his analysis of both *traditionale Herrschaft* and bureaucracy, can be rather misleading in this respect. For although bureaucratic regulation is undeniably a major form of the routinisation of conduct in contemporary society, such an emphasis might tempt us to forget the degree to which even heavily bureaucratised organisations are chronically innovatory when compared to more traditional types of group or community. A rather similar comment is in order with regard to Weber's formulation of the nature of charismatic movements. Although, as Weber uses it, 'charisma' aptly captures the de-routinising potential of social movements, it is not especially helpful in spotlighting the differences between movements that arise at the second level of de-routinisation noted above, and those distinctive to the contemporary era.

Critique of unfolding models of change

Any attempt to grasp the parameters of change in the modern age must of course acknowledge the basic significance of what I have earlier referred to as the extension of social systems in space and time; historicity and de-routinisation are essential elements of such extension. Consciousness of history as a progression of change, rather than as the constant re-enactment of tradition, and the availability of 'exemplars' located differentially in time or space for current processes of transformation, basically alter the overall conditions of social reproduction in the contemporary societies. As E. H. Carr says, 'One reason why history so rarely repeats itself is that the dramatis personae at the second performance have prior knowledge of the *dénouement*'[33] (or, as Marx put it, those who fail to learn from history in repeating it are apt to turn tragedy into farce).

With these considerations in mind, some critical comments can be offered about conceptions of social change that have hitherto been dominant in the social sciences. As I have tried to show elsewhere,[34] such conceptions have typically been heavily influenced by the context of their origin: the political and economic transformations experienced by the Western European societies from the late eighteenth to the early twentieth centuries. Both classical Marxism, and what I argue was its counterpart in nineteenth-century thought, the theory of industrial society, were deeply influenced by aspects of the European experience which have turned out to be in some degree specific to that experience, and which no longer have the same relevance to processes of change today. The nineteenth and early twentieth centuries in Western Europe marked a period in which political and economic revolution appeared closely tied together, with economic development appearing as the stimulating condition of political transmutation. The transfer of the mass of the population from an agrarian environment to an urban-industrial one seemed to occur as a progressive process internal to already established nation-states. In both the writings of Marx and of many liberal evolutionary thinkers, there are similar lacunae: an underestimation of the significance of the state in economic development and of military power as a coercive force; and a concentration upon internal processes of change. Marx certainly appreciated the world-historical impact of Western capitalism, its restless drive towards expansion and its corroding effect upon traditional cultures. He thus was able in some part to break with what I call an 'unfolding model' of social change. An unfolding model is one which treats social change as *the progressive emergence of traits that a particular type of society is presumed to have within itself from its inception.* Such a conception is particularly clear among those who have thought of social change in terms of some sort of biological analogy, with the 'maturation' of society being similar to the growth of an organism. In contemporary functionalism, where direct biological analogies have gone out of fashion, the leading unfolding models are characteristically posed in terms of the differentiation of functions: social change is examined as involving the progressive functional differentiation of institutions. These sorts of conceptions, in contrast to that of Marx and subsequent Marxists, have tended to see social development as a unified process, with the differentiation of institutions occuring in a co-ordinated way like parts of a growing body.

Rejecting an unfolding model of change does not necessitate, as Nisbet argues,[35] abandoning any talk of terms such as 'development' at all. Still less, when we are speaking of the contemporary world, does it involve taking the stance (as Nisbet does, following Teggart) that social change, of any significance, stems only from the intrusion of 'external events' upon societies or cultures. Such is more nearly the case in societies where tradition is dominant in social reproduction, although even there we can recognise the influence of incremental change. But it is clearly no longer so once historicity and de-routinisation have become far advanced. Industrial capitalism not only dislocates and absorbs other social forms, it operates through chronic economic mutation and technological innovation, which are certainly at the heart of that 'restless expansion' which Marx identified, and whose origins he diagnosed in the accumulation process. If unfolding models concentrate upon endogenous influences within societies or postulated types of society, 'exogenous' interpretations, like that of Nisbet, are in an odd way still likely to treat societies as internally closed systems (until disturbed by outside influence) – as well as to leave unexplicated the sources of the 'external intrusions' upon which the weight of their emphasis is placed. The events or episodes that Nisbet mentions as external phenomena – 'invasions, migratiòns, new trade routes opened, wars, explorations' – are all obviously 'internal' if we consider the societies in which they have their origin rather than those upon which they have their impact.

These conceptual inadequacies probably stem from two sources. One is the tendency to treat societies as unified wholes: in this respect as well as in tending to regard them as closed, exogenous conceptions resemble the unfolding models to which they are in other respects opposed.[36] If however societies are considered as involving relations of autonomy and dependence between groups that exist in various modes of conflict or tension with one another, we can acknowledge divisions on the 'inside' that may be in some respects as pronounced as those which separate what is 'outside'. The second inadequacy is one expression of something I have noted previously: a failure to theorise space as integral to social analysis. The words 'inside' and 'outside' are obviously spatial in character, but they are usually applied in the literature only in a vague way – and, in a certain sense, in a more metaphorical manner than they need to be. All of the episodes cited in the above quotation from Nisbet involve transition in physical space; their perpetrators come from outside the society or societies that feel their impact, in a directly spatial sense of 'outside' (although it should also be noted that most of them can also occur 'inside'). Such episodes therefore always involve movements of groups or populations both from and to somewhere: if we acknowledge the spatial attributes of such 'external intrusions' we are not likely to focus only upon the 'end-result' of their impact, but will rather see them, to adapt Hägerstrand's phrase, *as time–space paths involving collectivities rather than individuals*.

But there is perhaps a more important aspect of the second point than this – in relation at least to the contemporary world. This is the significance of control of space, as fixed and delimited territory, by the nation-state. It is apparent enough that, in much sociological writing, 'society' is used as equivalent to the nation-state. What gives this its justification, and what makes it necessary to go on referring to happenings 'inside' and 'outside' societies, is the coincidence of territorial boundaries with administrative centralisation.

The industrialised societies are not unified wholes in the sense supposed by unfolding models; but they do have definite boundaries that conjoin the social and the spatial within the politico-military system of the nation-state.

Social change in the contemporary society

A satisfactory approach to problems of social change in the contemporary world has to give prominence to the following notions:[37]

1. Relations of autonomy and dependence among societies or nation-states. On an abstract level this is simply a further generalisation of what I have argued is characteristic of all social systems, that they are constituted of regularised relations of autonomy and dependence (power relations). If we recognise that the territoriality of the nation-state is the most significant basis of dividing endogenous from exogenous sources of change, there is no difficulty in acknowledging that, at the same time, there are relations of autonomy and dependence that escape its clutches: collectivities nominally internal to states that are perhaps more strongly integrated into transnational networks (the most important contemporary instance of this being the giant transnational corporations).

On a more substantive level, relations of autonomy and dependence among nation-states have to be understood in the context of the formation of the capitalist world-economy. In *The Class Structure of the Advanced Societies,* I argued that the class structure of the industrial capitalist societies is expressive of a definite alignment of economy and polity in which (in various possible and differing ways in particular circumstances) major features of economic organisation are kept 'insulated' from the operations of the polity, and vice versa.[38] I think it plausible to claim that the counterpart to this in respect of international relations within the world-economy, and in no small part one of its props, is the existence of similar forms of 'insulation' *that operate externally as well as internally.* Such is in fact the main burden of Wallerstein's interpretation of the rise of the European world-economy from the late fifteenth century onwards. The world-economy initiated by the emergence and spread of Western capitalism, Wallerstein argues, differs in a very basic fashion from previous empires. In the latter, the connections between the metropolitan centre and its subordinate regions were primarily political, economic relations being administered by a tax-collecting bureaucracy. In the capitalist world-economy, the broad connections are primarily economic, while political decisions are largely confined to the areas where the nation-state has a monopoly of legal control and control of the means of violence. As Wallerstein puts it, 'capitalism as an economic mode is based on the fact that the economic factors operate within an arena larger than that which any political society can totally control'.[39] This thesis can be accepted without acquiescing in the whole of Wallerstein's analysis: for Wallerstein, like Nisbet but in a very different vein, tends to overplay the influence of the external organisation of the world-economy at the expense of 'internal' components of the capitalist accumulation process.[40]

It should also be pointed out that we do not live today just in a *world-economy*, but in a *world military order*, in the sense that the balance of military power between the two dominant blocs – and the various forms of covert and direct military assistance lent to established states and insurgent movements – is a major influence upon change in all parts of the globe.

2. The uneven development of different sectors or regions of social systems. This is another sense in which we can trace time–space paths of development, both within nation-states and in the relations of autonomy and dependence between them. As I have pointed out before, the prevalence of unfolding models of change in social theory in some part expresses peculiarities of the development of the Western European societies in the nineteenth century, especially that of Britain. Those elements of an unfolding model that can be discerned in Marx (the progressive emergence of conditions favouring revolutionary change, through the concentration of large masses of workers in factories and urban neighbourhoods; the relative emiseration of an ever-expanding proletariat; and the formation of militant workers' unions and political associations eventually destined to assume political power) also lean heavily upon the British example, or an interpretation of it. However Marx also had a 'second theory of revolution', not unconnected with the first but only ambiguously reconciled with it,[41] that anticipates a conception of uneven development – later expanded upon by Trotsky and Lenin. This 'second theory' involves the idea that the conditions intitiating revolutionary transformation are to be found in the conjunction of the retarded and the advanced: the sort of explosive

situation Marx saw to exist in Germany in the late 1840s, and in Russia some thirty years later. But uneven development is not of course confined to such dramatic circumstances, although there can be no doubt that conceptions of uneven development are basic to explaining the occurrence of political revolution in modern times: in respect both of the internal development of nation-states and, on a global level, the confrontation of the industrially advanced societies and the 'Third World'.

On each of these levels a conception of uneven development can be expressed in time–space paths, because the notion implies both differential rates of change in political or economic forms, and their location in different regions. To speak of 'regions', in something like its ordinary everyday sense, at first sight seems of little importance to social theory, since the term is such a commonplace and general one. But I have already pointed to its usefulness in respect of face-to-face interaction, and it can also be applied on a broader scale. It can be argued that there are three basic divisions that focalise schism and cohesion in the contemporary world: *class, ethnic differentiation and territorial claims.* Each tends to be regionalised in time–space. I have previously mentioned that class divisions are characteristically regionalised: in terms of large-scale regional sectors and of the distribution of neighbourhoods in urban areas. But regions within societies also often have cultural or ethnic significance, that can either cut across or can act to further class divisions. In terms of relations between nation-states, the influence of differential regional rates and modes of development is expressed in the fact that the term 'the West' – Japan notwithstanding – can still be used as more or less equivalent to 'the advanced capitalist societies'. The prevalence of unfolding models of change, as I have suggested, reflects an ethnocentrism that generalises from (suspect interpretations of) the political, military and economic dominance which the West has achieved over the rest of the world. It is significant that ideas directly connecting relations of autonomy and dependence with regionalised uneven development have emanated largely from areas that are subject to such dominance. Some of these ideas, coming from the periphery, have remained on the periphery of social theory as a whole: but they should be brought into its centre. The concept of internal colonialism, for example, as originated by Casanova, has been much criticised, but appropriately amended it can be illuminating when applied to the industrialised societies as to others. Moreover, we can readily see that interest in connecting relations of national autonomy and dependence to uneven development should not be confined to ties between the economically advanced societies and those that are 'underdeveloped'. As an illustration, we might single out the case of Mediterranean countries such as Spain or Greece. Such countries are not 'underdeveloped' in the usual sense of that term, but nor are they as fully industrialised as their neighbours to the North. Certain of their characteristics are due to their spatial proximity to the metropolitan centres of advanced capitalism, which have a direct impact on them that is lacking in societies more remote from those centres.

3. Critical phases of radical social change, in which the existing alignment of major institutions in a society becomes transformed, whether or not this involves processes of political revolution. This point is both methodological and substantive. It has methodological aspects, in the sense that it suggests the importance to the theory of social change of what some authors have called episodic studies, concentrating upon sequences of change which are of medium-term duration, but which have far-reaching consequences for the society or region in question.[42] Four sorts of such episode, which may be combined in varying ways, are obviously and intrusively significant in the modern world: (a) rapid processes of industrialisation, however these may be initiated; (b) political revolution, this being understood not just as the immediate events involved in the conquest or transfer of power, but as stretching over a period of 'precipitating circumstances' prior to the revolutionary take-over and of post-revolutionary social reorganisation; (c) processes of institutional decay or disruption produced by the encounter of traditional cultures with the economic imperialism of the advanced societies; (d) processes of institutional decay or disruption produced by the effects of war.

Looked at more substantively, the point has reference to dichotomous contrasts between the traditional and the modern that have characterised unfolding models of change. Such dichotomous conceptions dominated nineteenth-century thought, in various formulations: as status versus contract, *Gemeinschaft* versus *Gesellschaft*, or mechanical versus organic solidarity. But their influence has lasted well into the twentieth century, in spite of the numerous critical objections that have been registered against them. A mark of the far-reaching nature of their ascendancy within social theory is the fact that Parsons made the *Gemeinschaft/Gesellschaft* distinction the basis of his 'pattern-variables' – thus rendering a contrast founded upon specific traits of nineteenth-century European development as a set of supposedly universal features of all forms of human society.

Dichotomous conceptions of this sort are not necessarily unilluminating: their flaws really derive from their association with unfolding models, and from certain assumptions that this association has frequently brought in its train. Two such assumptions, often implicitly held rather than explicitly stated, are worth drawing particular attention to:[43] that the institutional character of a society is above all determined by its level of technological or economic advancement; and that therefore the most economically developed society or societies at any one time (however 'most economically developed' be defined) show other societies an image of their future in the present. If Britain in the nineteenth century was often looked to as a type case, in the twentieth century, in non-Marxist forms of social and political theory at any rate, it has been replaced in this role by the United States.

Now critics of dichotomous contrasts have talked instead of the various 'mixes' that are possible between tradition and modernity in specific societies. But while this usefully directs attention away from unfolding models and towards notions of dependency and uneven development, I wish to claim that recognition of the significance of 'critical phases' of change can add something further. For in critical phases, it can be suggested, there is established a kind of 'spot welding' of institutions that forms modes of integratioñ which may subsequently become resistant to further change. A theory of critical phases can thus in principle be applied to grasp both generic features of episodes, and modes in which differences become established between societies that are at similar levels of economic development. I have suggested elsewhere how this might be applied in elucidating certain chronic differences that can be seen to exist between class consciousness, industrial conflict and the labour movement in the United States, Britain and France.[44]

4. A 'leapfrog' idea of change, according to which the 'advanced' in one set of circumstances may inhibit further change at a later date; while on the other hand that which is 'retarded' at one point in time may later become a propitious basis for rapid advancement. This fourth point is really implied in the other three, and the first part of

the theorem can be aptly illustrated by considering the changing fortunes of Britain over the period of the past 150 years. Britain achieved its leading position in the middle to later part of the nineteenth century in some substantial part because it was the 'first industrial society', able also to exploit the fruits of world-wide imperial dominions. But today, in a post-imperial stage, the residues of Britain's early industrial development act to reduce its capabilities of achieving favoured goals of rapid economic growth, as compared to societies that have industrialised later and in different internal and external circumstances. The leapfrog effect can however apply just as much in respect of narrower technological imperatives as in regard of broad episodes of social change.

The leapfrog effect returns our attention to historicity – or to awareness of history as a fundamental feature of modern history – in societies in which the sources of de-routinisation are manifold. For leapfrog processes of change involve the awareness that some events in the past need not be repeated in the future: that *avoidable possible worlds* are the other face of future states of society to be striven for.

The social sciences and history: some observations

In closing this paper, a few remarks, which I shall make no attempt to defend in a detailed way, may be offered about the relations between history – as the writing of history – and the social sciences. It is not infrequently claimed, as part of a reaction against positivistic philosophies in the social sciences, that sociology should become, or should be regarded as being, 'historical' in character. But stated thus bluntly, this means very little at a time when historians are becoming more 'sociological', and where basic issues of the nature of historical investigation remain as contested as ever. As a minimal claim it can be said that what history is, or should be, cannot be analysed in separation from what the social sciences are, or should be. However, I should want to go much further than this. *There simply are no logical or even methodological distinctions between the social sciences and history – appropriately conceived.*

In speaking of the relations between social science and history, Braudel writes: 'By *structures*, observers of the social mean an organisation, coherence, relatively fixed relations between social realities and groups. For us historians, a structure is no doubt fabrication, architecture, but more than this a reality which time erodes only slowly....'[45] This, however, is a version of the system/structure distinction: if Braudel's use of 'structure' is not the same as mine, it is concerned with the 'binding' of time that I have emphasised in this book.

Braudel's conception of the concern of history with the *longue durée*, of course, finds only few echoes among Anglo-Saxon historians; and is even more distant from the types of historical example that philosophers have ordinarily discussed. The most prominent issues aired in the philosophy of history in the English-speaking world in recent years are those raised in the Hempel–Dray debate. I shall not attempt to discuss these issues here; rather I want to point to some problems that have received little attention from the two principals in the controversy.

It is worth noting that the debate has been posed in closely similar terms to positivist/anti-positivist debates in the social sciences. That is, the main problems at issue have concerned interpretations of human actions in terms of agents' reasons, versus interpretations in terms of universal laws that have the same logical form as laws in the natural sciences. But whatever else may have emerged from the controversy, it has failed to illuminate several key issues that are posed by attempts to explicate human conduct. First, the terms in which Dray has helped to frame the debate explicitly concern what he refers to as 'actions of individual agents'. He admits that 'individual actions as such are below the threshold of proper interest; they enter history only insofar as they have "societal significance"'.[46] But he does not discuss how 'societal significance' (a term borrowed from Mandelbaum) is to be defined, nor why it should be legitimate to consider historical explanation from such a limited aspect. Consequently, Dray skirts some important questions raised by his position. It will not do just to assert that agents' reasons, or 'the reasonableness of doing what this agent did' are of vital interest to history, however reasonable such a statement may be. For this avoids questions of how the reasonableness of behaviour, or what I have called the 'rationalisation of action', is to be connected with other main features of social life: namely, with other characteristics of agents besides their reasons for conduct; and with the unintended consequences of their intended behaviour.

Second, although the controversy is preoccupied with the relation between the rationalisation of action and laws of human conduct, nowhere in the debate *is this relation considered as itself an historical question*, concerning the sorts of knowledge that human beings have of the conditions of their action. The reasons that actors have for their acts, or the modes in which the reflexive monitoring of conduct is tied in to its rationalisation, *include* 'generalisations' or 'laws': the latter, whether expressed in causal form or not, are in no way at the exclusive command of historical or sociological observers.

Third, all such laws are themselves 'historical', in the sense that they hold under particular parameters of social reproduction, involving definite alignments of intended and unintended consequences of action[47] (although there are of course naturalistic laws of a universal type that affect the margins and the technical possibilities of human activity). To say that sociological laws are 'historical' is to claim that the relations they express are in principle unstable in the light of alterations in conditions of the rationalisation of action: such alterations include the incorporation of laws themselves. Consider an example that figures in the Hempel–Dray debate (although actually introduced into the controversy by other authors):[48] the generalisation, 'In seafights, 1653–1805, large formations were too cumbersome for effectual control', represented as relevant to explaining the defeat of Villeneuve at Trafalgar. One can remark about this: (a) that naturalistic laws are certainly implied in the 'technical boundaries' of seventeenth-century warfare, but as limiting conditions to the activities that actually occurred; (b) it might have made a considerable difference to Nelson's decision to engage battle, and to his reasons for attempting to direct the course of the encounter in a particular way, whether or not he knew about the generalisation in question: certainly whether or not he did know about it is important to establishing the nature of his reasoning; (c) the diffusion of the generalisation among naval officials is likely to have been one of the factors leading to changes in the form and tactics of sea battles subsequently.

Fourth, and finally, although the Hempel–Dray controversy is all about explanation, and each of the two main contributors recognises that there may be no single logical form to explanations in history, insufficient attention is given to the contextual character of inquiries and their resolution. The object of an explanation, as Dray rightly says, 'is to resolve puzzlement of some kind'; and he then adds, 'When a historian sets out to explain a historical action, his problem is usually that he does not know what reason the agent had for doing it.'[49] But this is only one among various other possible sources of puzzlement generating 'why-questions' – even if we were to suppose that the main tasks of historical explanation are to understand definite acts of particular individuals. Dray of course admits that history is about far more than the interpretation of 'historical actions', but one should note just how restrictive and artificial such a formulation is.

7

The Prospects for Social Theory Today

In this concluding paper, I shall try to place some of the issues discussed earlier in the book in the context of an overall analysis of the current prospects for social theory. The logical starting-point for such an analysis is the state of disarray that characterises social theory today – a matter of common awareness to anyone working within the social sciences. The past decade or so has seen the revival of traditionally established forms of theory (such as hermeneutics), the emergence of seemingly novel perspectives (including especially ethnomethodology), and the attempted incorporation within social theory of various approaches claimed to be drawn from formerly separate philosophical endeavours (the philosophy of the later Wittgenstein, ordinary language philosophy and phenomenology). To these we can add the important resurgence of Marxist theory. The latter however cannot always be clearly distinguished from trends in non-Marxist social science, since most of the same divisions appear, even if in rather different form, within Marxism: the contrasts between the various sorts of 'phenomenological Marxism', 'critical theory', 'Marxist structuralism', etc. are often as pronounced as those outside Marxism.

Now we must recognise that there are still fairly distinct 'national sociologies' – or, more accurately, types of intellectual tradition associated with major language communities, such as English, French and German. The degree of prominence of the different theoretical parameters indicated above varies between these communities: my remarks in this paper will be primarily directed to social science within the English-speaking world.

The orthodox consensus

In English-speaking sociology, the immediate origins of the disarray of social theory can be quite readily discerned. During the post-war period, up until at least the late 1960s, there was something like a consensus that held the 'middle ground' of sociology. This was not, to be sure, an unchallenged consensus; but it provided a focus of debate both for those who supported it and for those who were critical. This consensus, or so I would argue, involved two connected strands: sets of ideas whose antecedents can be traced back well into the nineteenth century, but which became elaborated in novel forms in the 1950s and 1960s. The first of these concerns what I have referred to generically as the theory of industrial society.[1] Those who contributed to the theory of industrial society – authors such as Lipset, Bell and Parsons in the United States, and Aron and Dahrendorf in Europe – held a range of broadly similar views. By opting for a bipolar contrast between 'traditional society' and 'industrial society', they were able to conclude that no form of socialist society could be distinctively different from a capitalistic one; socialism and capitalism are at most merely two partially distinct sub-types of industrial society. Such authors held to the view that, with the maturity of the industrial order, class conflict loses its transformative potential. Acute class struggles, they agreed with Durkheim,[2] are characteristic of the strains created during the early phase of development of industrial society; once class relations have become normatively regulated, class conflict becomes accommodated to the existing order. The 'institutionalisation of class conflict', which meant both the normative regulation of class struggles and at the same time their confinement to the separate spheres of industrial negotiation and political mobilisation, also supposedly entailed an end of ideology: Marxism, and other forms of radical socialist thought, were regarded as ideological expressions of the same strains which produced intense class conflicts in the initial stages of the formation of industrial society.

These views, which were developed in a political context of progressive liberalism, during a phase of relatively stable economic growth in Western capitalism, now appear almost archaic, following a period of heightened political and economic conflict. Indeed, they may now be interpreted as a cautionary tale of the perils of overgeneralisation in social analysis: a period of not much more than a decade or so was taken as evidence for the most general assertions and projections about profoundly rooted trends in 'industrial society'. (The salutary nature of this lesson should not be ignored by those who are prone to treat falterings in the smooth economic growth of the Western economies in current times as a basis for a reversion to a dogmatic type of orthodox Marxism.) The theory of industrial society has today probably lost most of the support it once enjoyed among sociologists and political theorists: even some of its most enthusiastic advocates have had second thoughts about their earlier views.

Since the theory of industrial society, as elaborated in the 1950s and 1960s, was closely bound up with certain interpretations of political and economic changes in the early post-war period in the West, some of its shortcomings can be quite easily identified in the light of subsequent developments in the advanced capitalist societies. (One may take as an illustration the wholesale expansion of higher education, which only a few years ago was made into a long-term trend deeply entrenched within 'industrial society'.)[3] Such is not the case with the other strand in the erstwhile consensus in sociology, which was of a more abstract character, and involved an overall appraisal of the logical form and likely achievements of the social sciences. We can distinguish in turn two features of this second strand of orthodox or mainstream sociology: the prevalence of *functionalism* and *naturalism*. It is these perspectives that I shall be concerned with in this paper.

Each of these features has had a long-standing association with the theory of industrial society: the traditions of thought which run from Comte and Durkheim through to Parsons and modern American sociology have been of primary importance in sustaining this connection. Functionalist thought, which has always been strongly associated with unfolding models of change based upon metaphors of biological growth or evolution, has in general accorded well with the theme of 'progress with order', a Comtean *motif* that has been echoed in some version or another by all proponents of the theory of industrial society.[4] 'Functionalism', of course, is only a loosely associated body of doctrines. Several related versions have been developed in this century: the 'anthropological functionalism' of Radcliffe-Brown and Malinowski, the 'normative functionalism' of Parsons, and the 'conflict functionalism' of Merton. It is not relevant here to attempt a direct characterisation of the principal traits of functionalist thought. But it is worth emphasising that functionalism has normally been closely associated with the idea that biology provides the proximate model for sociology, since both disciplines, it is argued, deal with systems rather than aggregates. I have tried to show elsewhere that models of biological systems, especially those tied to a notion of homeostasis, will not suffice to illuminate some of the key issues posed by the analysis of social systems.[5] This has also been in a certain sense acknowledged by Parsons, who has turned to cybernetic models of information control in his more recent writings.[6]

From Comte to Durkheim to modern American sociology, functionalism has been closely connected with a naturalistic standpoint in social philosophy, if naturalism is understood to refer to the thesis that the logical frameworks of natural and social science are in essential respects the same. No more comprehensive interpretation of this standpoint has been offered than that formulated by Comte, and I want to point to at least one important residue of the Comtean position that remained an integral element of mainstream sociology in the post Second World War period. Comte's 'hierarchy of the sciences' was intended to be applied both analytically and historically. That is to say, it provided a logical exposition of the relations between the sciences, including that between biology and sociology: each science is both dependent upon those below it in the hierarchy and yet has its own rigorously autonomous factual sphere of investigation (a notion that was later strongly reiterated by Durkheim). But if understood laterally rather than horizontally, the hierarchy of the sciences provided an historical understanding of the progression of scientific development – in combination, of course, with the 'law of the three stages'. Science develops first in relation to those objects and events furthest removed from human involvement and control. Mathematics and physics are hence the first fields to be established on a scientific basis; the subsequent history of science is that of approaching nearer and nearer to human society itself. Human conduct is most refractory to the scientific understanding, since it is most difficult of all for human beings to look at their own behaviour in a scientific light. Sociology is thus the last science to come into being. Now the significance of this general conception is that it ties a naturalistic formulation of the logical form of sociology *to an account of its youthful character as compared to the natural sciences.* Sociology is a 'late arrival', the completion of the extension of the positive spirit to the explanation of human social conduct.

The notion of the youthfulness of sociology, as compared to biology, but particularly to the fields of physics and chemistry, survived as an important element of the mainstream consensus. Its significance is precisely that it connects presumed logical features of social science to a specific self-understanding of the history of the discipline. If there appear to be certain differences between the natural and social sciences, in respect of such matters as the establishment of a set of precisely formulated laws of a universal character, such differences can be explained as resulting from the relatively limited amount of time that sociology has been established on a scientific footing. The thesis of naturalism is sustained by the assumption of a lag between the respective development of natural and social science.

The 1950s and 1960s saw a partial reunification, especially in the context of American sociology, of functionalism with positivistic philosophies of science, the latter as formulated by such authors as Carnap, Hempel and Nagel: this conjunction formed a major means whereby the naturalistic standpoint of the orthodox consensus was formulated. Many sociologists embraced such positivistic philosophies, which were essentially liberalised forms of logical empiricism,[7] with a fervour that blinded them to the fact that the logical empiricist view of science represents only one possible philosophy of science among other available philosophies. The logical empiricist philosophy of science came to be seen simply as what natural science *is*, and as showing what sociology should become. If the empiricist philosophers from their side were less hasty to consummate the union, and were for the most part sceptical of the logical status of functionalism, they none the less came to accept that functional analysis, as the shared concern of both biology and social science, could be made to conform to the exigencies of scientific method.[8]

Current dilemmas

The dissolution of the orthodox consensus has been succeeded by the Babel of theoretical voices that currently clamour for attention. One might distinguish three prevalent reactions to the seemingly disoriented situation of social theory. The first is a reaction of despair or disillusionment. There are some who are prone to argue that, since those concerned with the more abstract problems of social theory cannot agree even about the basic presumptions with which the study of human social conduct should be approached, such problems can effectively be ignored in the continuance of the practice of social research. Many of the issues dealt with as 'social theory', it is claimed, are really philosophical rather than sociological in character: the squabbles of 'social theorists' can hence be ignored in favour of a concentration upon the doing of social research. But such a stance does not withstand close scrutiny. Quite apart from the untenable character of the positivistic conception which holds that questions of philosophy can be clearly distinguished from the main body of social theory, we must insist that theoretical considerations cannot be without potential impact even upon the most sheerly 'empirical' types of social investigation. A second reaction might be described as a search for security at any cost: a reversion to dogmatism. This is surely the case for some of those who have turned back towards orthodox Marxist positions. There are clear senses in which such positions share similar perspectives to the erstwhile consensus in mainstream sociology; and are equally barren when confronted with issues raised by other theoretical standpoints.

The third response to the theoretical disarray of the social sciences today is almost exactly the opposite of the first. Rather than a reaction of despair, it is one of rejoicing: the diversity of theoretical perspectives is welcomed as testimony to the inherent fruitfulness of social theory. We cannot attempt to achieve a closure of this diversity, nor should we seek to. Even some of the principal figures once involved in the orthodox consensus have now come to veer towards such a view.[9] And it is a view which, appropriately expressed, has a good deal to commend it. For it can plausibly be argued that chronic debates and persistent dissensus about how the study of human social conduct is to be approached express something about the very nature of human social conduct itself; that deeply established disagreements about the nature of human behaviour are integral to human behaviour as such, and thus necessarily intrude into the heart of the discourse of philosophy and social theory. Admitting the significance of this point, however, should not entail advocating the desirability of creating as many divergent abstract perspectives upon human social behaviour as possible. We may acknowledge the likelihood of continuing disagreements about basic issues in the study of human action, while still stressing the importance both of establishing connections between divergent positions and of attempting to transcend them.

I therefore wish to reject each of these reactions to the theoretical Babel, and to propose instead that social theory stands in need of systematic reconstruction. I make this claim not in the anticipation of substituting a new orthodoxy for an old one, but in the hope of providing a more satisfactory ground for the discussion of central issues in social theory than that provided by the erstwhile consensus, or permitted by the hermetic isolation in which the diversity of current theoretical standpoints tend to exist. I want to argue that the orthodox consensus cannot be quietly forgotten, or dismissed as merely an ideological reflex of welfare-state capitalism, but that its weaknesses have to be identified if we are to declare its abandonment justified; and I want to say that these weaknesses can now be discerned without too much difficulty. I also wish to make the further argument that a diagnosis of the shortcomings of the pre-existing consensus indicates the necessity of theorising – of making a focus of theoretical analysis – issues that were ignored within that consensus. I propose to list five such shortcomings, or sets of shortcomings, that characterised the erstwhile consensus.

The origins of 'sociology'

The first I have briefly alluded to above: it is that mainstream sociology incorporated a *mistaken self-interpretation of its origins vis-à-vis* the natural sciences. As I have also mentioned above, this point has a twofold aspect: it involves assertions about the past development of social science, but also concerns logical implications that are drawn from that development concerning contrasts between the social and natural sciences.

There is no room here to undertake a proper documentation of the thesis that social science is a relative newcomer as compared either to biology or to the other natural sciences: the idea that 'sociology' has been the last discipline to be put on a scientific footing, breaking with speculative philosophy and the philosophy of history. But we have good reason to be sceptical of these claims if we consider how often they have been lodged: in fact, members of each generation of social thinkers since at least the early part of the eighteenth century have been inclined to assert that they were initiating a newly scientific study of man in society, in contrast to what went before.[10] Vico conceived himself to be founding a 'new science' of society. Montesquieu and Condorcet made similar claims, and held they were breaking with what went before. Comte said much the same thing in his time, acknowledging the contributions of these forerunners, but largely relegating them to the prehistory of sociology, which was only coming to be placed on a scientific basis through his own efforts. And so it continues: Marx argued much the same in respect of Comte; Durkheim in respect of Marx; and yet another generation later, Parsons of Durkheim and others. The fact that such claims have been lodged so persistently by successive generations of social thinkers does not in and of itself show that they cannot be sustained, but it does justify regarding them in a sceptical light. At any rate, I shall assert at this point that the notion that sociology is a newcomer as compared to the natural sciences is an error, whose source is to be found in the accepting of the declarations of one or other of these generations of authors (usually either Marx, or the '1890–1920 generation' to which Durkheim belonged) at their face value. Social science is as old as natural science is; both can be dated back to the post-Renaissance period in Europe, as recognisably 'modern' in form.

Of course, different sectors of both natural and social science have developed unevenly. To forestall possible misunderstandings, I must emphasise that rejection of the thesis of the youthful character of the social sciences does not involve denying that progress has been achieved within them; or that there have been important ruptures or dislocations between different phases of their development, as well as between rival intellectual traditions. Moreover we have to be careful with terminology: the invention of the term 'sociology' by Comte, and its subsequent successful propagation by Durkheim (who however regarded it as a 'somewhat barbaric term') has had more than a certain amount to do with the view that the 'great divide' in social thought can be located somewhere from the middle to the late nineteenth century. 'Sociology' meant something close to what became the orthodox consensus – *'progress with order' in respect of the maturation of industrial capitalism, naturalism in respect of the logical framework of social science,*

and functionalism. The term 'sociology' is thus a heavily comprom-
ised one, and I continue to use it only in the acknowledgement that
it is today in such wide currency that there is no hope of substituting
a more appropriate term.

Problems of nomology

If the idea of the youthful nature of sociology cannot be sustained,
neither can the implications that are drawn from it to explain the
apparently rudimentary level of development of social science as
compared with the natural sciences. Sociology is not in the process
of taking the first steps along paths already successfully trodden by
the natural sciences (to say this, as I should strongly emphasise, is
not to say that the achievements of the natural sciences are irrelevant to the social sciences).

The most characteristic difference between social and natural
science, which has inevitably preoccupied the advocates of naturalism, is the apparent lack, in the former, of sets of precisely formulated laws that are generally agreed upon by the members of a
professional community. Various qualifications obviously have to
be made in approaching this matter. The natural sciences are not a
unity; some disciplines, and sectors of disciplines, are more
nomologically 'advanced' than others. Nor are the social sciences, if
that term be interpreted to include economics, all of a piece either.
Those who work in the social sciences are probably prone to
underestimate the prevalence of profound disagreements among
physical scientists over quite fundamental problems within their
areas of endeavour. None the less, the contrasts between even the
less 'advanced' fields of natural science and the most 'advanced'
fields within the social sciences, in respect of nomology, are clear
and demonstrable.

Rejecting the thesis that social science is a latecomer means also
rejecting a 'lag' interpretation of this difference. What, then, are we
to make of the issues of the existence and logical form of laws in the
social sciences?

I want to propose that laws certainly do exist in the social
sciences, if 'laws' be understood in a comprehensive sense to refer to
generalisations of a causal character; there only appears to be a
dearth of laws in social science if such generalisations are dismissed

as unimportant or wanting by comparison with those to be found in certain areas of natural science. (This should not be taken to imply that the establishing of laws is necessarily the sole concern of either natural or social science.) But there are two principal reasons to suppose that social scientific laws, even in those areas where quantification is most feasible, will be differentiated from those characteristic of the various fields of the physical sciences. One does not refer to a logical contrast and, although not trivial, I shall treat it as essentially uninteresting; the other type is logical in character, and more significant for purposes of my present discussion.

The first concerns the underdetermination of theories by facts. It has become a well-established principle of the philosophy of science that theories are underdetermined by facts: that no amount of accumulated fact will in and of itself determine that one particular theory be accepted and another rejected, since by the modification of the theory, or by other means, the observations in question can be accommodated to it. There is good cause to suppose that the level of underdetermination of theories by facts is likely to be greater in most areas of social science than in most areas of natural science. The factors involved are well-enough known, and there is no need to elaborate upon them at any length: they include difficulties of the replication of observations, the relative lack of possibilities of experimentation, the paucity of 'cases' for comparative analysis with regard to theories concerned with total societies, etc.

The second reason is more important, at least to the present discussion, because it concerns a deep-rooted difference in logical form between laws in the social sciences as compared to those found in natural science. Although the character of natural scientific laws is still controversial and much debated, there is little basis to doubt that most such laws are putatively universal in form within the domains of their application;[11] all laws operate within certain boundary conditions, but the causal relations that they specify are immutable given the occurrence of those conditions. This is how-ever not the case with laws in the social sciences in which, as I have tried to show elsewhere,[12] the causal relations involved always refer to 'mixes' of intended and unintended consequences of reproduced acts. Laws in the social sciences are *historical* in character and in principle *mutable* in form. All forms of regularised social conduct, as I have argued earlier, can be analysed as involving typical sets of connections between the unacknowledged conditions of action, the rationalisation of action in the context of its purposive reflexive monitoring, and the unintended consequences of action.[13] The boundary conditions involved with laws in the social sciences include as a basic element the knowledge that actors, in a given institutional context, have about the circumstances of their action. Change in typically established connections tying unacknowledged conditions, the rationalisation of action, and unintended consequences, into modes of social reproduction results in potential alteration of the causal relations specified by a law or laws: and such alteration can stem from coming to know about such a law or laws. Once known – by those to whose conduct they relate – laws may become applied as rules and resources in the duality of structure: the very double meaning (and origin) of 'law' as both precept of action and generalisation about action draws our attention to this. To say that all laws in the social sciences are historical and in principle mutable is not, of course, to deny that there may be laws of universal form concerning physical aspects of the human organism which might be relevant to the study of social conduct.

The orthodox consensus was familiar with the mutability of laws in the social sciences in the form of 'self-fulfilling' and 'self-negating prophecies'.[14] But here the relation between the reflexive appropriation of knowledge and the conditions of action is apprehended, first, only as a 'problem' confronting the social investigator; and second, only as affecting the mobilisation of evidence for generalisations, rather than as broaching epistemological issues relevant to the very character of those generalisations themselves. Self-fulfilling or self-negating prophecies, in other words, are seen as predictions which, by the fact of their announcement or propagation, serve to create the conditions which render them valid, or alternatively produce the contrary consequence. The 'problem' they pose is that of marginalising the noxious effect which such nuisances have upon the testing of hypotheses. But if the mutable character of all social scientific generalisations is acknowledged, we must conclude that such a standpoint is quite inadequate. Rather than attempting to marginalise, and treat purely as a 'problem', the potential incorporation of social scientific theories and observations within the reflexive rationalisation of those who are their 'object' – human agents – we have to treat the phenomenon as one of essential interest and concern to the social sciences. For it becomes clear that every generalisation or form of study that is concerned with an existing society constitutes *a potential intervention within that society*: and this leads through to the tasks and aims of sociology *as critical theory*.

Ordinary language and social science

The second set of shortcomings that characterised the erstwhile consensus concern its reliance upon a now *outmoded and defective philosophy of language*. As I shall try to demonstrate, the implications of this point link directly with considerations I have just discussed. Orthodox sociology took for granted an old-established view of language: an old-established view, however, that received a new impetus from the work of Russell, the early Wittgenstein, and subsequently from logical empiricism. According to this conception, language is above all a medium of describing the world (physical or social). Language should be studied as a medium of descriptions, and an isomorphy can be discovered between the structural form of language, or certain basic features of language, and the object-worlds to which language gives access. The most developed and sophisticated version of this standpoint is to be found in Wittgenstein's *Tractatus*, according to which the basic units of language are 'pictures' of corresponding units in reality.

Wittgenstein's own rejection of his former views is only one element in a convergence of philosophies otherwise quite distinct from one another: ordinary language philosophy, Schutzian phenomenology, and contemporary hermeneutics. All these have come to the view that it is erroneous to treat language as being most aptly characterised as a medium of descriptions. Description is only one among many other things that are carried out in and through language. Language is a medium of social practice, and as such is implicated in all the variegated activities in which social actors engage. Austin's famous example is still as good as any to illustrate the point. The words uttered in a marriage ceremonial do not constitute a description of that ceremonial: they *are* part of that ceremonial. In another equally well-known example: language has as many uses, and therefore as many facets, as the tools in a tool-box.[15]

Since the orthodox consensus accepted the traditionally-established view of language, those working within it dismissed the relation between ordinary language – the language employed in the course of day-to-day conduct – and the technical metalanguages of social science as of no particular interest or importance. The object of concepts introduced or invented by the sociologist, they presumed, is to improve upon or correct, where necessary, the inadequacies of ordinary language. Ordinary language is often fuzzy and imprecise: these deficiencies can be overcome by moving over to metalanguages that embody clear and precisely formulated concepts.[16] But the assumption that the relation between ordinary language and the technical languages of social science poses no questions of any particular interest or difficulty cannot be maintained if we understand the significance of the newer philosophical conceptions of language. Ordinary or lay language cannot be just dismissed as corrigible in the light of sociological neologisms, since lay language enters into the very constitution of social activity itself.

This point has been recognised by those working from the standpoint of post-Wittgensteinian philosophy, as well as by phenomenological authors. At least two distinct interpretations of how the connections between ordinary language and the technical concepts of the social sciences should be grasped can be discerned in the literature. One is that formulated by Schutz in relation to what, borrowing a term from Weber, he calls the *postulate of adequacy*. Schutz holds that the relevances presumed by the concerns of the social scientist are different from those of lay actors in their day-to-day behaviour. In social science, we are interested in generalised, context-free knowledge; the stocks of knowledge employed by social actors in social life, on the other hand, are forms of 'cookery book knowledge', in which the emphasis is upon the practical mastery of the demands of everyday activities. The concepts invented by the social scientist thus may differ from those employed in ordinary language, because two different orders of relevances are involved. But the former have to meet a criterion of adequacy in respect of the latter. Schutz's various formulations of the postulate of adequacy are not wholly unambiguous. He seems, however, to assert that concepts of social science can only be declared to be adequate in so far as they can be translated in principle into the everyday language of lay actors.[17] If this is in fact what Schutz means, it is hardly a defensible viewpoint. In what sense does the notion of 'liquidity preference' have to be capable of translation into the ordinary language concepts of actors engaged in economic activities? There seems no reason to suppose that an evaluation of the adequacy of the concept to economic theory has anything to do with whether or not such a translation can be effected. The shortcomings of Schutz's view are also indicated by considering the behaviour of very small children, to which we might very well want to apply technical terminologies of action; if the children in question are too young to have mastered more than rudimentary linguistic skills, there would obviously be no possibility of testing the adequacy of such terminologies in terms of a translation process.

Schutz's postulate of adequacy is therefore not a satisfactory mode of approaching the connections between lay language and the concepts of social science. An alternative view is set out by Winch, and I shall suggest that this is more nearly correct. Winch holds that there is a 'logical tie' between ordinary language and the specialised languages of the social sciences, and indicates that the nature of this tie is the reverse of that entailed by Schutz's postulate of adequacy. It exists not because sociological concepts have to be capable of transposition into lay ones, but rather the opposite: because the concepts invented by the social scientist presume mastery of concepts applied by social actors themselves in the course of their conduct. Winch does not spell this out satisfactorily, and does not make it sufficiently clear that such lay concepts are typically only partially available discursively to actors; nor does he really explain why distinctive social scientific languages are needed at all, as Schutz tries to do.[18] But his main point is clear enough, and valid: a term like liquidity preference only applies to the behaviour, and consequences of behaviour, of actors who have mastered, in the sense of practical consciousness, notions like 'risk', 'profit', 'investment', etc.: notions embedded in the contexts of use of ordinary language.

The question of why social scientific metalanguages are necessary at all I shall leave to the next section, since answering it involves looking at issues to be discussed there. We cannot, however, leave matters where Winch leaves them in respect of the relation between lay language and the terminologies of social science. The 'tie' between the two is not only logical in character: it has *practical implications* which relate to the significance of reflexivity, introduced earlier. It is not just that the social analyst is dependent upon 'mutual knowledge' – founded in ordinary language categories – in order to generate characterisations of his field of investigation. There is a two-way relation involved between lay language and the language of social science, because any of the concepts introduced by sociological observers can in principle be appropriated by lay actors themselves, and applied as part of 'ordinary language' discourse. Thus it may happen that terms (a good example is the term 'economic') are appropriated by technical specialists from lay discourse, new meanings given to them, and these new meanings later returned to lay discourse. Such a phenomenon is not just of interest to the history of ideas. Again it opens out to issues that cannot effectively be marginalised in social science, in the manner normally suggested within the orthodox consensus. For the latter typically assumed an instrumental connection between sociological findings and practical 'applications' of them, a connection presumed to be logically the same as that pertaining between natural science and technology.

Revelation, mutual knowledge, common sense

To carry this discussion further, however, there is another source of weakness in the erstwhile consensus which must be analysed. This I shall identify by saying that orthodox sociology relied upon an *oversimple revelatory model of social science*, based upon naturalistic presumptions. The essentials of this model are as follows. The findings of natural science, it is assumed, are revelatory or demystifying in respect of common-sense beliefs about the physical world. What science does is to 'check up' upon common-sense views of and attitudes towards the world, showing some of them to be mistaken, and using others as a point of departure from which to develop more detailed and profound explanations of objects and events than were available in lay knowledge. The progress of science punctures the delusions of customary habitual beliefs. Now under some circumstances, it is pointed out, the findings claimed by scientists are resisted by those who choose to cling on to their established beliefs or conceptions. Those findings are rejected or ignored, either because of vested interests that are threatened by them, or because of the inertia of habit or prejudice. There are those who continue to hold that the earth is flat, no matter how conclusive the evidence to the contrary might appear to others to be.

In the orthodox consensus, this view was transferred *en bloc* to sociology. There are strong reasons to suppose (following particularly the arguments developed by Husserl in *The Crisis of European Sciences*) that this is an inadequate approach even in respect of the relation between natural science and 'common sense'; I shall be concerned here, however, only with its implications when transposed to the social sciences.

According to the revelatory model just described then, 'resistance' to the findings of social investigators takes the same form as that found in respect of some of the claims of natural science: a 'refusal to listen' in favour of an obdurate affiliation to pre-existing beliefs or ideas. But anyone who works within the social sciences is likely to be familiar with a quite different form of resistance to the claimed findings of social science. Far from resisting the findings of sociological investigations because they convey claims that people are disinclined to want to know about, such findings are resisted *on the basis that they are already well known and familiar.* Sociology, it is often argued, simply tells us what we already know – albeit often wrapped up in esoteric jargon, such that it might initially appear to be something novel. This could be called the *lay critique of sociology.*

Now sociologists are not prone to take the lay critique of their claims seriously, usually attributing it to the influence of engrained habits of thought, or prejudice. Resistance to the findings of social science they see as including resistance to the very idea of studying human social conduct in a scientific manner. But lay objections to social science are so prevalent that a more plausible defence against them is needed; and this can also be found by an elaboration of the revelatory model. The object of sociology is to check up on common-sense beliefs. Where social research reveals that what actors believe about the conditions of their own action, or other features of their society, is in fact the case, its findings will necessarily appear banal or unilluminating. It is just such instances, it is proposed, that are fastened upon by the lay critics of sociology. But there will be other instances in which social analysis will show that common-sense beliefs are in fact invalid; in such circumstances, social science will appear revelatory.

If the practitioners of social science have not been inclined to give serious attention to the lay critique of sociology, some philosophers have done so. Louch, for example, has argued that the concepts of sociology are 'unnecessary and pretentious'.[19] To explain human social activity, we need only to inquire into the reasons actors have for acting as they do. Once we have ascertained what those reasons are or were, which can be done in ordinary language, there is nothing more that can be asked. While anthropology, Louch says, can provide for us a collection of 'travellers' tales', sociology is a redundant exercise – indeed, worse than that, since the introduction of technical concepts in place of ordinary language terms can serve to obscure what was formerly evident enough to everybody, and hence can be used by the powerful as a means of dominating the less powerful. Winch flirts with the same conclusion, although he evidently regards anthropology as of more importance than Louch does. Given that he does not clearly explicate the role of technical concepts in social science, and that he precludes the possibility of formulating causal laws in respect of social conduct, it is not easy to see what a 'Winchean sociology' would look like.[20]

I wish to suggest that we should indeed take the lay critique of sociology seriously, even if in the end it cannot be sustained. For it is correct to claim that every member of society must know (in both the practical and discursive modes) a great deal about the workings of that society by virtue of his or her participation in it: or, more accurately put, that such knowledge is incorporated as an element in the production and reproduction of that society via the duality of structure. It is not at all as easy as the orthodox consensus presumed to puzzle out the conditions under which the social sciences can deliver enlightenment to the members of a society that is made the subject of study. Explanation of human social conduct in terms of reasons can certainly not be ignored by sociologists: the rationalisation of action is the fundamental component of social activity that orthodox sociology discounted. On the other hand, it should be emphasised just as strongly that the rationalisation of action is always bounded, in every sort of historical context; and it is in exploring the nature and persistence of these bounds that the tasks of social science are to be found. As I have proposed in an earlier paper, there are three types of circumstance relevant here: unconscious elements in action, practical consciousness, and the unintended consequences of action, all of which combine within the reproduction of social systems.

One further aspect of these issues must be mentioned. It is a notable feature of the 'rediscovery of ordinary language and common sense' that it has frequently eventuated in a sort of *paralysis of the critical will.* Having come to see that ordinary language and the world of the natural attitude cannot merely be disregarded or corrected by the social analyst, some authors have been tempted to conclude that no kind of critical evaluation of beliefs or practices is possible where such beliefs and practices form part of an alien cultural system. The debate surrounding Winch's discussion of Zande sorcery is, of course, well known, as is that stimulated by Garfinkel's principle of 'ethno-methodological indifference'. In these controversies, I want to argue, both sets of proponents have right on their side: but each has failed to make a vital distinction. It is right to claim that the condition of generating valid descriptions of a form of life entails being able in principle to participate in it (without necessarily having done so in practice). To know a form of life is to know a language, but in the context of the practices that are organised through the 'common sense' or tacit presuppositions against the background of which discourse is carried on. In this sense, hermeneutic tasks are integral to the social sciences. But it does not follow from such a conclusion that the beliefs and practices involved in forms of life cannot be subjected to critical assessment – including within this the critique of ideology. We must distinguish between *respect for the authenticity of belief,* as a necessary condition of any hermeneutic encounter between language-games; and the *critical evaluation of the justification of belief.* Expressed in less cumbersome fashion, we must differentiate what I call 'mutual knowledge' from what might simply be called 'common sense'.

Mutual knowledge is a necessary medium of access in the mediation of frames of meaning, and brackets the factual status of the tacit and discursive understandings shared by an observer with those whose conduct he or she seeks to characterise. It is largely because the bracketing involved in the application of mutual knowledge is usually itself tacit mutual knowledge, employed in a routine fashion, that the need to respect the authenticity of belief is not always apparent to sociological investigators. But the difference that such an orientation makes is easily seen in circumstances where it is absent. Thus according to 'physiological' views of schizophrenia, the utterances of schizophrenics are often to be regarded as merely meaningless babble. If Laing is right, however, the language of schizophrenics is meaningful, so long as we see that some of the notions that are taken for granted by the majority of the population are questioned or expressed in quite different form by schizophrenic individuals. The development of dialogue with schizop-hrenic persons, as a hermeneutic endeavour, is only possible if we accept that their utterances and behaviour may be treated 'methodologically' as authentic. To treat such utterances and be-haviour as authentic means to hold in abeyance their possible validity or falsity.

What I earlier called the 'rediscovery of ordinary language and common sense' is in these terms *the discovery of the significance of mutual knowledge*: mutual knowledge is not corrigible to the sociological observer. It is only the methodological bracketing mentioned above that separates mutual knowledge from what I want to suggest can be called 'common sense'. By 'common sense' I refer to the un-bracketing of mutual knowledge: the consideration of the logical and empirical status of belief-claims involved (tacitly and discursively) in forms of life. Common sense is corrigible in the light of claimed findings of social and natural science. The distinc-tion between mutual knowledge and common sense can be illus-trated by allusion to the Zande witchcraft controversy. Winch is right to hold that accurate characterisations of the beliefs and practices connected with Zande sorcery are 'rational' – in so far as that term means in this context that there exist internally coherent frames which both a sociological observer and the Azande draw upon in generating descriptions of witchcraft. But he is wrong in so far as he seems to infer from this that acknowledgement of the 'rationality' or authenticity of Zande witchcraft and oracular divi-nation precludes critical evaluation of the beliefs and the activities thus characterised or identified. Mutual knowledge is the necessary medium of identifying what is going on when a sorcerer places a malicious spell upon an individual in order to procure that person's death. But this is no logical bar at all to critical inquiry into the empirical grounding that can be marshalled to support the validity of the belief-claims held in relation to this practice, or into their possible ideological ramifications.

Of course, I do not want to say this provides a solution to problems of 'rationality'; it would be more accurate to say that it is where those problems begin, in respect of the rational justification of belief. However, this is not the point in the particular context of my argument here. Winch and others have demonstrated entirely convincingly the naïveté of the views of the orthodox consensus about the revelatory character of social science. I am only concerned at this juncture to propose that we should not therefore succumb passively to a paralysis of the critical will. There are many threads involved in connecting the rational justification of belief to critical theory, and I shall attempt to provide a detailed discussion of these in the book to follow this one. However, I do want to make what seems to me an important logical point, which I think shows that the critical evaluation of beliefs and practices is an inescapable feature of the discourse of the social sciences. This is that the critical assessment of common-sense beliefs does not just logically presume drawing upon mutual knowledge; *the reverse is in fact also the case*. For any characterisations of beliefs or practices made by a sociological observer logically presuppose the possibility of their justification, offered in response to the potential critical evaluation by others of the accuracy or appropriateness of those characterisations themselves.

The theory of action

As a fourth type of shortcoming of the erstwhile consensus, we may say: *orthodox sociology lacked a theory of action*. But I also want to claim that this was directly linked to a failure to make questions of power central to social theory. The lack of a theory of action, by which I mean a conception of conduct as reflexively monitored by social agents who are partially aware of the conditions of their behaviour, is first of all to be attributed to the dominance of naturalism as a philosophy of social science. In the cruder versions or applications of naturalism in sociology, conduct is explained merely as the outcome of social causes. As the most thoroughgoing attempt to produce a synthesis of a theory of action with functionalism, Parsons's 'action frame of reference' has justly been the most influential overall theoretical scheme in (English-speaking) sociology. Critics have often pointed out that, in spite of the action terminology which Parsons uses, recognisably human agents seem to elude the grasp of his scheme: the stage is set, the scripts written, the roles established, but the performers are curiously absent from the scene.[21] But the critics have not always recognised why this is so. In *The Structure of Social Action*, Parsons identifies action theory with 'voluntarism', by which he refers primarily to the purposive character of human conduct, and to the capability of actors to

choose between different goals or projects.[22] Voluntarism is interpreted against the backdrop of the 'Hobbesian problem of order', as
posing the question of how purposiveness or a diversity of wills is
compatible with 'order'. The reconciliation of the Hobbesian problem and voluntarism thus becomes the main issue that the action
frame of reference is called into existence to resolve, and this
reconciliation is achieved through regarding values simultaneously
as the basis of social consensus and as the motivational components
of the personalities of members of society. Apart from the difficulties raised by this thesis in respect of the nature and significance of
values – and of 'order'[23] – this approach does not serve to draw
attention to the importance of reasons in human conduct: that
human beings reflexively monitor their conduct via the knowledge
they have of the circumstances of their activity. Although Parsons
separates 'cognitive' from 'cathectic' symbols in his scheme, *his
social actors are not capable, knowledgeable agents.*

Of course neither naturalism nor functionalism reigned unchallenged in the post-war period. Within American sociology, those
writing from a perspective of symbolic interactionism have diverged
significantly from the emphases of the orthodox consensus, especially in respect of being concerned with the theory of action, as I
have specified it above. But 'symbolic interactionism' – Blumer's
term for a diffuse set of influences emanating from G. H. Mead – has
from the beginning been hampered by an inadequate theoretical
grasp of problems of institutional analysis and transformation. The
importance of Mead's conceptions of the development of reflexivity, of the gesture and symbol, overshadowed the fact that his
treatment of society, as represented by the 'generalised other', is a
rudimentary one. Mead's social philosophy (like Piaget's developmental psychology) lacks an understanding of the broader society as
a differentiated and historically located formation. Moreover, although Mead successfully places reflexivity at the centre of the
concerns of social philosophy and social theory, the origins of the 'I'
in the dialectic of 'I' and 'me' remain obscure and unexplained. The
major part of his concern is with the emergence of the 'me', or social
self. Hence it is perhaps not surprising that, amongst some of his
followers, the reflexive relation of 'I' and 'me' largely disappears
from view in favour of a concentration upon the social self. Once
this movement has taken place, given the dearth of an adequate
conceptualisation of institutions and institutional change, the way is

opened for the idea that symbolic interactionism and functionalism can be helpfully conjoined to one another. The former is held to deal with 'micro-sociological' issues to do with small-scale social relationships, while 'macro-sociological' issues, concerned with aspects of the institutional character of society, are left to functionalism.

In 'Agency, Structure' I have argued that the successful introduction of a theory of action into sociology cannot be achieved without a complementary re-working of the idea of structure. Such a re-working is immediately relevant to questions of ordinary language and the lay critique of sociology. The notion of the *duality of structure*, which I have accentuated as a leading theme of this book, involves recognising that the reflexive monitoring of action both draws upon and reconstitutes the institutional organisation of society. The recognition that to be a ('competent') member of society, every individual must know a great deal about the workings of that society, is precisely the main basis of the concept of the duality of structure. The thesis that the notion of human agency cannot be adequately explicated without that of structure, and vice versa, necessarily connects with the claim that temporality has to be treated as integral to a conceptual grasp of the constitution of social life. Whatever the incompatibilities between structuralist thought and history, one of the specific contributions of structuralism from Saussure onwards has been to illuminate the temporal ordering of social reproduction. The social totality cannot be best understood, as in functionalist conceptions of the whole, as a given 'presence', but as relations of presence and absence recursively ordered. The strictures of structuralist authors against philosophies and forms of social theory that accord primacy to the subject may be readily understandable against the background of Cartesianism; and it is essential to grasp the importance of the thesis that we have to reject any conception of a subject that is 'transparent to itself'. But here we also approach the limitations of structuralist theories, which are riddled with dualisms inherited from Saussure. One of these dualisms is that between structure and event, usually overlapping directly with that of unconscious/conscious. The prominence of these oppositions has effectively foreclosed the possibility of generating a satisfactory account of human agency from within structuralist thought. The supersession of the dualism of structure and event, within sociological theory at any rate, is most readily approached –

or so I want to claim – by introducing a distinction between system and structure, the former being ordered in terms of the reproduction of spatially and temporally situated events, the latter being both the medium and outcome of such reproduction. This is immediately connected to the rejection of the polarity of unconscious/conscious, since a theory of agency must recognise the basic significance of practical consciousness in social reproduction. Practical consciousness is not 'consciousness' as ordinarily understood in structuralist theories; but it is also easily distinguishable from the unconscious in any sense of that term.

Structuralism and functionalism betray their common origins in respect of concepts of power with which they have often been associated. For many authors working within those traditions, if a concept of power has been developed at all, power is regarded as a phenomenon of a society or collectivity confronting the individual. This was already clear in Durkheim, who in the places where he addressed problems of power, tended to do so in terms comparable to those in which he sought to analyse the constraining influence of social facts.[24] Those authors writing within the philosophy of action, on the other hand, have either regarded power as the capability of an individual agent to accomplish his will, or (especially in the literature influenced by Austin and the later Wittgenstein) have largely ignored issues of power altogether. In this regard, there is a point of direct contact between the philosophy of action and 'normative functionalism', *each of which, in rather different ways, have tended to treat norms or conventions as exemplifying 'the social'.* Weber's definition of power, as the chance of an agent to secure his will even against the resistance of others, has probably been the most frequently utilised in the literature. I criticise this in two respects. On the one hand, it reflects Weber's subjectivist methodological position, and leads to the dualism of action and structure that I have insisted has to be overcome; on the other, considered solely from the point of view of the connection between power and agency, it does not bite deeply enough. For the notion of human action logically implies that of power, understood as transformative capacity: 'action' only exists when an agent has the capability of intervening, or refraining from intervening, in a series of events so as to be able to influence their course. The introduction of a theory of action into sociology thus entails regarding power as just as essential and integral to social interaction as conventions are.

But the same considerations which apply to the theory of agency generally also apply to power: we have to relate power as a resource drawn upon by agents in the production and reproduction of interaction to the structural characteristics of society. Neither aspect of power is more 'basic' than the other.

The social and natural sciences

The fifth type of shortcoming of the orthodox consensus has been much discussed in recent years, but I want to claim that its implications cannot be adequately understood apart from the issues I have referred to in the preceding sections. This fifth point, which connects back to themes I introduced at the beginning of the paper, is: orthodox sociology *was closely tied to a positivistic model of natural science*. The term 'positivism' has become so indiscriminately employed[25] that it is important to point out that, in the context of the ideas informing the erstwhile consensus, it can be used in a fairly definite sense: to refer to what some philosophers have labelled the 'received model' of natural science. The received model was strongly conditioned by liberalised versions of logical positivism, as worked out by Carnap and others; but it was further consolidated and elaborated by members of the 'Berlin group' (especially Hempel), and by indigenous currents of American philosophy (as represented, for instance, by Nagel).

I have already pointed to the important, if never entirely happy, conjunction that was effected between this approach to the philosophy of science and functionalism. But the influence of naturalistic standpoints, of course, has stretched considerably more broadly than this: many authors who have been either sceptical about, or directly critical of, functionalism have presumed that the received model of natural science is appropriate for sociology. Logical empiricist conceptions of natural science, particularly the hypothetico-deductive method as originally advocated by Hempel and Oppenheim, achieved widespread acceptance.[26] Such conceptions were employed to suggest that social science should aim towards the (admittedly distant) goal of formulating deductively related hierarchies of laws; and that explanation in both natural and social science consists in the deductive subsumption of an observation or event under a law.[27] But the first cannot be regarded as an appropriate general interpretation of the nomological form of the natural sciences, and has even less relevance to sociology, given the historical character of laws of human social conduct: the laws of the social sciences are in principle open to the 'environment' to which they refer. In the light of these considerations, the emphasis that explanation is the deductive relating of an event to a law appears as peculiarly dogmatic and restrictive – even if applied in respect of the natural sciences, but particularly within the sphere of the social sciences.

Explanation, most broadly conceived, can be more appropriately treated as the clearing up of puzzles or queries; seen from this point of view, explanation is the making intelligible of observations or events that cannot be readily interpreted within the context of an existing theory or frame of meaning. The distinction between description and explanation then becomes in some part contextual in character: the identification or description of a phenomenon, by its incorporation within a given frame of meaning, is explanatory where that identification helps to resolve a query. Such a broad notion of explanation relates explanatory queries in science quite closely to everyday queries. In neither case is there a logically closed form assumed by explanation: that is to say, *all attempts to satisfy queries presuppose a contextual 'etcetera clause'*, whereby an inquiry is deemed to be concluded 'for present purposes'.

Now this of course explains very little about the nature of explanation. In particular, it does not show what are the characteristics of a 'satisfactory' or valid' explanation of a phenomenon, as compared to others that might be judged to be defective.[28] I do not intend to take up this issue here. What I do want to stress is that the claim that explanation is contextual does not, as proponents of the orthodox consensus might suppose, imply advocating a 'soft' or humanistic version of sociology. In particular, there can be no reversion to the opposition of *verstehen* and *erklären* which, in the hermeneutic tradition, served to differentiate the tasks of the social sciences from those of the natural sciences. For it is a notable feature of the development of hermeneutics that most authors who have proposed that the social or human sciences are distinctively concerned with 'meanings' or 'cultural products', have accepted a positivistic model of natural science. Dilthey, as is well known, was strongly influenced by J. S. Mill's *Logic,* and accepted the latter's overall characterisation of natural science as a foil for his conception of the human sciences. In more recent times, Winch's account of the philosophical basis of the social science appears to rely upon the view of natural science developed by the logical empiricists; and Habermas's elaboration of his notion of knowledge-constitutive interests still seems to retain elements of a positivistic model of science, thus in some part recapitulating the *verstehen/erklären* differentiation.[29]

The main implication of the ideas I have set out in this paper is that, in the current phase of social theory, we are involved in rotating two axes simultaneously: that of our understanding of the character of human social activity, and that of the logical form of natural science. *These are not entirely separate endeavours, but feed from a pool of common problems.* For just as it has become apparent that hermeneutic questions are integral to a philosophical understanding of natural science, so the limitations of conceptions of the social sciences that exclude causal analysis have become equally evident. We cannot treat the natural and social sciences as *two independently constituted forms of intellectual endeavour,* whose characteristics can be separately determined, and which then subsequently can be brought together and compared. Philosophers and practitioners of sociology must remain attentive to the progress of the natural sciences; but any philosophy of natural science in turn presupposes a definite stance towards problems of social theory.

Notes and References

Introduction

1. Anthony Giddens, *Capitalism and Modern Social Theory* (Cambridge University Press, 1971).
2. Anthony Giddens, *New Rules of Sociological Method* (London: Hutchinson, 1976).
3. Anthony Giddens, *Studies in Social and Political Theory* (London: Hutchinson, 1977).
4. William James, *A Pluralistic Universe* (New York: Longman, 1943) p. 254.
5. For a discussion, see Alvin I. Goldman, *A Theory of Human Action* (Englewood Cliffs: Prentice-Hall, 1970) pp. 123–4.
6. See also Giddens, *New Rules of Sociological Method*, pp. 144ff.
7. Giddens, *Studies in Social and Political Theory*, pp. 23–4.

Chapter 1

1. The nature and extent of the influence of Durkheim over Saussure has been a matter of some dispute. See, for example, E. F. K. Koerner, *Ferdinand de Saussure* (Braunschweig: Hunold, 1973) pp. 45–71.
2. Cf., for example, Barthes: 'I have been engaged in a series of structural analyses, all of which are concerned to define a number of extra-linguistic "languages"...' Roland Barthes, *Essais critiques* (Paris: Seuil, 1964) p. 155.
3. *New Rules of Sociological Method* (London: Hutchinson, 1976); 'Functionalism: après la lutte', in *Studies in Social and Political Theory* (London: Hutchinson, 1977).
4. Ferdinand de Saussure, *Course in General Linguistics* (London: Peter Owen, 1960) p. 14.
5. There has been much subsequent debate about this issue. Some have accepted Saussure's view of the relation of semiology and linguistics; others have reversed it, taking semiology to be derivative of linguistics.

Except when referring to Saussure, I shall use the term 'semiotics' rather than 'semiology'.

6. Saussure, *Course in General Linguistics*, p. 68.

7. Ibid., p. 120.

8. Ibid., pp. 83 and 85.

9. However, critical editions of the *Cours* produced by de Mauro, Engler and Godel have demonstrated, among other things, that Saussure did not claim a priority for synchronic linguistics over historical linguistics.

10. Cf. for a relevant recent discussion, David Lewis, *Convention* (Cambridge, Mass.: Harvard University Press, 1969).

11. Saussure, *Course in General Linguistics*, p. 67.

12. Emile Benveniste, 'The nature of the linguistic sign', *Problems in General Linguistics* (Florida: University of Miami Press, 1971) p. 44.

13. Cf. Paul Ricoeur, *Interpretation Theory: Discourse and the Surplus of Meaning* (Fort Worth: Texas Christian University Press, 1976) pp. 6ff.

14. Frederic Jameson, *The Prison-House of Language* (Princeton University Press, 1974) pp. 32–3.

15. C. K. Ogden and I. A. Richards, *The Meaning of Meaning* (London: Routledge, 1960) pp. 5–8.

16. Noam Chomsky, *Current Issues in Linguistic Theory* (The Hague: Mouton, 1964) p. 23.

17. For Lévi-Strauss's early thoughts on Durkheim, see his article 'French sociology', in Georges Gurvitch and Wilbert E. Moore, *Twentieth Century Sociology* (New York: Philosophical Library, 1945). On Durkheim and Lévi-Strauss, cf. Simon Clarke, 'The origins of Lévi-Strauss's structuralism', *Sociology*, vol. 12 (1978). See also Yvan Simonis, *Claude Lévi-Strauss ou la passion de l'inceste* (Paris: Aubier, 1968) pp. 81ff.

18. Claude Lévi-Strauss, *Structural Anthropology* (London: Allen Lane, 1968) p. 62.

19. Ibid., p. 280. Compare also Jean Piaget, *Structuralism* (London: Routledge, 1971) upon which Lévi-Strauss has commented approvingly.

20. Lévi-Strauss, *The Elementary Structures of Kinship* (Boston: Beacon Press, 1969) p. 98.

21. *Structural Anthropology*, p. 82.

22. Interview with Lévi-Strauss, *Le Monde*, 13 Jan 1968. See also *The Raw and the Cooked* (New York: Harper and Row, 1969) pp. 31ff.

23. Cf. Ino Rossi, 'Structuralism as a scientific method', in Rossi, *The Unconscious in Culture* (New York: Dutton, 1974) p. 77.

24. Lévi-Strauss, *The Savage Mind* (University of Chicago Press, 1966) p. 252. See also the comments on psychoanalysis in *L'Homme nu* (Paris: Plon, 1971) pp. 561ff.

25. *The Savage Mind*, p. 256.

26. Lévi-Strauss nevertheless frequently emphasises the inescapability of beginning from historical study: 'Even the analysis of synchronic structures . . . requires constant recourse to history. By showing institutions in the process of transformation, history alone makes it possible

to abstract the structure which underlies the many manifestations and remains permanent throughout a succession of events.' *Structural Anthropology*, vol. I (London: Allen Lane, 1968) p. 21. This is said partly in criticism of Malinowski. See also Lévi-Strauss's inaugural lecture, in the second volume of *Structural Anthropology* (London: Allen Lane, 1977) where frequent nods are made to the historians. A typical later statement is the following: 'I am not therefore rejecting history. On the contrary, structural analysis accords history a paramount place, the place that rightfully belongs to that irreducible contingency without which necessity would be inconceivable.' *From Honey to Ashes* (London: Cape, 1973) pp. 474–5. On the other hand, Lévi-Strauss has never ceased to hold that it is the aim of anthropology 'to elucidate, by a kind of backward course, all that ... |myths| owe to historical process and to conscious thought' (vol. I, p. 23). Characteristic is Lévi-Strauss's reading of Marx's aphorism: 'Men make their own history, but not under conditions of their own choosing' which, Lévi-Strauss says, 'justifies, first, history, and, second anthropology' (ibid.); that is to say, the conscious and the unconscious. But another reading would be that human social life is enacted under conditions of bounded and alienated understanding, as expressed in both unacknowledged conditions and unintended consequences of action.

27. Ibid., p. 236, Cf. also G. Charbonnier, *Conversations with Claude Lévi-Strauss* (London: Cape, 1969) pp. 39ff.
28. Lévi-Strauss, 'J.-J. Rousseau, fondateur des sciences des hommes', in *Jean-Jacques Rousseau* (Neuchâtel: Editions de la Baconnière, 1962).
29. 'Functionalism: après la lutte'.
30. *L'Homme nu*, p. 572.
31. Ibid., p. 560.
32. *The Raw and the Cooked*, p. 11.
33. For a relevant discussion, cf. Maurice Godelier, 'Mythe et histoire: réflexions sur les fondements de la pensée sauvage', *Annales*, vol. 26 (1971).
34. Pierre Bourdieu, *Outline of a Theory of Practice* (Cambridge University Press, 1977) p. 5; cf. Jean-Paul Sartre, *Critique of Dialectical Reason* (London: New Left Books, 1976) pp. 479ff.
35. Cf. Paul Ricoeur, 'Structure and hermeneutics', in *The Conflict of Interpretations* (Evanston: Northwestern University Press, 1974). Ricoeur remains one of the most penetrating critics of structuralism. On the other hand, even in his later publications he confines his remarks on structuralism mainly to Saussure, the Formalists and Lévi-Strauss. Ricoeur, it seems to me, gives too much and too little to structuralism, thus defined. Too much, because he seems prepared to accept major features of structuralist thought *en bloc*, within defined limits; too little, because in trying to fit structuralist analysis within a more encompassing hermeneutics, he does not sufficiently take into account the radical nature of the challenge that structuralist thought poses for hermeneutic phenomenology. Some of the differences between phenomenologists and structuralists were aired at a symposium

at Cerisy-la-Salle in 1966, reported in J. Ricardou, *Les chemins actuels de la critique* (Paris: Plon, 1967).

36. George Steiner, *After Babel. Aspects of Language and Translation* (Oxford University Press, 1975); cf. also Dufrenne, who confronts 'the problem posed by the extraordinary diversity of languages', pointing out that 'the arbitrary character of language, having been shown to be of comparatively little significance at the level of the elements of a language, reasserts itself quite definitely at the level of the language taken as a whole', Mikel Dufrenne, *Language and Philosophy* (New York: Greenwood, 1968) p. 35.

37. Paul Ricoeur, *Interpretation Theory: Discourse and the Surplus of Meaning*, p. 86.

38. *The Raw and the Cooked*, p. 13.

39. Jonathan Culler, *Structuralist Poetics* (London: Routledge, 1975) p. 48; cf. also Tzvetan Todorov, *Poétique de la prose* (Paris: Seuil, 1971) p. 247.

40. Cf. Stanley Diamond, 'The myth of structuralism', in Rossi, *The Unconscious in Culture*.

41. R. Jakobson, 'Principes de phonologie historique', in N. S. Trubetskoy, *Principes de phonologie* (Paris: Klincksieck, 1964). According to Lévi-Strauss, the distinction between synchrony and diachrony 'is the very aspect of the Saussurian doctrine from which modern structuralism, with Trubetskoy and Jakobson, has most resolutely diverged, and about which modern documents show that the master's thought has at times been forced and schematised by the editors of the *Course*'. *Structural Anthropology*, vol. 2, p. 16.

42. Lévi-Strauss frequently seems to assimilate the diachronic and syntagmatic. There are examples of this in *Structural Anthropology*, and in the *Mythologiques* volumes.

43. Roland Barthes, *Elements of Semiology* (London: Cape, 1967) pp. 27ff.

44. Lévi-Strauss, *Tristes Tropiques* (New York: Atheneum, 1967) p. 62.

45. *Le Cru et le cuit* (Paris: Plon, 1964) p. 20.

46. Jacques Derrida, *L'Écriture et la différence* (Paris: Seuil, 1967) p. 411.

47. Derrida, *Positions* (Paris: Éditions de Minuit, 1972) p. 28.

48. Derrida, *Speech and Phenomena* (Evanston: Northwestern University Press, 1973).

49. On 'pyramid', an allusion taken from Hegel, and 'tomb', see Derrida, 'Le puits et la pyramide', in *Marges de la philosophie* (Paris: Minuit, 1972).

50. Ibid., p. 48.

51. Derrida, *L'Écriture et la différence*, p. 50. Derrida writes approvingly of Lévi-Strauss's criticisms of those who have accorded history an undue place in social science and philosophy. History here 'has always been the accomplice of a teleological and eschatological metaphysics: that is to say, paradoxically, of that philosophy of presence to which it is believed that history can be opposed' (ibid., p. 425). On the other hand, Derrida adds, Lévi-Strauss only replaces one type of

metaphysics of presence by another: in spite of the latter's disclaimers, a type of classical formalism.

52. Julia Kristeva, *Semiotike: Recherches pour une sémanalyse* (Paris: Seuil, 1969).

53. Kristeva, *La révolution du langage poétique* (Paris: Seuil, 1974) p. 33.

54. Ibid., pp. 114ff.

55. Cf. Stanley Cavell, *Must We Mean What We Say?* (Cambridge University Press, 1975) p. xix and passim.

56. Ricoeur, 'Structure, word, event', in *The Conflict of Interpretations.*

57. See 'Signature, événement, contexte', whose title echoes that of Ricoeur's article, in Derrida, *Marges de la philosophie* (Paris: Éditions de Minuit, 1972); this is translated in *Glyph*, vol. I (1977). (See also footnote 67).

58. Cf. Derrida's comment, made in the course of discussing trends in philosophy in France, that the object of contemporary philosophy is 'neither to abolish nor to destroy meaning. It is rather a question of determining the possibility of *meaning* deriving from a "formal" organisation that itself has no meaning...', *Marges de la philosophie*, p. 161.

59. In this sense, Wittgenstein is not well served by some of his followers, who have effectively translated his emphases into a type of idealism: most notably, Winch.

60. Cf. the various discussions in Gareth Evans and John McDowell, *Truth and Meaning: Essays on Semantics* (Oxford: Clarendon Press, 1976). But see also Putnam's analysis in *Meaning and the Moral Sciences* (London: Routledge, 1978) pp. 97ff.

61. 'Signature, événement, contexte', pp. 181–2.

62. Ibid., p. 183.

63. Derrida says (*L'Écriture et la différence*, p. 413) that it is because we cannot finally escape metaphysics altogether that the signified cannot be done away with: 'For the *paradox* is that the metaphysical reduction of the sign needs the opposition [of signifier/signified] which it reduces.' Cf. also Derrida's comments in an interview with Lucette Finas, in Lucette Finas *et al., Écarts* (Paris: Fayard, 1973) pp. 303–12.

64. Ricoeur, 'The question of the subject', in *The Conflict of Interpretations*, p. 244.

65. Jacques Lacan, 'The agency of the letter in the unconscious', *Écrits* (London: Tavistock, 1977) p. 166.

66. Julia Kristeva (interview with J.-C. Coquet), 'Sémanalyse: conditions d'une sémiotique scientifique', *Semiotica*, vol. 4 (1972) pp. 328–9.

67. Cf. Searle's comments on Derrida's discussion of Austin in 'Signature, événement, contexte', in 'Reiterating the differences: a reply to Derrida', *Glyph*, vol. I, p. 202.

68. Cf. my *New Rules of Sociological Method*, pp. 81–4, for further discussion.

69. As expounded by Gadamer in particular. Hans-Georg Gadamer, *Truth and Method* (London: Sheed and Ward, 1975). Gadamer, however, rejects the thesis (which he associates with Valéry) that

'every encounter with [a] work has the rank and justification of a new production. This seems to me an untenable hermeneutic nihilism ... [Valéry] transfers to reader and interpreter the authority of absolute creation which he himself no longer desires to exert' (p. 85).

70. *The Raw and the Cooked*, p. 18. The latter phrase is strikingly reminiscent of Gadamer.

71. 'Signature, événement, contexte', p. 182.

72. One focus of debate is that involving Gadamer, Betti and Hirsch. For Hirsch's latest contributions, see E. D. Hirsch, *The Aims of Interpretation* (Chicago University Press, 1976).

73. Culler, *Structuralist Poetics*, p. 126.

74. Ward Goodenough, *Description and Comparison in Cultural Anthropology* (Chicago: Aldine, 1970).

75. Goodenough, 'Cultural anthropology and linguistics', in Dell Hymes (ed.), *Language in Culture and Society* (New York: Harper, 1964) p. 36.

76. *New Rules of Sociological Method*.

77. Kristeva writes: 'The text is not a linguistic *phenomenon*; in other words, structured signification does not appear in a linguistic corpus as a single level of structure ... The process of meaning generation can be grasped in two ways: 1. the creation of the material of language, and 2. the creation of the "I" which is in a position to make meaning appear.' *Semiotike*, p. 280.

78. Michel Foucault, 'What is an author?', in *Language, Counter-Memory, Practice* (Oxford: Blackwell, 1977) p. 116; cf. Williams's remarks on the origins of the term 'author', in Raymond Williams's, *Marxism and Literature* (Oxford University Press, 1977) pp. 192–3.

79. Relevant to this is the somewhat comic exchange between Derrida and Searle in *Glyph*, vols. I and II, in which Derrida goes through absolute contortions in order to defend himself against Searle without having to employ the terminology, 'What I meant was . . .'.

80. Cf. Frederic Jameson, 'Imaginary and symbolic in Lacan: Marxism, psychoanalytic criticism, and the problem of the subject', *Yale French Studies*, no. 55/6 (1977), p. 382 and *passim*.

81. Cf. 'Functionalism: après la lutte'.

82. Cf. Henri Lefebvre, *L'idéologie structuraliste* (Paris: Anthropos, 1971). Still one of the more interesting discussions of structuralism and Marxism is Lucien Sebag, *Marxisme et structuralisme* (Paris: Payot, 1964).

83. Charbonnier, *Conversations*, p. 39.

84. Umberto Eco, *A Theory of Semiotics* (London: Macmillan, 1977) pp. 4ff.

Chapter 2

1. Most of the concepts I discuss here have been introduced in a preliminary way in *New Rules of Sociological Method*, and in 'Notes on the theory of structuration', in *Studies in Social and Political Theory*.

2. See, for instance, G. E. M. Anscombe, *Intention* (Oxford: Blackwell, 1963); Theodore Mischel, *Human Action* (New York: Academic Press, 1969); Richard Taylor, *Action and Purpose* (Englewood Cliffs: Prentice-Hall, 1966); Arthur C. Danto, *Analytical Philosophy of Action* (Cambridge University Press, 1973).

3. Emile Durkheim, *The Rules of Sociological Method* (London: Collier-Macmillan, 1964) pp. xlvii– xlix.

4. Talcott Parsons, *The Structure of Social Action* (Glencoe: Free Press, 1949); cf. 'Durkheim's contribution to the theory of integration of social systems', in Kurt H. Wolff, *Emile Durkheim* (New York: Harper, 1964).

5. In Hollis's terms, however, the 'action frame of reference' would constitute a form of 'weak actionism', defined as a view which 'takes the actor to be plastic and his actions to be caused by the normative structures requiring them'. Martin Hollis, *Models of Man* (Cambridge University Press, 1977) p. 85.

6. Louis Althusser and Etienne Balibar, *Reading Capital* (London: New Left Books, 1970) p. 180.

7. E. Paci, *The Function of the Sciences and the Meaning of Man* (Evanston: Northwestern University Press, 1972). For an attempt to place Paci's writings in a general sociological context, see Barry Smart, *Sociology, Phenomenology and Marxian Analysis* (London: Routledge, 1976).

8. In non-Marxist sociology, Berger and Luckmann's *Social Construction of Reality* (London: Allen Lane, 1967) is closest to this type of standpoint. Their approach, however, completely lacks a conception of the critique of ideology. Moreover, notwithstanding the interest of some of their formulations, their work remains close to Parsonianism in stressing the centrality of 'internalisation' of values as crucial to the existence of 'order'.

9. Marx, *Grundrisse* (Harmondsworth: Pelican, 1973) p. 712.

10. Charles M. Sherover, *Heidegger, Kant and Time* (Bloomington: Indiana University Press, 1971) p. 284.

11. See *New Rules of Sociological Method*, chap. 2.

12. This is pointed out by Schutz. Alfred Schutz, *The Phenomenology of the Social World* (London: Heinemann, 1972) pp. 8ff. For the conception of *durée*, see Henri Bergson, *Time and Free Will* (London: Swan Sonnenschein, 1910).

13. *New Rules of Sociological Method*, p. 75; I have slightly amended the original formulation.

14. See, for example, R. S. Peters, *The Concept of Motivation* (London: Routledge, 1958) pp. 12ff.

15. A mistake which I made; *New Rules of Sociological Method*, p. 75. I did not see that the view that the 'could have done otherwise' of agency is logically distinct from the obverse of any condition of social constraint or compulsion contradicts the case I made later that the concept of action logically entails that of power.

16. J. L. Austin, 'Three ways of spilling ink', *The Philosophical Review*, vol. 75 (1966).

17. Peter Marsh, Elisabeth Rosser and Rom Harré, *The Rules of Disorder* (London: Routledge, 1978) p. 15.

18. Cf. Harold Garfinkel, *Studies in Ethnomethodology* (Englewood Cliffs: Prentice-Hall, 1967).

19. For a discussion of this in the context of Durkheim's sociology, see my 'The "individual" in the writings of Emile Durkheim', in *Studies in Social and Political Theory*.

20. Garfinkel, *Studies in Ethnomethodology*: see also Garfinkel's contribution to Roy Turner, *Ethnomethodology* (Harmondsworth: Penguin, 1974) pp. 15–18.

21. Cf. Jerome Neu, 'Genetic explanation in *Totem and Taboo*', in Richard Wollheim, *Freud, a Collection of Critical Essays* (New York: Doubleday, 1974).

22. Cyril Barrett, *Wittgenstein: Lectures and Conversations* (Oxford: Blackwell, 1967) pp. 42ff.

23. A well-known example discussed by Davidson is a good case in point. I move a switch, turn on a light, illuminate the room, and at the same time alert a prowler. Davidson's interest in this is purely confined to the problem of action descriptions: do I do four different things, or only one that can be described in different ways? 'Actions, reasons and causes', *The Journal of Philosophy*, vol. 60 (1963). One of the few philosophical discussions of action that approaches a concern with unintended consequences is Alvin I. Goldman, *A Theory of Human Action* (Englewood Cliffs: Prentice-Hall, 1970) pp. 22ff, where he analyses the 'generation' of acts by other acts or 'act-tokens'.

24. 'Functionalism: après la lutte', pp. 106–9.

25. In some circumstances it is important to recognise a distinction between unintended and unacknowledged consequences of action. But this distinction concerns the agency/structure relation primarily in so far as what is unintended 'returns' to form conditions of action that operate 'prior' to practical or discursive consciousness. The distinction between 'intended' and 'known' consequences of action is of course covered in the differentiation between the reflexive monitoring and the rationalisation of conduct.

26. R. K. Merton, 'Manifest and latent functions', in *Social Theory and Social Structure* (New York: Free Press, 1957); for comments see 'Functionalism: après la lutte'.

27. For example, Lévi-Strauss's formulation of the major features of structural analysis in *Structural Anthropology*, vol. I.

28. Raymond Firth, *Elements of Social Organisation* (London: Watts, 1956) pp. 30 and 39 (italics not in original).

29. *Structural Anthropology*, vol. I, p. 271.

30. The conception of structure I advance seems to me close to that advocated by Bauman, save that he uses 'structure' as more or less synonymous with 'culture'. Zygmunt Bauman, *Culture as Praxis* (London: Routledge, 1973).

31. See, for instance, John R. Searle, *Speech Acts* (Cambridge University Press, 1969), pp. 33ff. Raymond D. Gumb, *Rule-governed Linguistic*

Behaviour (The Hague: Mouton, 1972) reaches the same conclusion that I do, in respect of language rules: 'all linguistic rules have both a regulative and a constitutive aspect' (p. 25). For other relevant considerations, see Joan Safran Ganz, *Rules, a Systematic Study* (The Hague: Mouton, 1971); and Hubert Schwyzer, 'Rules and practices', *Philosophical Review*, vol. 78 (1969).

32. See Paul Ziff, *Semantic Analysis* (Ithaca: Cornell University Press, 1960); also Pierre Bourdieu, *Outline of a Theory of Practice* (Cambridge University Press, 1977). It might be noted that the notion of rule appears frequently in the symbolic interactionist literature, but with very little cross-referencing to the parallel literature in philosophy to do with rules. See, for instance, the various contributions to George J. McCall *et al.*, *Social Relationships* (Chicago: Aldine, 1970).

33. Michael Oakeshott, *Rationalism in Politics* (London: Methuen, 1967).

34. Wittgenstein, *The Blue and Brown Books* (Oxford: Blackwell, 1972) p. 25.

35. Wittgenstein, *Philosophical Investigations* (Oxford: Blackwell, 1972) pp. 80–1.

36. Cf. Georg Lukács, *Die Zerstörung der Vernunft* (Berlin: Aufbau-Verlag, 1965).

37. The nature of Weber's conceptualisation of power is still a matter of some controversy. Weber says 'Macht bedeutet jede Chance, innerhalb einer sozialen Beziehung den eigenen Willen auch gegen Widerstreben durchzusetzen, gleichviel worauf diese Chance beruht' (*Wirtschaft und Gesellschaft* (Tübingen: Möhr, 1956) p. 28). Although most English translations render *Chance* as 'capacity', it has been argued that, understood as 'chance' or 'possibility', the definition is less individualistic than appears to be the case. See Niklas Luhmann, *Macht* (Stüttgart: Enke, 1975).

38. '"Power" in the writings of Talcott Parsons', in *Studies in Social and Political Theory*.

39. Ernst Bloch, *A Philosophy of the Future* (New York: Herber, 1970) p. viii.

40. Georges Gurvitch, *Déterminismes sociaux et liberté humaine* (Paris: Presses Universitaires, 1955).

41. G. L. S. Shackle, *Decision, Order and Time* (Cambridge University Press, 1969).

42. Cf. Howard S. Becker, *Sociological Work* (London: Allen Lane, 1971).

43. See Nicholas Abercrombie and Bryan S. Turner, 'The dominant ideology thesis', *British Journal of Sociology*, vol. 29 (1978).

44. For one of the most acute pieces of research reporting around this theme, see Paul Willis, *Learning to Labour* (Westmead: Saxon House, 1977).

45. Alfred Schutz, *Reflections on the Problem of Relevance* (New Haven: Yale University Press, 1970) pp. 120ff and *passim*.

46. Amitai Etzioni, *The Active Society* (New York: Free Press, 1968).

47. Talcott Parsons, *The Social System* (London: Routledge, 1951).

48. Ludwig von Bertalanffy, *General System Theory* (London: Allen Lane, 1968) p. xvii. See also John W. Sutherland, *Systems: Analysis, Administration, and Architecture* (New York: Van Nostrand, 1975).

49. For comments on this, see Russell L. Ackoff, 'General system theory and systems research: contrasting conceptions of system science', in Mihajlo D. Mesarovic (ed.), *Views on General Systems Theory* (New York: Wiley, 1964).

50. Cf. Jürgen Habermas and Niklas Luhmann, *Theorie der Gesellschaft oder Sozialtechnologie?* (Frankfurt: Suhrkamp, 1973). Bertalanffy stresses the importance of approaching systems theory with 'humanistic concerns' in mind, recognising the very real 'fear that system theory is indeed the ultimate step towards mechanisation and devaluation of man and towards technocratic society' (*General System Theory*, p. xxi). See also Bertalanffy, *Perspectives on General System Theory* (New York: Brazillier, 1975).

51. Richard Taylor, 'Comments on a mechanistic conception of purposefulness', and 'Purposeful and non-purposeful behaviour: a rejoinder', *Philosophy of Science*, vol. 17 (1950).

52. See, for example, W. Ross Ashby, *An Introduction to Cybernetics* (London: Chapman and Hall, 1956).

53. Walter Buckley, *Sociology and Modern Systems Theory* (Englewood Cliffs: Prentice-Hall, 1967).

54. See M. L. Minsky, *Computation, Finite and Infinite Machines* (Englewood Cliffs: Prentice-Hall, 1967).

55. F. G. Varela *et al.*, 'Autopoiesis: the organisation of living systems, its characterisation and a model', *Systems*, vol. 5 (1974). See also M. Gardner, 'On cellular automata, self-reproduction, the Garden of Eden, and the game "life"', *Scientific American*, no. 224 (1971); M. Zeleny and N. A. Pierre, 'Simulation of self-renewing systems', in E. Jantsch and C. H. Waddington (eds), *Evolution and Consciousness* (Reading: Addison-Wesley, 1976).

56. G. Spencer Brown, *The Laws of Form* (London: Allen and Unwin, 1969). I have also drawn upon an unpublished paper by Hayward R. Alker, 'The new cybernetics of self-renewing systems', Center for International Studies, MIT.

57. David Lockwood, 'Social integration and system integration', in George K. Zollschan and W. Hirsch, *Exploitations in Social Change* (London: Routledge, 1964). I do not, however, understand the differentiation in the same way as Lockwood.

58. 'Functionalism: après la lutte', pp. 114ff.

59. Cf. Buckley, *Sociology and Modern Systems Theory*.

60. Anthony Giddens, *Class Structure of the Advanced Societies* (London: Hutchinson, 1973).

61. Cf. 'A theory of suicide', in *Studies in Social and Political Theory*.

62. See, in particular, Erving Goffman, *Frame Analysis* (Harmondsworth: Penguin, 1975).

63. In previous discussions, I called the third dimension of interaction a 'moral' one, having in mind Durkheim's analysis of moral obligations.

I now regard this as better described in terms of 'normative sanctions'. treating moral norms as one type of norms.

64. Peter Winch. *The Idea of a Social Science* (London: Routledge. 1958) pp. 32–3.

65. Alasdair MacIntyre, 'The idea of a social science', *Aristotelian Society Supplement*, vol. 41 (1967).

66. Cf. Astri Heen Wold, *Decoding Oral Language* (London: Academic Press, 1968).

67. Ziff. *Semantic Analysis*. See also Ziff. 'About what an adequate grammar could not do'. in *Philosophical Turnings* (Ithaca: Cornell University Press. 1966); Yehoshua Bar-Hillel. *Language and Information* (Reading: Addison-Wesley, 1964) pp. 175–6.

68. Cf. Andrew McPherson *et al.*, 'Social explanation and political accountability: two related problems with a single solution' (unpublished paper, Centre for Educational Sociology, University of Edinburgh).

69. Parsons, *The Social System*.

70. Cf. 'The "individual" in the writings of Emile Durkheim'. in *Studies in Social and Political Theory*.

71. *New Rules of Sociological Method*.

72. Cf. Bertrand Russell, *Power: a New Social Analysis* (London: Allen and Unwin) p. 25.

73. Dahl's earliest version of this view was that 'A has power over B to the extent that he can get B to do something that B would not otherwise do' (Robert A. Dahl, 'The concept of power'. *Behavioural Science*. vol. 2 (1957)). But this was subsequently amended and elaborated.

74. Peter Bachrach and Morton S. Baratz, 'The two faces of power', *American Political Science Review*, vol. 56 (1962); 'Decisions and non-decisions: an analytical framework', *American Political Science Review*, vol. 57 (1963); *Power and Poverty* (New York: Oxford University Press, 1970).

75. Steven Lukes, *Power, a Radical View* (London: Macmillan. 1974).

76. W. B. Gallie. 'Essentially contested concepts'. *Proceedings of the Aristotelian Society*, vol. 56 (1955–6). Gallie gives (pp. 171–2) five criteria of 'essential contestedness'.

77. Lukes. *Power, a Radical View*. pp. 21–2.

78. Lukes discusses this only cursorily, and to my mind inadequately, on p. 33 of his book. For an attempt to use Lukes's work without connecting power logically to interest, cf. Peter Abell, 'The many faces of power and liberty: revealed preference, autonomy and teleological explanation', *Sociology*, vol. 11 (1977); and commentary in K. Thomas, 'Power and autonomy: further comments on the many faces of power', *Sociology*, vol. 12 (1978).

79. 'Power and structure' in Lukes, *Essays in Social Theory* (London: Macmillan, 1977).

80. Ibid., pp. 6 – 7.

81. Ibid., p. 18.

82. *New Rules of Sociological Method*, pp. 110 – 13 and *passim*.

83. It is important to separate the approach suggested here from that of

exchange theory (especially Blau). Exchange theory analyses relations of autonomy and dependence in interaction in terms of resources which alter possesses that ego requires to reach his/her goals. This however does not incorporate power within a theory of the duality of structure, and tends to remain tied to a framework of utilitarian individualism.

84. Karl Popper, *The Open Society and its Enemies*, vol. 2 (London: Routledge, 1966) p. 98.

85. As Lukes argues. Steven Lukes, 'Methodological individualism reconsidered', *British Journal of Sociology*, vol. 19 (1968).

86. An idiosyncratic contribution to these issues has recently been offered by Cutler *et al.* in their *Marx's 'Capital' and Capitalism Today* (London: Routledge, 1977). 'There is nothing', they say, 'in the concept of agent to ensure that all agents must be conceived as human subjects . . .' (p. 266). Thus the capitalist is recognised as an agent in company law: however such a category is not limited to human individuals, but can include the business firm. 'The joint-stock company is a legal agent and a locus of economic decision distinct from its shareholders . . . As for the other attributes required of an entity if it is to function as an agent of capitalist possession, it is clear that these do not require that the agent be a human individual' (p. 277). These comments are unobjectionable, but also wholly unenlightening; they do not address the philosophical problem of agency at all. It is perfectly true that a corporation can be an agent in law. But laws have to be interpreted, and applied; it takes human agents to do that, as well as to frame them in the first place. In the sections where the authors do confront the issue of agency more directly, they make claims that simply seem to me wrong. Thus they say that, if we impute any universal attributes to human subjects, it follows that social relations 'are relations between subjects and they exist in and through the will and consciousness of subjects' (p. 268). But it does not follow at all; although certainly no approach which *ignores* the will and consciousness of human subjects is likely to be of much use in social theory.

Chapter 3

1. A. R. Radcliffe-Brown, 'On social structure', *Journal of the Royal Anthropological Institute*, vol. 70 (1940) p. 9.

2. Cf. Dean MacConnell, 'The past and future of "symbolic interactionism"', *Semiotica*, vol. 16 (1976): 'the symbolic interactionist version of meaning reduces to a social psychology of meaning, and it does not lead to research on the logic and order in the relations between signs' (p. 101). The symbolic interactionist view is the closest in social theory to intentionalist theories of meaning as developed by philosophers (Grice, *et al.*).

3. Raymond Williams, *Marxism and Literature* (Oxford University Press, 1977) pp. 38ff.

4. Umberto Eco, *A Theory of Semiotics*, p. 9.
5. See Giddens, *New Rules of Sociological Method*, pp. 104–7.
6. Cf. the interesting and important discussion in Edmond Wright, 'Sociology and the irony model', *Sociology*, vol. 12 (1978) pp. 528ff.
7. Eco, *Theory of Semiotics*, p. 49.
8. Cf. Edmund Leach, *Culture and Communication* (Cambridge University Press, 1976) pp. 52ff.
9. Cf. my discussion in 'Classical social theory and the origins of modern sociology', *American Journal of Sociology*, vol. 81 (1976).
10. Ralf Dahrendorf, *Class and Class Conflict in Industrial Society* (Stanford University Press, 1958).
11. Various papers reprinted in *Studies in Social and Political Theory*.
12. Talcott Parsons, *The Structure of Social Action*.
13. Talcott Parsons and Robert F. Bales, *Family, Socialisation and Interaction Process* (New York: Free Press, 1955) p. 54.
14. Eco, *Theory of Semiotics*, p. 50.
15. Paul Ricoeur, 'Existence and hermeneutics', in *The Conflict of Interpretations* (Evanston: Northwestern University Press, 1974) pp. 12–13. See also subsequent emendations of his position in *Interpretation Theory: Discourse and the Surplus of Meaning*.
16. Cf. Jung: 'a symbol is a term, a name, or even a picture that may be familiar in daily life, yet that possesses specific connotations in addition to its conventional obvious meaning'. Carl G. Jung *et al.*, *Man and His Symbols* (London: Pan, 1978) p. 3.
17. Cf. Donald A. Schon, *Displacement of Concepts* (London: Tavistock, 1963).
18. Cf. Max Weber, *Economy and Society*, vol. 2 (New York: Bedminster, 1968) pp. 901–10.
19. Alan Wells, *Social Institutions* (London: Heinemann, 1970) p. 133.
20. *The Class Structure of the Advanced Societies*.
21. Max Weber, *Economy and Society*, vol. 1, pp. 302ff.
22. Robert K. Merton, *Social Theory and Social Structure*.
23. 'Functionalism: après la lutte'.
24. Cf. David Lockwood, 'Social integration and system integration', Zollschan and Hirsch, *Social Change*.
25. Nicos Poulantzas, *Political Power and Social Classes* (London: New Left Books, 1973) p. 44. For a critical discussion of functionalism in recent Marxist literature, see R. W. Connell, 'Complexities of furies leave . . . a critique of the Althusserian approach to class', *Macquarie University Paper* (June 1978).
26. See, for example, Manuel Castells, *The Urban Question* (London: Arnold, 1977) especially pp. 461ff.
27. For a fuller development of this proposition, see 'Functionalism: après la lutte'.
28. Cf. Pierre Bourdieu and J. C. Passerron, *Reproduction in Education, Society and Culture* (London: Sage, 1977).
29. *The Class Structure of the Advanced Societies*.
30. Parsons, *Sociological Theory and Modern Society* (New York: Free Press, 1967) p. 11.

31. For German discussions, mainly revolving around Dahrendorf's *Homo Sociologicus*, see for example, Friedrich H. Tenbruck, 'Zur Deutschen Reception der Rollenanalyse', *Kölner Zeitschrift für Soziologie*, vol. 1 (1961); in English, Margaret A. Coulson, 'Role: a redundant concept in sociology?', in J. A. Jackson, *Role* (Cambridge University Press, 1972).

32. Erving Goffman, *Where the Action Is* (London: Allen Lane, 1969) p. 41.

33. Cf. Stanford Lyman and B. M. Scott, *The Drama of Social Reality* (New York: Oxford University Press, 1975).

34. R. K. Merton, 'Continuities in the theory of reference groups and social structure', in *Social Theory and Social Structure*, p. 370.

35. Ibid., p. 380.

36. Jacques Lacan, *The Four Fundamental Concepts of Psychoanalysis* (London: Hogarth Press, 1977) p. 43.

37. Lacan, *Écrits*, p. 26.

38. 'The agency of the letter in the unconscious', *Écrits*. Cf. also Anika Lemaire, *Jacques Lacan* (London: Routledge, 1977); Anthony Wilden, *The Language of the Self* (New York: Dell, 1975).

39. For example, he frequently elides 'signified' and 'object signified' in *Écrits*. Ricoeur's arguments, I think, are relevant to the standpoint I wish to advocate. The statement, 'the unconscious is structured like a language', he says, 'must not be divorced from Benveniste's remark that the Freudian mechanisms are both infra- and supra-linguistic. The mechanisms of the unconscious are not so much particular linguistic phenomena as they are paralinguistic distortions of ordinary language' (p. 404). Moreover, in stressing the 'economic' aspect of the closure of the discourse of the unconscious, Ricoeur emphasises the relation between repression and the energetics of practice.

40. As in the books published in 1908, each called *Social Psychology*, by William MacDougall and E. A. Ross.

41. S. Freud, *Group Psychology and the Analysis of the Ego* (London: Hogarth Press, 1959).

42. Gustave Le Bon, *The Crowd* (London, 1925) p. 7. Le Bon however held that the unconscious is composed primarily of an 'archaic heritage' of a racial character.

43. Ibid., p. 11.

44. Ibid., p. 12.

45. Bruno Bettelheim, *The Informed Heart* (Glencoe: Free Press, 1960).

46. Ibid., p. 169.

47. William Sargant, *Battle for the Mind* (London: Pan, 1959).

48. The book has a strong Cold Warish tone (it was first published in 1957). Sargant is more concerned with processes of radical alteration of belief than with critical situations as I conceptualise them; and he seeks to explain the responses he analyses primarily in physiological terms.

49. Sargant, *Battle for the Mind*, p. 192.

50. Freud, *Group Psychology*, p. 37.

51. Cf. Sargant, *Battle for the Mind*, pp. 95–6, who claims that it is easiest to resist the impact of religious conversion ceremonials if one is indifferent or adopts a joking attitude towards them; a strongly defined hostile attitude, on the other hand, may produce a conversion experience.
52. Cf. Jerome S. Bruner, 'The organisation of early skilled action', in Martin P. Richards, *The Integration of a Child into a Social World* (Cambridge University Press, 1974).
53. Daniel Bertaux, *Destins personnels et structure de classe* (Paris: Presses Universitaires, 1977), in which the author argues for a version of class theory incorporating 'social trajectories'.

Chapter 4

1. Marx, 'Critique of Hegel's dialectic', in T. B. Bottomore, *Karl Marx, Early Writings* (New York: McGraw-Hill, 1964) p. 198.
2. 'Economic and philosophical manuscripts', ibid., p. 144.
3. 'Contribution to the critique of Hegel's Philosophy of Right', ibid., pp. 58–9.
4. Marx and Engels, *Selected Works* (London: Lawrence and Wishart, 1968) pp. 182–3.
5. It is often remarked that Marx's comments on the decay of Rome parallel Weber's later, more detailed, discussion. Cf. 'Marx, Weber and the development of capitalism', in *Studies in Social and Political Theory*, pp. 197–8.
6. Gary Young, 'The fundamental contradiction of capitalist production', *Philosophy and Public Affairs*, vol. 5 (1976) p. 196.
7. 'Manifesto of the Communist Party', in Marx and Engels, *Selected Works*, p. 40.
8. *Capital*, vol. 1, p. 763.
9. 'The barrier to *capital* is that this entire development proceeds in a contradictory way, and that the working out of the productive forces, of general wealth, etc., knowledge, etc., appears in such a way that the working individual *alienates* himself; relates to the conditions brought out of him by his labour as those not of his *own*, but of an *alien wealth* and his own property.' *Grundrisse* (Harmondsworth: Pelican, 1973) p. 451.
10. Young, 'Fundamental contradiction of capitalist production', p. 201.
11. *Grundrisse*, p. 77.
12. Maurice Godelier, 'Structure and contradiction in *Capital*', in Robin Blackburn, *Ideology in Social Science* (London: Fontana, 1972).
13. Ibid., p. 350.
14. Ibid., p. 353.
15. I introduced a differentiation between conflict and contradiction in *The Class Structure of the Advanced Societies*; the interpretation I offered there of contradiction, however, I now see as limited and defective.

16. See Pierre van den Berghe, 'Dialectic and functionalism. Toward a theoretical synthesis', *American Sociological Review*, vol. 28 (1963).

17. Op. cit., p. 367. See also van den Berghe, *Rationality and Irrationality in Economics* (London: New Left Books, 1972).

18. Jon Elster, *Logic and Society, Contradictions and Possible Worlds* (Chichester: Wiley, 1978).

19. Elster specifically criticises Althusser and Godelier on p. 90, saying that the term contradiction should not be used to refer to the capital/wage-labour relation. However he attributes more terminological consistency to Marx than is warranted, mistakenly claiming that Marx never refers to contradiction (*Widerspruch*) between capital and wage-labour.

20. It should be mentioned that Elster rejects the conception that either the persistence or change in a social item can be explained in terms of functional need, an emphasis with which I am in entire agreement. 'If ... one can demonstrate that the apparent neutrality of the state in modern capitalist societies actually is better suited to capitalist purposes than an overtly biased government would have been, then a well-known Marxist-functionalist argument tends to conclude that this beneficial effect *explains* the neutrality of the state' (p. 121). It does not, unless it is shown how the neutral posture of the state actually comes about and is reproduced; 'the feedback must be *demonstrated* rather than merely postulated' (p. 122). Cf. also Elster's discussion of an example from the work of E. P. Thompson, pp. 119ff.

21. Ibid., p. 113. Elster argues however that Marx made a mistake about this by himself committing the fallacy of composition. 'From the fact that a given innovation is labour-saving when all other things are constant, Marx illegitimately concludes that this remains true when all innovations are considered simultaneously' (p. 118).

22. Engels, 'Socialism: utopian and scientific', in Marx and Engels, *Selected Works*, p. 421.

23. This formulation I think superior to that proposed in *New Rules of Sociological Method*, p. 125, and again in 'Functionalism: après la lutte', pp. 127–8, in which I still had not separated contradiction as fully from opposition of interest as I should have done.

24. Cf. Mao, 'On contradiction', *Selected Works of Mao-Tse-Tung* (Peking: Foreign Languages Press, 1967) pp. 331ff.

25. Set out in a general way in Weber, *Economy and Society*, vol. 1. But cf. various of the pieces in *Gesammelte politische Schriften* (Tübingen: Möhr, 1958), which are almost as important.

26. For useful background discussion, see Martin Albrow, *Bureaucracy* (London: Pall Mall, 1970).

27. Herbert Marcuse, 'Industrialism and capitalism in the work of Max Weber', in Otto Stammer, *Max Weber and Sociology Today* (Oxford: Blackwell, 1971).

28. Marcuse, *One-dimensional Man* (London: Sphere, 1968).

29. Harry Braverman, *Labour and Monopoly Capital* (New York: Monthly Review Press, 1974).

30. Cf. Wolfgang Mommsen, *The Age of Bureaucracy* (Oxford: Blackwell, 1974).
31. Michel Crozier, *The Bureaucratic Phenomenon* (London: Tavistock, 1964).
32. Cf. Laurie Taylor and Stanley Cohen, *Escape Attempts* (London: Allen Lane, 1976).
33. This was the basis of my distinction between conflict consciousness and revolutionary consciousness in *The Class Structure of the Advanced Societies.*
34. Cf. Richard Sennett and Jonathan Cobb, *The Hidden Injuries of Class* (Cambridge University Press, 1977).
35. Albert Camus, *The Myth of Sisyphus* (New York: Knopf, 1955).
36. See 'A theory of suicide', in *Studies in Social and Political Theory.*
37. *The German Ideology* (London: Lawrence and Wishart, 1965). (I have amended this and certain other translations below.)
38. 'Economic and philosophical manuscripts', in Bottomore, *Karl Marx: Early Writings*, p. 164.
39. *The Poverty of Philosophy* (London: Lawrence and Wishart, n.d.) p. 92.
40. *The German Ideology*, p. 39.
41. Ibid., pp. 37-8.
42. *The Communist Manifesto*, in Marx and Engels, *Selected Works*, p. 35.
43. Marx and Engels, *Selected Works*, pp. 182-3.
44. I abstract as far as possible from Althusser's broader philosophical standpoint. For an example of the vagaries to which that standpoint can give rise, cf. the perambulations of Hirst and Hindess through their various works: Barry Hindess and Paul Q. Hirst, *Pre-capitalist Modes of Production* (London: Routledge, 1975); *Mode of Production and Social Formation* (London: Macmillan, 1977); Anthony Cutler, Barry Hindess, Paul Hirst and Athar Hussain, *Marx's 'Capital' and Capitalism Today*, 2 vols (London: Routledge, 1977 and 1978).
45. Louis Althusser, *For Marx* (London: Allen Lane, 1969) p. 113.
46. Louis Althusser and Etienne Balibar, *Reading Capital* (London: New Left Books, 1970) pp. 186ff.
47. Ibid., pp. 188-9.
48. Ibid., p. 180.
49. J. Laplanche and J.-B. Pontalis, *The Language of Psycho-analysis* (London: Hogarth Press, 1973) pp. 292-3.
50. For recent remarks by Althusser on this issue, see Louis Althusser, *Essays in Self-criticism* (London: New Left Books, 1976) pp. 176ff.
51. Cf. Miriam Glucksmann, *Structural Analysis in Contemporary Social Thought* (London: Routledge, 1974) pp. 129ff.
52. Cf. *Essays in Self-criticism*, pp. 126-31.
53. Theodor Adorno, *The Positivist Dispute in German Sociology* (London: Heinemann, 1976).
54. See especially Lewis Mumford, *The Myth of the Machine* (London: Secker and Warburg, 1967).

Chapter 5

1. See, for example, George Lichtheim, *The Concept of Ideology and Other Essays* (New York: Vintage, 1967); Martin Seliger, *Ideology and Politics* (London: Allen and Unwin, 1976); Bhikhu Parekh, 'Social and political thought and the problem of ideology', in Robert Benewick, *Knowledge and Belief in Politics* (London: Allen and Unwin, 1973).
2. Noted by Lichtheim, *Concept of Ideology*, p. 154; and by Alvin W. Gouldner, *The Dialectic of Ideology and Technology* (New York: Seabury Press, 1976) pp. 11ff.
3. Cf. Hans Barth, *Wahrheit und Ideologie* (Zürich, 1945).
4. Cf. Sarah Kofman, *Camera obscura. De L'idéologie* (Paris: Éditions Galilée, 1973) for a discussion of the cultural importance of the camera obscura. Cf. also J. Mepham, 'The theory of ideology in *Capital*', *Radical Philosophy*, vol. 2 (1972) for comments on ideology in Marx's early and later writings.
5. Marx and Engels, *The German Ideology* (London: Lawrence and Wishart, 1965) p. 37.
6. Ibid., p. 61.
7. Many subsequent commentators on Marx's notion of ideology rely heavily upon the opening sections of *The German Ideology*, ignoring the bulk of the book – which after all is a prolonged attack upon certain *ideologists*.
8. Both quotes from Karl Mannheim, *Ideology and Utopia* (New York: Harcourt, Brace and World, 1936) p. 76; See also *Essays on the Sociology of Knowledge* (London: Routledge, 1952).
9. Mannheim, *Ideology and Utopia*, p. 78.
10. This point is made by Seliger in *The Marxist Conception of Ideology* (Cambridge University Press, 1977) pp. 136–7.
11. Mannheim, *Ideology and Utopia*, p. 168.
12. At other times he preferred to repudiate it. Cf. Gunter W. Remmling, *The Sociology of Karl Mannheim* (London: Routledge, 1975) pp. 74–5.
13. For one of Marx's few comments on such issues, see his brief discussion of why Greek literature retains an interest and appeal today. *Grundrisse*, pp. 110–11.
14. Mannheim, 'Historicism', in Gunter W. Remmling, *Towards the Sociology of Knowledge* (London: Routledge, 1973).
15. R. K. Merton, 'Karl Mannheim and the sociology of knowledge', in *Social Theory and Social Structure* (Glencoe: Free Press, 1963) pp. 491ff.
16. Merton, ibid., pp. 501ff.
17. *Ideology and Utopia*, p. 188.
18. Ibid., p. 186.
19. Cf. A. Neusüss, *Utopia, Bewusstein und freischwebende Intelligenz* (Meisenheim, 1968).
20. Jürgen Habermas, *Strukturwandel der Öffentlichkeit* (Neuwied: Luchterhand, 1962).

21. Habermas, 'Technology and science as ideology', in *Towards a Rational Society* (London: Heinemann, 1971) p. 99.
22. Ibid.
23. Cf. my 'Habermas's critique of hermeneutics', in *Studies in Social and Political Theory*.
24. H.-G. Gadamer, *Truth and Method* (London: Sheed and Ward, 1975).
25. Habermas, 'Was heisst Universalpragmatik?' in K.-O. Apel, *Sprachpragmatik und Philosophie* (Frankfurt: Suhrkamp, 1976).
26. This theme is developed in Alvin W. Gouldner, *The Dialectic of Ideology and Technology* (London: Macmillan, 1976).
27. Cf. Habermas's Introduction to the fourth German edition of *Theory and Practice* (London: Heinemann, 1974).
28. Louis Althusser, *For Marx* (London: Allen Lane, 1969) p. 235 (I have modified the translation). However, Althusser's use of 'ideology' does not always appear consistent. For a relevant discussion, see Gregor McLennan *et al.*, 'Althusser's theory of ideology' in *Working Papers in Cultural Studies*, vol. 10 (Centre for Contemporary Cultural Studies, 1977).
29. Althusser, 'Ideology and the state ideological apparatuses', in *Lenin and Philosophy and Other Essays* (London: New Left Books, 1977). Comparison of Lacan's interpretation of *Wo es war, soll Ich werden*, with that adopted by Habermas, is relevant here (see pp. 120–1).
30. Saul Karsz, *Théorie et politique: Louis Althusser* (Paris: Maspero, 1974) p. 82.
31. *For Marx*, pp. 234–5 (amended translation).
32. Cf. McLennan, 'Althusser's theory of ideology'.
33. *Ideology and Utopia*, p. 3.
34. E. Husserl, *The Crisis of European Sciences and Transcendental Phenomenology* (Evanston: Northwestern University Press, 1970).
35. Cf. *New Rules of Sociological Method*, p. 162.
36. Cf. 'Positivism and its critics', in *Studies in Social and Political Theory*, pp. 57ff.
37. See, for instance, Lewis S. Feuer, *Ideology and the Ideologists* (Oxford: Blackwell, 1975). For a survey and analysis of uses of ideology, see Norman Birnbaum, 'The sociological study of ideology (1940–1960)', *Current Sociology*, vol. 9 (1960); George A. Huaco, 'On ideology', *Acta Sociologica*, vol. 14 (1971).
38. Brian Barry, *Political Argument* (London: Routledge, 1965) p. 174.
39. S. I. Benn, 'Interests in politics', *Proceedings of the Aristotelian Society*, vol. 60 (1960).
40. This formulation is *prima facie* close to that offered by Barry, and some of the qualifications he makes to its use (*Political Argument*, pp. 178ff) are relevant here, although I shall not discuss them. However, Barry appears for the most part to understand wants in terms of 'empirical wants', which is definitely not my position; and he also confines the notion of wants to those concerning the 'private wants' of the individual, which brings his view back towards a form of utilitarianism. For a critique, cf. William E. Connolly, *The Terms of Political Discourse* (Lexington: D. C. Heath, 1974) pp. 53ff.

41. Norbert Elias, *The Civilising Process* (Oxford: Blackwell, 1978).
42. Clifford Geertz, 'Ideology as a cultural system', in David Apter (ed.), *Ideology and Discontent* (New York: Free Press, 1964).
43. Macpherson *et al.*, 'Social explanation and political accountability'. One should note the differences between Macpherson's position and that taken by the theorists of 'citizenship and social class'. See especially T. H. Marshall, *Citizenship and Social Class* (Cambridge University Press, 1949); Reinhard Bendix, *Nation-building and Citizenship* (Berkeley: University of California Press, 1977)
44. *The Class Structure of the Advanced Societies.*
45. For an interesting analysis of Adorno's criticisms of Lukács in this respect, see Gillian Rose, *The Melancholy Science* (London: Macmillan, 1978) pp. 40ff. (See also Lukács's own comments upon his work in the 1967 Preface.)
46. Georg Lukács, *History and Class Consciousness* (London: Merlin, 1971) pp. 93–4.
47. Zygmunt Bauman, *Towards a Critical Sociology* (London: Routledge, 1976) pp. 34–5.
48. Daniel Bell, 'Ideology: a debate', *Commentary*, vol. 38 (Oct 1964) p. 70.
49. For relevant contributions, see Chaim I. Waxman, *The End of Ideology Debate* (New York: Funk and Wagnall, 1968).

Chapter 6

1. Cf. the comments of Gluckman on 'data and theory', in Max Gluckman, *Politics, Law and Ritual in Tribal Society* (Oxford: Blackwell, 1965).
2. Cf. Gellner: 'How can one say, as some anthropologists seemed to say almost with one breath, that the past of a tribal society is unknown, *and* that is known to be stable?' Ernest Gellner, *Thought and Change* (London: Weidenfeld, 1964) p. 19.
3. Cf., however, R. N. Bellah, 'Durkheim and history', *American Sociological Review*, vol. 24 (1959).
4. J. A. Barnes, 'Time flies like an arrow', *Man*, vol. 6 (1971).
5. J. G. A. Pocock, *Politics, Language and Time* (London: Methuen, 1972).
6. Ibid., p. 255.
7. For a conservative analysis of the development of hermeneutics, and a critique of Enlightenment, see H.-G. Gadamer, *Truth and Method*. On writing and culture, see particularly Jack Goody, *The Domestication of the Savage Mind* (Cambridge University Press, 1977). Cf. Paul Ricoeur, *The Conflict of Interpretations*, pp. 288ff.
8. Cf. Wilbert E. Moore, *Man, Time and Society* (New York: Wiley, 1963); Georges Gurvitch, *The Spectrum of Social Time* (Dordrecht: Reidel, 1964).
9. Cf. however, Shils: 'Time provides not only a setting which permits the

state of one moment to be compared heuristically with that of another moment. Time is also a constitutive property of society. Society is only conceivable as a system of varying states occurring at moments in time. Society displays its characteristic features not at a single moment in time but in various phases assuming various but related shapes at different and consecutive moments of time.' Edward Shils, *Center and Periphery* (Chicago University Press, 1975) p. xiii.

10. Cf. 'Functionalism: après la lutte'.

11. Harvey Sacks and Emmanuel A. Schegloff, 'A simplest systematics for the organisation of turn-taking in conversation', *Language*, vol. 50 (1974).

12. Garfinkel, *Studies in Ethnomethodology*.

13. Cf. Paul Ricoeur, 'The model of the text: meaningful action considered as a text', *Social Research*, vol. 38 (1971), which explores some of these similarities.

14. Marshall McCluhan, *The Gutenberg Galaxy* (Toronto University Press, 1962).

15. Cf. Whitman: 'It seems that, however accurate the repetitive control elements of the clock may be, one can never arrive at a concept of standard time-duration without prior reference to space congruence. In fact, the more accurate the clock, the more complex are the spatio-temporal physical laws which have to be known and utilised.' Michael Whitman, *Philosophy of Space and Time* (London: Allen and Unwin, 1967) p. 71.

16. On the development of time and space concepts with the decay of feudalism, see Agnes Heller, *Renaissance Man* (London: Routledge, 1978) pp. 170–96.

17. Alan Pred, 'The choreography of existence: comments on Häger-strand's time-geography and its usefulness', *Economic Geography*, vol. 53 (1977) p. 208.

18. Only fairly recently has a literature begun to develop which treats these issues with some sophistication. See especially the writings of Harvey and Castells.

19. John Rex and Robert Moore, *Race, Community and Conflict* (London: Oxford University Press, 1967),

20. Erving Goffman, *The Presentation of Self in Everyday Life* (New York: Doubleday, 1959); for the same author's more recent views on some overlapping issues, see Goffman, *Frame Analysis*.

21. Kathleen Archibald, *Wartime Shipyard* (Berkeley: University of California Press, 1947) p. 159.

22. Cf. David Lockwood, *The Black-coated Worker* (London: Allen and Unwin, 1969) for a discussion in the context of broader issues of class theory.

23. Cf. R. E. Pahl and J. T. Winkler, 'The economic elite: theory and practice', in Philip Stanworth and Anthony Giddens, *Elites and Power in British Society* (Cambridge University Press, 1974).

24. Lewis Mumford, *Interpretations and Forecasts* (London: Secker and Warburg, 1973) p. 272.

25. Cf. 'Functionalism: après la lutte'.
26. Elster, *Logic and Society*, pp. 121–2, makes this point forcibly.
27. R. K. Merton. *Social Theory and Social Structure* (Glencoe: Free Press, 1963) pp. 64–5. Italics in original.
28. 'Functionalism: après la lutte', pp. 111–12.
29. E. E. Evans-Pritchard, *Witchcraft, Oracles and Magic among the Azande* (Oxford University Press, 1950); also Bryan Wilson, *Rationality* (Oxford: Blackwell, 1970), and numerous other contributions.
30. Pierre Bourdieu. *Outline of a Theory of Practice* (Cambridge University Press, 1977) p. 83.
31. Cf. Raymond Williams, *Keywords* (London: Fontana, 1976).
32. For a rather different view of these matters, and a variant use of the term 'historicity'. see Alain Touraine. *The Self-production of Society*.
33. E. H. Carr, *A History of Soviet Russia*, vol. I (London: Macmillan, 1969) p. 88.
34. *Studies in Social and Political Theory*, pp. 14ff: 'Classical social theory and the origins of modern sociology'. *American Journal of Sociology*.
35. Cf. Nisbet's criticisms of metaphors of growth, linked to 'immanent causation, continuity, differentiation, necessity and uniformitarianism [*sic*]'. Robert A. Nisbet, *Social Change and History* (New York: Oxford University Press, 1969) p. 251 and *passim*.
36. For a relevant discussion, see Herminio Martins, 'Time and theory in sociology', in John Rex, *Approaches to Sociology* (London: Routledge, 1974).
37. *Studies in Social and Political Theory*, pp. 19–20.
38. *The Class Structure of the Advanced Societies*.
39. Immanuel Wallerstein, *The Modern World-system* (New York: Academic Press, 1974) p. 348.
40. For one critique along these lines. see Robert Brenner. 'The origins of capitalist development: a critique of neo-Smithian Marxism'. *New Left Review*, no. 104 (July–August, 1977).
41. Cf. *The Class Structure of the Advanced Societies*, pp. 38–40.
42. Gellner. *Thought and Change*.
43. *The Class Structure of the Advanced Societies*, pp. 19–22, and *passim*.
44. Ibid., pp. 211ff.
45. Fernand Braudel, *Écrits sur l'histoire* (Paris: Flammarion, 1969) p. 50.
46. William Dray, 'The historical explanation of actions reconsidered', in Sidney Hook, *Philosophy and History: A Symposium* (New York University Press, 1963) p. 105.
47. *New Rules of Sociological Method*, pp. 153–4 and *passim*.
48. N. Rescher and O. Helmer, 'On the epistemology of the inexact sciences', *Management Science*, vol. 4 (1959).
49. Dray, 'The historical explanation of actions reconsidered', p. 108.

Chapter 7

1. *Studies in Social and Political Theory*, pp. 14–20; 'Classical social theory and the origins of modern sociology', *American Journal of Sociology*, vol. 81 (1976).

2. Cf. my *Durkheim* (London: Fontana, 1978) pp. 21–33.
3. Cf. Jerome Karabel and A. H. Halsey, *Power and Ideology in Education* (New York: Oxford University Press, 1977).
4. It is a mistake, as I have tried to show elsewhere, to link functionalism mainly to conservative standpoints in politics. 'Four myths in the history of social thought', in *Studies in Social and Political Theory*.
5. Cf. 'Functionalism: après la lutte', in *Studies in Social and Political Theory*.
6. For Parsons's views on cybernetics, see 'The relations between biological and socio-cultural theory', and other papers in Parsons, *Social Systems and the Evolution of Action Theory* (New York: Free Press, 1977).
7. See 'Positivism and its critics', ibid., pp. 44–57.
8. See in particular Carl G. Hempel, 'The logic of functional analysis', in *Aspects of Scientific Explanation* (New York: Free Press, 1965).
9. See the interesting essay by Robert K. Merton, 'Structural analysis in sociology', in Peter M. Blau, *Approaches to the Study of Social Structure* (New York: Free Press, 1975).
10. Cf. 'Classical social theory and the origins of modern sociology'.
11. For an important emendation of traditional views of scientific laws, see however Mary Hesse, *The Structure of Scientific Inference* (London: Macmillan, 1974).
12. *New Rules of Sociological Method.*
13. Ibid., pp. 153–4 and *passim.*
14. These accounts have their origin in R. K. Merton, 'The self-fulfilling prophecy', in *Social Theory and Social Structure* (New York: Free Press, 1957).
15. Ludwig Wittgenstein, *Philosophical Investigations* (Oxford: Blackwell, 1972) para. 11.
16. See, for instance, C. W. Lachenmeyer, *The Language of Sociology* (New York: Colombia University Press, 1971).
17. The concepts of social science 'must be constructed in such a way that a human act performed within the life-world by an individual actor in the way indicated by the typical construct would be understandable for the actor himself as well as for his fellow-men in terms of common-sense interpretations of everyday life.' Alfred Schutz, *Collected Papers* (The Hague: Mouton, 1967) p. 44.
18. Peter Winch, *The Idea of a Social Science* (London: Routledge, 1963).
19. A. R. Louch, *Explanation and Human Action* (Oxford: Blackwell, 1966) p. 160.
20. See especially pp. 83ff in Winch, *Idea of Social Science.*
21. See some of the contributions to Max Black, *The Social Theories of Talcott Parsons* (Englewood Cliffs: Prentice-Hall, 1961).
22. Talcott Parsons, *The Structure of Social Action* (Glencoe: Free Press, 1949) pp. 737ff and *passim.*
23. Cf. *New Rules of Sociological Method*, p. 98.
24. See especially 'Deux lois de l'évolution pénale', *Année sociologique*, vol. 4 (1899–1900).
25. 'Positivism and its critics', in *Studies in Social and Political Theory.*

26. Carl G. Hempel and P. Oppenheim, 'Studies in the logic of explanation', *Philosophy of Science*, vol. 15 (1948).
27. Cf. George Homans, *The Nature of Social Science* (New York: Harcourt Brace, 1967).
28. This point is made with some vigour in Alan Ryan, *The Philosophy of the Social Sciences* (London: Macmillan, 1970) pp. 48–9.
29. 'Habermas's critique of hermeneutics', in *Studies in Social and Political Theory*.

Index